TEXTBOOK OF SYRIAN SEMITIC INSCRIPTIONS

TEXTBOOK OF SYRIAN SEMITIC INSCRIPTIONS

VOLUME II

ARAMAIC INSCRIPTIONS
including inscriptions in the dialect of Zenjirli

BY

JOHN C. L. GIBSON

READER IN HEBREW AND SEMITIC LANGUAGES
UNIVERSITY OF EDINBURGH

OXFORD
AT THE CLARENDON PRESS
1975

Oxford University Press, Ely House, London W. 1
GLASGOW NEW YORK TORONTO MELBOURNE WELLINGTON
CAPE TOWN IBADAN NAIROBI DAR ES SALAAM LUSAKA ADDIS ABABA
DELHI BOMBAY CALCUTTA MADRAS KARACHI LAHORE DACCA
KUALA LUMPUR SINGAPORE HONG KONG TOKYO

ISBN 0 19 813186 0

Printed in Great Britain
at the University Press, Oxford
by Vivian Ridler
Printer to the University

PREFACE

THE present volume is devoted to written remains in Aramaic on stone, potsherd, and papyrus dating from the first six to seven centuries of the I millennium B.C., when such remains constitute our primary source for the study of the language. It comprises (chapter I) nearly all the extant inscriptions in Old Aramaic dialects belonging to the period of Aramaean political dominance in the 9 and 8 centuries; (chapter II) the two large inscriptions in the Semitic dialect closely related to Aramaic which was during that period the vernacular of the area of Zenjirli (anciently Sam'al); and (chapters III and IV) a representative selection of inscriptions, ostraca, and papyri in Official or Imperial Aramaic, which ousted the various Old Aramaic dialects and became the lingua franca of the Near East during the ensuing periods of Assyrian, Babylonian, and Persian hegemony. With the splitting of the lingua franca into a number of younger local dialects after the fall of the Persian empire, a new phase of Aramaic studies begins, in which epigraphic texts play only a subsidiary role alongside the vast Jewish, Syriac, and Mandaic literatures. Because of the different problems that are posed, it has seemed to me appropriate not to include material from this phase in the Textbook, though for the benefit of students interested in taking the subject further I give some guidance on it in the Bibliographical Notes.

I am grateful to the Clarendon Press for agreeing to the inclusion of a generous selection of photographs and sketches, and for allowing several additional plates and figures to be devoted to texts from volume I (*Hebrew and Moabite Inscriptions*), where the absence of illustrations was widely regretted. In response to many requests I have also numbered the inscriptions serially so as to facilitate cross references. A similar numbering has been undertaken for the second impression of volume I, and is given later in this volume (with some corrigenda and addenda) for the convenience of those who already possess a copy of the first impression. References to Phoenician and Punic inscriptions, which will form the subject-matter of volume III, are meanwhile given according to the enumeration in Donner and Röllig's *Kanaanäische und aramäische Inschriften*. The only other substantial change from volume I is in the disposition of the bibliographies, which are now appended to each inscription instead of being gathered together at the end.

My cordial thanks are due to all the authors, editors, and publishers whose illustrations are reproduced or have been used as the basis of my own sketches, in particular to Dr. S. A. Birnbaum, Professor Edda Bresciani, Dr. D. Diringer, Professor H. Donner, Professor Sir Godfrey

Driver, Professor A. Dupont-Sommer, Professor H. Ingholt, Mr. A. R. Millard, Professor J. B. Pritchard, l'Abbé J. Starcky, Professor Y. Yadin, the University of Chicago Press, l'Académie des inscriptions et belles-lettres, the trustees of the late Sir Henry Wellcome, and the editors of the *Bulletin of the American Schools of Oriental Research* and the *Israel Exploration Journal.* I am further indebted to Sir Godfrey Driver for the loan of his annotated copy of G. A. Cooke's *A Textbook of North-Semitic Inscriptions*, and for advice on a number of points of detail; and to Mr. Millard for drawing my attention to several books and articles I would otherwise have missed.

J. C. L. GIBSON

New College, Edinburgh
Autumn 1972

CONTENTS

LIST OF ILLUSTRATIONS

Figures 2–4 and all the Plates are reproduced, and Figures 1 and 5–28 sketched by myself from the sources indicated below. The Figures should not be relied upon by themselves where exact work is required; the same warning applies in the case of the Tables of scripts. Figures 15–28 and Plates X–XII are of Hebrew and Moabite inscriptions; see volume I for text and comment. Inscriptions not illustrated are, with a few exceptions, included in Pritchard's *The Ancient Near East in Pictures* (1954) or the *Supplementary volume* (1969).

FIGURES (pp. 189–92)

1 No. **1** Barhadad, line 2, representing the readings of (*a*) Albright (*b*) Cross (*c*) Donner [S. A. Birnbaum, *The Hebrew Scripts*, Part Two (London: Palaeographia, 1954–7), no. 010].

2 No. **5** Zakir B, C [H. Pognon, *Inscriptions sémitiques de la Syrie, de la Mésopotamie et de la région de Mossoul* (Paris: Imprimerie nationale, 1907), pls. XXXV, XXXVI].

3 No. **7** Sefire i A 1–16 [*Les Inscriptions araméennes de Sfiré* = *Mémoires présentées par divers savants à l'Académie des inscriptions et belles-lettres*, Tome XV (Paris, 1958), 197–351, pl. III].

4 No. **9** Sefire iii [*Bulletin du Musée de Beyrouth* 13 (1956), 23–41, pls. II and V].

5 No. **10** Tell Halaf [G. R. Driver, *Semitic Writing* (London: The British Academy, 1948), fig. 73 at p. 120].

6 No. **2** Hazael [S. A. Birnbaum, op. cit., no. 011].

7 No. **6** Hamath graffito i [H. Ingholt, *Rapport préliminaire sur sept campagnes des fouilles à Hama en Syrie* = *Det Kgl. Danske Videnskabernes Selskab. Archaeologisk-kunsthistoriske Meddelelser*, III, 1 (Copenhagen, 1940), pl. XXXIX, 1].

8 No. **11** Luristan i [*Iranica Antiqua* 4 (1964), pl. XXXIV].

9 No. **25** Tell el Maskhuta [*Journal of Near Eastern Studies* 15 (1956), pl. VII].

10 No. **32** Nebi Yunis ostracon [*Israel Exploration Journal* 14 (1964), pl. 41, H].

11 No. **16** Barrakkab ii [*Mitteilungen des Instituts für Orientforschung*, Berlin, 3 (1955), Abb. 1 at p. 74].

PLATES (at end)

ABBREVIATIONS OF JOURNALS AND WORKS CITED

AANL	*Atti della Accademia Nazionale dei Lincei.*
AfO	*Archiv für Orientforschung.*
AION	*Annali dell'Istituto Universitario Orientale di Napoli.*
AJSL	*The American Journal of Semitic Languages and Literatures.*
Altheim and Stiehl, *Sprache*	F. Altheim and R. Stiehl, *Die aramäische Sprache unter den Achaimeniden*, vol. I, *Geschichtliche Untersuchungen* (Frankfurt, 1964). A second volume on Old Aramaic is announced.
ANEP	J. B. Pritchard (ed.), *The Ancient Near East in Pictures* (Princeton, 1954). Supplementary vol.; see *ANET*.
ANET	J. B. Pritchard (ed.), *Ancient Near Eastern Texts Relating to the Old Testament*, 2 edn. (1955), and with continuing pagination, Supplementary vol. of texts and pictures (Princeton, 1969).
ARAB	D. D. Luckenbill, *Ancient Records of Assyria and Babylonia*, 2 vols. (Chicago, 1926–7).
BA	*The Biblical Archaeologist.*
BASOR	*Bulletin of the American Schools of Oriental Research.*
Birnbaum, *Scripts*	S. A. Birnbaum, *The Hebrew Scripts*, 2 vols. (London, 1954–7; 1971).
CIS	*Corpus Inscriptionum Semiticarum* (Paris, 1881 f.).
Cowley (with number of text)	A. E. Cowley, *Aramaic Papyri of the Fifth Century* B.C. (Oxford, 1923).
CRAIBL	*Comptes rendus des séances de l'Académie des inscriptions et belles-lettres* (Paris).
Degen, *Grammatik*	R. Degen, *Altaramäische Grammatik der Inschriften des 10–8 Jh. v. Chr.* (Wiesbaden, 1969).
Diringer, *Alphabet*	D. Diringer, *The Alphabet: A Key to the History of Mankind* (London, 1948).
DOTT	D. Winton Thomas (ed.), *Documents from Old Testament Times* (London, 1958).
Driver (with number of text)	G. R. Driver, *Aramaic Documents of the Fifth Century B.C.* (Oxford, 1954). Abridged edn., 1957.
Driver, *Writing*	G. R. Driver, *Semitic Writing: From Pictograph to Alphabet* (London, 1948). A revised edition is being prepared.
Dupont-Sommer, *Araméens*	A. Dupont-Sommer, *Les Araméens* (Paris, 1949).
EA (with number of text)	J. A. Knudtzon, *Die El-Amarna Tafeln* (Leipzig, 1915).
EHO	F. M. Cross and D. N. Freedman, *Early Hebrew Orthography: A Study of the Epigraphic Evidence* (New Haven, 1952).

Garbini, 'Antico'	G. Garbini, 'L'aramaico antico', *AANL*, *Memorie*, Serie VIII, vol. VII, fasc. 5 (1956), 235–85.
Gevirtz, 'Curses'	S. Gevirtz, 'West Semitic curses and the problem of the origins of Hebrew Law', *VT* 11 (1961), 137–58.
Ginsberg, 'Problems'	H. L. Ginsberg, 'Aramaic dialect problems', *AJSL* 50 (1933–4), 1–9; 52 (1935–6), 95–103.
Hanson, 'Inscrs.'	R. S. Hanson, 'Aramaic funerary and boundary inscriptions from Asia Minor', *BASOR* 192 (1968), 3–11.
IEJ	*Israel Exploration Journal.*
JAOS	*Journal of the American Oriental Society.*
Jean–Hoftijzer, *Dictionnaire*	C. F. Jean and J. Hoftijzer, *Dictionnaire des inscriptions sémitiques de l'Ouest* (Leiden, 1965).
JNES	*Journal of Near Eastern Studies.*
JSS	*Journal of Semitic Studies.*
KAI (with number of text)	H. Donner and W. Röllig, *Kanaanäische und aramäische Inschriften*, 3 vols. (Wiesbaden, 1962–4). 2 edn., 1966–9.
Koopmans, *Chrest.* (with number of text)	J. J. Koopmans, *Aramäische Chrestomathie: Ausgewählte Texte* (Inschriften, Ostraka und Papyri) (Leiden, 1962).
Kraeling (with number of text)	E. G. Kraeling, *The Brooklyn Museum Aramaic Papyri* (New Haven, 1953).
Leander, *Ägyptisch*	P. Leander, *Laut- und Formenlehre des Ägyptisch-Aramäischen* (Göteborg, 1928).
Lidzbarski, *Ephem.*	M. Lidzbarski, *Ephemeris für semitische Epigraphik*, 3 vols. (Giessen, 1902–15).
Moscati, *Comparative*	S. Moscati and others, *An Introduction to the Comparative Grammar of the Semitic Languages* (Wiesbaden, 1964).
Naveh, 'Inscrs'.	J. Naveh, 'Old Aramaic inscriptions (1960–64)', *AION* 16 (1966), 19–36.
Naveh, 'Script'	J. Naveh, 'The development of the Aramaic script', *Proceedings of the Israel Academy of Sciences and Humanities*, V, 1 (Jerusalem, 1970).
NSE (with page number)	M. Lidzbarski, *Handbuch der Nordsemitischen Epigraphik* (Weimar, 1898).
NSI (with number of text)	G. A. Cooke, *A Textbook of North-Semitic Inscriptions* (Oxford, 1903).
PEQ	*Palestine Exploration Quarterly.*
RA	*Revue d'assyriologie et d'archéologie orientale.*
Rosenthal, *Forschung*	F. Rosenthal, *Die aramäistische Forschung seit Th. Nöldeke's Veröffentlichungen* (Leiden, 1939).
Rosenthal, *Grammar*	F. Rosenthal, *A Grammar of Biblical Aramaic* (Wiesbaden, 1961).
Rosenthal, *Handbook* (with number of text)	F. Rosenthal (ed.) *An Aramaic Handbook*, 2 vols. (Wiesbaden, 1967).
RSO	*Rivista degli studi orientali.*

Tallqvist, *Names*	K. Tallqvist, *Assyrian Personal Names* (Helsingfors, 1918).
VT	*Vetus Testamentum.*
WZKM	*Wiener Zeitschrift für die Kunde des Morgenlandes.*
ZA	*Zeitschrift für Assyriologie und verwandte Gebiete.*
ZAW	*Zeitschrift für die Alttestamentliche Wissenschaft.*
ZDMG	*Zeitschrift der deutschen morgenländischen Gesellschaft.*
ZDPV	*Zeitschrift des deutschen Palästina-Vereins.*

SIGLA USED IN TRANSCRIBING AND TRANSLITERATING

° over a letter indicates that it is doubtful.

– indicates the presence of an undecipherable letter.

1, *5*, *10*, etc., indicate numerical signs.

. or ׀ indicates a separating dot or stroke.

[ ] in Semitic text enclose restorations; thus ומ̊[ן ׀ י]הגע.

. . . . indicate a missing piece of uncertain size, or a stretch of faded writing of uncertain length.

[ ] in English text enclose translations of restored portions.

( ) in English text enclose additions to improve the sense.

[ ] in the commentary enclose phonological reconstructions; thus מראה = [mār'ēh].

Personal and place-names occurring in the Bible are, where their structure is not in question, given in English form; thus חמת as Hamath and not [ḥmāt].

Other Syrian Semitic names occurring frequently are given in a similar conventional form, though some attention is paid in these cases to structure; thus Baalshamayn; Luʿath. I have been guided here by the practice followed in *ANET*.

Aramaic names of an Akkadian structure are given as in Tallqvist, *Names*, with some simplification; thus בלטר as Bel-etir and not Bēl-ēṭir.

Aramaic names of an Egyptian or Anatolian structure are given in straight transliteration; thus תחפי as TḤPY. Syrian Semitic and Akkadian names, whose structure is problematic, are also indicated in this way.

NOTE ON THE PHONOLOGY OF EARLY ARAMAIC

I. CONSONANTS

The Phoenician writing system taken over by the Aramaeans had no symbols for five consonantal sounds possessed by the Old Aramaic dialects and the earliest stage of the Official dialect (chaps. I–III). These had to be represented by symbols for neighbouring sounds, such symbols consequently performing a dual role (in one case a triple role). The five sounds were

voiceless interdental [ṯ];
voiced interdental [ḏ];
emphatic voiceless interdental [ṯ̣];
a velarized consonant corresponding to the emphatic voiced interdental [ḏ̣] of Proto-Semitic, transcribed here as [ġ];
a dental fricative, probably lateralized (i.e. [sl] or the like), but transcribed here by the traditional [ś].

During the Persian period (chap. IV) the first four of these sounds merged with other sounds, for which symbols were already available in the system, although the changes are often obscured by the conservatism of scribes in using the older symbols, especially within common words. In the case of the fifth sound a similar change took place at a later stage (cp. Syriac). The following table shows the reconstructed development from Proto-Semitic. The bracketed consonants in the Ugaritic column are less frequent variants. In the (classical) Arabic column the emphatic sounds are given the traditional transcriptions; their precise character varies from dialect to dialect.

Proto-Sem.	Ugar.	Phoen./Hebr.	Old Aram.	Later Aram.	Arab.
[ṯ]	[ṯ]	ש = [š]	ש = [ṯ]	ת = [t]	[ṯ]
[ḏ]	[d]([ḏ])	ז = [z]	ז = [ḏ]	ד = [d]	[ḏ]
[ṯ̣]	[ṯ̣]([ġ])	צ = [ṣ]	צ = [ṯ̣]	ט = [ṭ]	[ẓ]
[ḏ̣]	[ṣ]([ṯ̣])	צ = [ṣ]	ק = [ġ]	ע = [ʿ]	[ḍ]
[sl]	—	ש = [ś] (Hebr. only)	ש = [ś]	ס = [s]	—

See further on these matters Leander, *Ägyptisch*, 7 f.; Moscati, *Comparative*, 29, 36; Degen, *Grammatik*, 32 f., 36.

2. VOWELS

These are reconstructed from later vocalized stages of Aramaic writing (e.g. Palestinian Aramaic, Syriac) by a similar method to that adopted in vol. I; see, *mutatis mutandis*, my article, 'Stress and vocalic change in Hebrew: a diachronic study', *Journal of Linguistics* 2 (1966), 35–56. The main differences from Hebrew are two

(*a*) In Aramaic Proto-Semitic short vowels changed under the stress by the following system

[a] was retained.
[i] to [ē], though sometimes [i] was retained; thus biblical Aram. [yintēn], 'he shall give', but [sgid], 'he prostrated himself'.
[u] to [ō], though sometimes [u] was retained; thus biblical Aram. [qšōṭ], 'truth', but [pruq], 'break off' (imper.).

This system is found in Hebrew also; thus (classical)

[gabr], 'man'; [sētr] or [sitr], 'shelter'; [ʿōrp] or [ʿurp], 'back',

but, e.g., in so-called First declension nouns, a second system, which does not exist in Aramaic and in which [a] went to [ā], operates; thus

[dabār], 'word'; [kabēd], 'heavy'; [ʿamōq], 'deep'.

(*b*) Against the practice in Hebrew, where Proto-Semitic short vowels were retained in open syllables in the immediate pre-stress position, such vowels were reduced in Aramaic to zero (Shewa); thus

Hebr. [ḥakām], 'wise'; Aram. [ḥkam].

Note: as in vol. I, the stress is not marked unless it falls on a penultimate syllable; nor is the Shewa vowel, which need not normally be distinguished from absence of vowel or zero.

I

INSCRIPTIONS IN OLD ARAMAIC DIALECTS

1. Damascus: Barhadad Fig. 1 (a, b, c)

THE stele, containing the inscr. on its bottom half, was discovered in 1939 at Breidj, some 7 km. north of Aleppo. The top half has a relief of the god to whom it was dedicated, Melcarth, the chief deity of Tyre. The whole measures 1·15 m. high by 0·43 m. broad. It is now housed in the National Museum at Aleppo.

Writing and date

The figure of the god is carved in a style of Hittite derivation widespread in northern Syria at the beginning of the 1 millennium B.C. A similar style was used on the earliest stone monuments from Zenjirli before Assyrian influence made itself felt. This suggests a date for the inscr. not later than the 9 cent. The writing points more precisely to the first half of the cent. It is not greatly different from that of the Phoen. inscrs. from Cyprus (*KAI* no. 30) and Nora (*CIS* i 144 = *KAI* no. 46), which belong to 900 B.C. or shortly afterwards, and seems to predate that of the two Kilamuwa inscrs. (*KAI* nos. 24, 25; *c.* 825 B.C.). The כ in 3 and the two examples of ז in 4 (with a curl on the top bar) provide a possible link with Old Hebr. writing. A date around 860 B.C. is a reasonable deduction. On early Aram. stone writing see further Naveh, 'Script', 7 f.

Words are sometimes separated by strokes and sometimes run together; no pattern emerges.

Historical circumstances

If the name in 1 and the title in 3 go together (which is not absolutely certain), it is difficult to see who else could have erected the stele than the Barhadad of Damascus (biblical Benhadad), who entered a league with Asa of Judah against Baasha and later led an Aramaean invasion of Israel in the reign of Ahab; 1 Kgs. xv 16 f.; xx 1 f. The title king of Aram was held by the rulers of Zobah in the 10 cent. (cp. 2 Sam. viii 3 f.; x 16; see further at no. **6** Hamath, Graffiti), and probably devolved on the dynasty of Damascus early in the following cent., when it took over Zobah's hegemony in the struggles of the Aramaean states with Israel. Later in the 9 and during the 8 cents. it signified a position of leadership in the defence of Syria against Assyrian expansion. Thus in 853 we find Barhadad's successor Hadadezer at the head of a confederacy of Syrian states (including

Israel by this time), which was worsted by Shalmaneser at the battle of Qarqar (*ANET*, 278 f.; *DOTT*, 46 f.). If this alliance was forged by Barhadad towards the end of his reign, we have a plausible explanation of his presence in the region of Aleppo around 860. The veneration by an Aramaean monarch of a Tyrian deity is not surprising when we recall events in contemporary Israel, where Ahab contracted a marriage with Jezebel and introduced the cult of the Tyrian Baal into his capital; 1 Kgs. xvi 31–2. The primary reason in both cases would be the fostering of commercial relations with the rich mercantile cities of the coast. No doubt this led in Damascus as in Israel to Canaanite religious practices becoming even more popular than usual, but it is unlikely that the official worship of Hadad or Yahweh was modified.

Language

The wording of the inscr. is paralleled in many Phoen. and Punic votive texts; e.g. Idalion (*CIS* i 90 = *KAI* no. 38); Carthage (*CIS* i 181, etc.); and particularly Malta (*CIS* i 122 = *KAI* no. 47). A Phoen. model was clearly being followed. It would, however, be unwise to deduce from this that the language was affected. The ז = [ḏ] in נזר (4; Phoen. נדר), the emph. ending in נצבא (1), and the word מרא, 'lord', which does not occur in Phoen. or Hebr., are sufficient to establish the dialect of this inscr. as Old Aramaic. Because it was found so far from Barhadad's home territory is no reason for not regarding it as representing the dialect of Damascus; he would hardly have employed an alien scribe to compose so personal a declaration of faith.

Bibliography

M. Dunand, 'Stèle araméenne dédiée à Melqart', *Bulletin du Musée de Beyrouth* 3 (1939), 65–76; see also 6 (1942–3), 41–5.
W. F. Albright, 'A votive stele erected by Ben-Hadad I of Damascus to the god Melcarth', *BASOR* 87 (1942), 23–9.
G. Levi della Vida, 'Some notes on the stele of Ben-Hadad', *BASOR* 90 (1943), 30–2 (with addendum by Albright).
H. L. Ginsberg, 'Psalms and inscriptions of petition and acknowledgement', *Louis Ginzberg Jubilee Volume* (New York, 1945), 159–71.
A. Herdner, 'Dédicace au dieu Melqart', *Syria* 25 (1946–8), 329–30.
EHO, 24.
A. Jepsen, 'Zur Melquart-Stele Barhadads', *AfO* 16 (1952–3), 315–17.
Garbini, 'Antico', 224 f.
Koopmans, *Chrest.* no. 4.
KAI no. 201.
Degen, *Grammatik*, 8 and index.
F. M. Cross, 'The stele dedicated to Melcarth by Ben-Hadad of Damascus', *BASOR* 205 (1972), 36–42.

Translations

ANET, 655; *DOTT*, 239 f.

Plates and figures

Dunand, loc. cit.; Albright, loc. cit.; Diringer, *Alphabet*, fig. 126; Driver, *Writing*, fig. 76; *ANEP*, no. 499; Birnbaum, *Scripts*, no. 010; *DOTT*, pl. XV; Cross, loc. cit.

1 נצבא'זי'שם ברה

2 דד'בר טב֯ר֯[מ]ן֯ ב֯ר֯'[חז]י֯ן֯

3 מלך ארם למראה'למלקר

4 ת'זי נזר לה֯ ושמע'לק֯ל

5 ה

2. Alternative reading דד'בר ע֯ז֯ר֯'ד֯מ֯ש֯ק֯י֯[א] ב֯[ר]

1. Statue which Barhadad,
2. son of Tobrimmon, son of Hezion,
3. king of Aram, raised for his lord Melcarth,
4, 5 to whom he had made a vow when he listened to his voice.

Alternative:

1. Statue which Barhadad,
2. son of Ezer, the Damascene, son of
3. the king of Aram, raised . . .

NOTES

1. **נצבא** = (nṣība'). **זי** = [d̲ī]; later **די** = [dī]; cp. Arab. [d̲ū], 'possessor of'. **שם** = [śām].
2. This is the crux of the inscr. I give in Fig. 1 (a) my adaptation of Albright's brilliant restoration (see 1 Kgs. xv 18), and in Fig. 1 (b) of Cross's more recent reading of the line; both should be checked against the photograph in *ANEP*. The whole second half is very faint, but Albright's reading can be traced except for the מ, where there seems to be a stroke leaning to the right, and the ח. Similarly, there are marks to fit in with Cross's reading except in the case of א and the final ר, where he overlooks a shape that may well be נ; and he has difficulty with the stroke ignored by Albright in reading מ, being uncertain whether to regard it as a score on the stone or part of ד. With the description 'the Damascene' cp. vol. I no. **16** Mesha 1. If the ד is omitted, recourse has to be made to the old and very dubious derivation of the name Damascus from Aram. די plus משק; cp. no. **14** Panammu 18, where the full word דמשק occurs; but in both these early texts (י)ז would be expected. There are also historical objections to Cross's restoration. The Barhadad, son of Ezer (עזר = [ʿd̲ar], '(my) help', a shorter form of Hadadezer), who Cross argues was regent like Jotham of Judah during his father's illness (2 Kgs. viii 7 f.; xv 5), is nowhere else heard of. Moreover, he assumes an equation between the Benhadad of the Elisha cycle and the Hadadezer of the Assyrian annals; but, though we

may think of a throne-name and a personal name, we have also to remember the character of the Elisha stories; historical accuracy is not their strength, and the name Benhadad, like so much else in them, could have been transferred from the Elijah cycle, which they frequently plagiarize. The historical objection against Albright's restoration is not so serious; in the past some scholars distinguished between the Benhadad of 1 Kgs. xv 18 and the one who was the enemy of Ahab (1 Kgs. xx); but if we follow him here, that is no longer possible, since epigraphically the inscr. can hardly be dated before Ahab's reign. To my mind, therefore, the simplest succession of kings of Damascus is a single Barhadad (not two), followed by Hadadezer (carelessly called Benhadad in the Bible), followed by the usurper Hazael; and on this historical ground I admit to preferring Albright's reading. טברמן = [ṭāb rammān], 'Good is Rimmon'; Hebr. [ṭōb rimmōn]. The deity's name means 'thunderer', and originates in Mesopotamia, the base RMN not being found in Syrian Sem.; it stands here for Hadad, with whom the Mesopotamian Rammānu was identified. חזין = [ḥadyān]; Hebr. [ḥa/ezyōn]; Arab. [ḥadwā], 'lop-eared'. If in spite of their attractiveness, we remain sceptical about these two restorations, we may with *KAI* (Fig. 1 (c)) read the sequence בר (Albright) or משק (Cross) as עבד, i.e. 'Barhadad, son of . . . , servant of . . . , king of Aram'. Barhadad then becomes merely the son of a high official in the employ of some unknown monarch, presumably from the region of Aleppo, who bore the title king of Aram between the rulers of Zobah and Damascus. (See now Addenda, p. 166.)

3. מראה = [mār'ēh]. מלקרת = Phoen. [milqart] from [milk qart], 'king of the city'; contrast Hebr. and Aram. [malk], [mlak]; [qiryā]; but Hebr. also has קרת = [qart] (Prov. viii 3, etc.). Melcarth was equated by the Greeks with Hercules.
4. נזר = [ndar]; later נדר; Hebr. נזר (Niph.); Arab. [nadara]. From a related base come Hebr. (Qal) and Phoen. נדר; Ugar. *ndr* may reflect either Proto-Sem. NḎR or NDR. לה = [lēh]. ושמע לקלה = [wašmaʿ lqālēh]; cp. כשמע קל (*CIS* i 90, 2 = *KAI* no. 38); Yehaumilk 8 (*KAI* no. 10). The use of ו for Phoen. כ (= [kī]) seems awkward, but cp. in Hebr. Isa. xxxix 1 with 2 Kgs. xx 12.

2. Damascus: Hazael — Fig. 6

The fragmentary ivory plaque was discovered in 1928 at Arslan Tash (the ancient Hadattu, near Edessa), and was probably carried there by Adadnirari III after his subjection of Damascus in 802 B.C.; *ANET*, 281 f.; *DOTT*, 51 f. It is made up of three small pieces, one containing the first three letters, the other two joining to give the longer stretch of text. Hazael usurped the throne of Damascus *c.* 842 B.C. (2 Kgs. viii 7 f.), and occupied it till nearly the end of the cent. The writing demands a date at the beginning of his reign. The plaque would be attached originally to a statue or painting or other artefact. In Hebr. cp. Nimrud (vol. I no. **6**).

The inscr. was published with plates in F. Thureau-Dangin and others, *Arslan Tash* (Paris, 1931), 135 f.; see also Dussaud's review in *Syria* 13 (1932), 388 f.; Dupont-Sommer, *Araméens*, 49, n. 22; Koopmans, *Chrest.* no. 5; *KAI* no. 232. Other pictures in Driver, *Writing*, fig. 74; Birnbaum, *Scripts*, no. 011.

..... זׄת . ח .... בר[.]עמא . למראן . חזׄאל . בשנת .....

This ...... has ...... son of Amma engraved for our lord Hazael in the year ......

NOTES

זת = [zāt], an archaic form of the fem. demonstrative pronoun, later זא = [zā] (no. **13** Hadad 19; no. **7** Sefire i A 35, etc.). The elision of ['] is not unexpected; cp. the equivalent Hebr. form [זאת = [zōt]), where it took place in the Proto-Hebr. stage prior to the shift [ā] to [ō]; the omission of the letter in the writing is, however, strange in so early a text. The following verb may have been חרש (cp. Hebr. and Phoen. [ḥārāš], 'engraver, artificer') or חקק (cp. Isa. xxii 16; Ezek. xxiii 14). Even if the first fragment is laid contiguous to the second, there is room for more than two letters, so prob. the personal name of the workman intervened. עמא = ['amma']; contracted from a name beginning with עם, 'the uncle (god)'; cp. Hammurabi; Hebr. עמרם; עמיאל, etc. In Hebr. the ending appears as א in the Samaria ostraca, later as ה = [ā]; thus אחא (vol. I no. **2** ostracon li); אלא (1 Kgs. iv 18); אבה (Cowley vi 16); אלה (1 Kgs. xvi 6). מראן = [mār'an]; this is the only example of the 1 plur. suffix in an Old Aram. text; the shorter form is general in Egyp. Aram. and the longer [nā] in biblical and the later Western dialects. בשנת was most likely followed by a numeral and the phrase 'of his reign'; cp. 2 Kgs. xxv 1; on the use of the constr. see the note to Samaria ostracon i (vol. I no. **2**). A more general reference as in no. **14** Panammu 1; Isa. vi 1 is, however, also possible.

3, 4. Damascus: Ein Gev and Dan

Inscr. no. **3** is written across the shoulder of a store jar discovered in 1961 during preliminary excavations at Ein Gev, an Israeli kibbutz on the eastern shore of the Sea of Galilee. Inscr. no. **4** is written round the base of a bowl, 10·5 cm. in diameter, which came to light in a fragmentary condition during the 1960s at the digging of a trench on Tell Dan, the former Tell el-Kadi and the site of the biblical Dan.

The scripts are early, probably belonging to the first half of the 9 cent.; if so, the utensils witness to the Aramaean occupation of north Israelite towns by Barhadad in the time of Baasha; 1 Kgs. xv 20; but not impossible is a date later in the cent. during Hazael's reign; see 2 Kgs. xiii 22 f.

The inscr. from Ein Gev was published by B. Mazar and others in *IEJ* 14 (1964), 27–9; for that from Dan see N. Avigad, *PEQ* 100 (1968), 42–4.

לשקיא No. **3**

לטב[ח]יא No. **4**

NOTES

The editors of no. **3** vocalized שקיא as a sing., i.e. [šāqya'], lit. 'cup-bearer', regarding it as a title of a high Aramaean official; they compared the Akkad.

Rabshakeh (2 Kgs. xviii 17 f.) and Hebr. משקה (Gen. xl 1; Neh. i 11). The plur. of the second text makes it likely, however, that it is also a plur., i.e. (šāqayya'], and that the purpose of the utensils was more humble. טבחיא = [ṭabbḥayya']; the ח is restored, a portion of the bowl being missing at that point. We may translate in the case of the jar 'for the use of the wine butlers', and in the case of the bowl 'for the use of the butchers or cooks'. Although in the Bible טבח is, like משקה, attested in a metaphorical sense of 'guardsman' (Gen. xxxvii 36; Dan. ii 14), the coincidence of utensil and trade in both inscrs. argues strongly in favour of the straightforward explanation.

5. Hamath: Zakir

Pl. I (A); Fig. 2 (B, C)

The stele, now in the Louvre, was discovered in four pieces in 1903, though the exact site, Afis, some 45 km. SW. of Aleppo, was not revealed until much later; see Dussaud in *Syria* 3 (1922), 175 f.; restored, it measures just over 2 m. high and 0·27–0·30 m. broad. The face (A) held a relief, most of which is missing, of the god mentioned in the first line of the inscr.; this begins under the relief and is continued on the right side (B), finishing with two lines on the left side (C).

Historical circumstances

Zakir, the king of Hamath who erected the stele, was a successor of the Irhuleni, who accompanied Hadadezer of Damascus at the battle of Qarqar. Irhuleni is a non-Semitic name, and Zakir's description of himself in A2 suggests he was an Aramaean usurper, who ousted an older neo-Hittite dynasty. The chief events which the inscr. celebrates are his accession to the throne of the neighbouring state of Luʿath, probably after conquest, and his victory over a coalition of sixteen (?) Syrian monarchs led by the king of Damascus. The latter is named as Barhadad (i.e. II), son of Hazael, who succeeded his father towards the end of the 9 cent. The territories of seven of the kings are not given; these may have been minor princes within Damascus's sphere of control, although they are mentioned at the end of the list, whereas Damascus comes first. The territories of nine kings are named, or were, since two are missing due to lacunas: one is Damascus; the other six all lay to the north of Hamath. The inscr. makes clear (3–4) that it was Zakir's acquisition of Luʿath that led to the confederacy being formed and to the siege of Hadrach, its capital; his ambition upset the balance of power among the Syrian states and they moved to redress it, as it happened, unsuccessfully. There is nothing to support the view sometimes held that Zakir, like several of the kings of Zenjirli, owed his position to Assyrian intervention, or was tempted in his isolation to seek help from that quarter. The most likely period for his rise to power is in fact the opening decades of the 8 cent., when the Assyrian armies, having devastated Damascus in a campaign in 802 (*ANET*, 281 f.; *DOTT*, 51), were fully engaged nearer home. Jehoash of Israel further to the south seems also to have taken advantage of Damascus's defeat to recover territories previously lost to it; see nos. **3** and **4** Ein Gev, Dan; 2 Kgs. xiii 25. If the short report in 2 Kgs. xiv 25 is to be accepted as it stands, his successor Jeroboam II felt strong enough to invade Damascus's domains, and even to extend his frontiers beyond them at the expense of Hamath. A suitable date for the siege of Hadrach would be late in Jehoash's reign or early in Jeroboam's, when Damascus had enjoyed a period of respite in which to recoup her forces after the Assyrian invasion, but before she collapsed again as Israel advanced northwards, i.e. during the decade 790–80 B.C. To allow for the building operations described in B, the making of the inscr. should be placed a few years later, i.e. 780–775. The stele is dedicated to the local god, and concludes with an execration against anyone tampering with it.

Writing

The style of writing does not contradict this date. The ח and כ connect the inscr. with the Kilamuwa (*KAI* nos. 24, 25) rather than the later Zenjirli inscrs. (below, nos. **13–17**), but they are paralleled at Sefire (nos. **7–9**), and the ז, looking like a European 'z', is not found elsewhere before the time of the Panammu and Barrakkab inscrs. This prevents us assigning it a date much before the second quarter of the 8 cent.; the Hadad and Sefire inscrs. belong to the middle of that cent., and both have the earlier ז with perpendicular middle bar. Words are divided by strokes, which can be restored in the few places where they have faded. There is one instance of an internal *mater lectionis*, the ו in שורא (A 17); cp. שר (10). The ו in the divine name אלור (A 1) and in מחנות (A 9) and the י in אית (B 5, etc.) are consonantal. See further on the writing Naveh, 'Script', 7 f.

Language

The phonological system and the system of endings in nouns place the language of the inscr. firmly among the Old Aram. dialects. Further than this, we have in phonology reduction of the diphthong [ay] in ענה (A 2) and in יענני (A 11). There is no such evidence of a change [aw] to [ō], but if it had occurred, the ו in המו (A 9) is possibly to be vocalized [ō] as in biblical Aram. The emph. ending is א in the inscr., but ה in a graffito (no. **6**, i), suggesting that a final ['] has lapsed. In grammar, the pronoun אל (A 9, etc.) is the same as at Zenjirli, though it also occurs once in the biblical dialect. The object marker is אית as in Phoen., but this form also appears at Sefire. The most interesting isogloss, however, is what seems to be a number of instances of Waw consecutive with the imperf. in A 11 f., a construction known elsewhere only from Hebr. and Moabite. I confess to some scepticism about this, however; there are several examples of imperfs. with past meaning in biblical Aram., which offer a way of explaining the feature within Aramaic. In the vocabulary there is one verb which is not certainly attested elsewhere (הגע, B 16; but see p. 157), and one noun (אשר, B 15 f.), where the required meaning is recorded only for Arabic. The use of אית in the description of the building operations (B 5 f.), but not in the previous historical section, provides a parallel in syntax with the Mesha stele (see vol. I 74).

Bibliography

H. Pognon, *Inscriptions sémitiques de la Syrie, de la Mésopotamie et de la région de Mossoul* (Paris, 1907–8), 156 f.

J. Halévy, 'Inscription de Zakir roi de Hamat', *Revue sémitique* 16 (1908), 243 f., 255 f., 357 f.

J. A. Montgomery, 'Some gleanings from Pognon's ZKR inscription', *Journal of Biblical Literature* 28 (1909), 57–70.

Lidzbarski, *Ephem.* III, 1 f.

C. C. Torrey, 'The Zakar and Kalamu inscriptions', *JAOS* 35 (1915–17), 353 f.

A 1 [נ]צבא׀זי׀שם׀זכ֯ר׀מלך [׀ח]מת׀ולעש׀לאלור [׀מראה׀]

2 א֯נה׀זכר׀מלך׀חמת׀ולעש׀אש׀ענה׀אנה׀ו[חצל]

3 [נ]י׀בעלשמין׀וקם׀עמי׀והמלכני׀בעלשמ[ין׀ב]

4 [ח]זר֯ך׀והוחד׀עלי׀ברהדד׀בר׀חז֯אל׀מלך׀ארם׀ש

5 [שת]׀עשר׀מלכן׀ברהדד׀ומחנתה׀וברגש׀ומחנתה׀ו[מ]

6 [לך׀] קוה׀ומחנתה׀ומלך׀עמק׀ומחנתה׀ומלך׀גרג[ם׀]

7 [ומח]נתה׀ומלך׀שמאל׀ומ[חנת]ה׀ומלך׀מלז֯׀[ומ]ח[נתה׀ומלך׀]

8 [---׀ומחנתה׀ומלך׀----׀ו]מ֯[ח]נ֯ת֯[ה׀] ו֯שבעת֯ [׀אחרן׀]

9 ה]מ֯ו׀ומחנות׀הם׀ושמו׀כל[׀]מלכיא[׀]אל׀מצר׀על׀חזר֯[ד׀]

10 ו֯הרמו׀שר׀מן׀שר׀חזרך׀והעמקו׀חרץ׀מן׀חר֯[צה׀]

11 ו֯אשא׀ידי׀אל׀בעלש[מי]ן׀ויענני׀בעלשמי[ן׀וימל]

12 [ל׀] בעלשמין׀אלי׀[ב]יד׀חזין׀וביד׀עדדן֯[׀ויאמר׀]

13 [לי׀] בעלשמין׀אל׀תזחל׀כ֯י֯[׀]אנה׀המל[כתך׀ואנה׀א]

14 [ק]ם׀עמך׀ואנה׀אחצלך׀מן׀כל׀[מלכיא׀אל׀זי׀]

W. F. Albright, 'Notes on early Hebrew and Aramaic epigraphy', *Journal of the Palestine Oriental Society* 6 (1926), 85 f.
M. Noth, 'Laʿasch und Hazrak', *ZDPV* 52 (1929), 124–41.
EHO, 24 f.
Garbini, 'Antico', 251 f.
Gevirtz, 'Curses', 144 f.
M. Liverani, 'Bar-Gush e Bar-Rakib', *RSO* 36 (1961), 185 f.
Koopmans, *Chrest.* no. 8.
KAI no. 202.
J. Friedrich, 'Zu des altaramäischen Stele des ZKR von Hamat', *AfO* 21 (1966), 83.
Rosenthal, *Handbook*, sect. I, 1.
Degen, *Grammatik*, 5–7 and index.

Translations

ANET, 655 f.; *DOTT*, 242 f.

Plates and figures

Pognon, loc. cit., pls. IX–X, XXXV–XXXVI; Diringer, *Alphabet*, fig. 126 (A); Birnbaum, *Scripts*, no. 015 (A); *KAI* Taf. XIII–XIV.

A 1. The stele, which Zakir, king of Hamath and Luʿath, set up for Ilwer, [his lord].
2. I am Zakir, king of Hamath and Luʿath. A pious man was I, and Baalshamayn [delivered]
3. me, and stood with me; and Baalshamayn made me king in
4. Hadrach. Then Barhadad son of Hazael, king of Aram, organized against me an alliance of
5. [six]teen kings—Barhadad and his army, Bargush and his army, the
6. [king] of Kue and his army, the king of Umq and his army, the king of Gurgum
7. and his army, the king of Sam'al and his army, the king of Melitene and his army, [the king
8. of . . . . . and his army, the king of . . . . . and his army], and seven [others]
9. together with their armies. All these kings laid siege to Hadrach;
10. they put up a rampart higher than the wall of Hadrach, and dug a trench deeper than its moat.
11. But I lifted up my hands to Baalshamayn, and Baalshamayn answered me, and Baalshamayn [spoke]
12. to me through seers and messengers; and Baalshamayn [said
13. to me], Fear not, because it was I who made you king, [and I
14. shall stand] with you, and I shall deliver you from all [these kings who]

15 מחאו' עליך' מצר' וי̊אמר' ל[י' בעלשמין -----']
16 כ̊ל' מלכיא' אל' זי' מחאו̊[' עליך' מצר'] . . . . . c. 9 . . . .
17 [--]'ושורא' זנה' ז[י' הרמו'] . . . .

B 1 [-----'] חז̊ר̊ך̊[']ק[----]
2 [-----']לרכב'[ו]לפרש'
3 [-----]מלכה' בגוה' אנ̊
4 [ה' בני]ת' חזרך' והוספ
5 [ת' לה]' אית' כל' מחגת[']
6 [חסני]א' ושמ̊תה' מל[כתי']
7 [ושמ]תה' אר̊[קי' ובנית']
8 [כל' ח]סניא' אל[']בכ̊ל' גב[ל]
9 [י' וב]נית[']בתי' אלהן' בכ[ל']
10 [ארק]י' ובנית' אית['---'ו]
11 [בנית'] א̊ית' אפ̊ש' ו[הושבת']
12 [אית' אלה]יא' בית[' אלור']
13 [באפש' ו]שמת' קדמ̊[' אל]
14 [ור'] נצבא' ז̊נה' וכ[תב]
15 [ת' ב]ה' אית[']אשר' ידי[']וכ
16 ל']מן' יהגע' אית' א[שר']
17 [ידי'] זכר' מלך' חמ[ת' ול]
18 ע̊ש' מן' נצבא' זנה[']ומ̊[ן']
19 [י]הגע' נצבא' זנה' מן' [ק]
20 [ד]ם' אלור̊' ויהנסנה' [מן']
21 [אש]רה' או' מן' ישלח[']ב[ר]
22 [ה'-----]ת̊ה . . . . c. 8 . . . .

15. have forced a siege upon you. Then [Baalshamayn] said to me, (Destroyed shall be)

16. all these kings who forced [a siege upon you] . . . .

17. . . . . . and this rampart which [they put up] (shall be cast down).

B 1. . . . . . Hadrach . . . . .

2. . . . . . for rider and horse

3. . . . . . its king in its midst. I

4. (then) [rebuilt] Hadrach, and I added

5. [to it] a whole circle of

6. [strongholds]; and I established it (once more) as my kingdom,

7. and established it as [my land. I built

8. all] these strongholds throughout my whole territory,

9. and I built temples for gods throughout my whole

10. [land]. Then I rebuilt . . . . . . [and

11. I rebuilt] Afis; and [I gave a resting-place to

12. the gods] in the temple of [Ilwer

13. in Afis]; and I have set up

14. this stele before [Ilwer], and [written]

15. thereon the story of my achievements.

16. Now, whoever effaces the story

17. [of the achievements] of Zakir, king of Hamath and

18. Luʿath, from this stele, and whoever

19. removes this stele from

20. Ilwer's [presence], and drags it away [from

21. its place], or whoever sends

22. [his son] . . . . . . ,

23 [יקתלו·בע]לשמין·ואל̊

24 [ור·ו---·] ושמש·ושהר[·]

25 [ו----]·ואל̊הי·שמי[ן·]

26 [ואלה]י·ארק·ובעל[·]ע

27 [---·אית·] אשא·ואית·[ב]

28 [רה·ואית·כל·] ש[ר]שה·

C 1 [---·יהוי·עד·על]

2 [ם·] שם[·]ז̊כר·ושם [·ביתה·]

NOTES

A 1. **נצבא** = [nṣība'] or with ['] suppressed (nṣībā]. **זכר**; traditionally the name has been vocalized as a passive partic. = [d̲kīr], but a commoner structure is a perf. [d̲kar] with a god's name omitted; cp. **חזאל** (4); **זכר** and **זכריה** (1 Chron. viii 31; ix 37). **חמת** = [ḥmāt]. **לעש** = [lū'at̲]; the vocalization depends on an identification with the Nukhashshe of the El Amarna letters and the *n-g-s* of Amenhotep III's list of Asiatic countries (*ANET*, 243). For the consonantal equations cp.

Egyp. *k-p-n* with **גבל** (Byblos); Akkad. *Gubli.*
Egyp. *g-d̲-t* with **עזה** (Gaza); Akkad. *Ḫazati.*
Egyp. *'-s-t-r-t* with **עשתרת** (Ashtoreth); Akkad.
Aštarti (cp. Ugar. *'t̲trt*, the goddess Astarte).

חמת and **לעש** are also named on ivories found at Nimrud, possibly carried there as booty after an Assyrian expedition to Syria (Millard, *Iraq* 24 (1962), 42). **אלור** = ['ilwēr], ['līwēr] or the like. A deity Ilumer, equated with Hadad, is known from Assyrian lists of gods, so the name like Rimmon (no. **1** Barhadad 2) is of Mesopotamian origin; for the consonantal equation cp. **שוש** = Akkad. *Šamaš-ai* on a cuneiform tablet with Aramaic endorsement (Delaporte, *Épigraphes araméens* (Paris 1912), no. 61). With the restoration in the lacuna cp. no. **1** Barhadad 3. Also possible (cp. vol. I no. **16** Mesha 3) is **באפש**; B 11.

2. **ענה** = ['nē]; prob. an adjective in the form of the passive partic. from 'NY = Proto-Sem. 'NW, lit. 'humble, poor, afflicted'; Hebr. **ענו**; **עני**; the plur. occurs in Dan. iv 24. Most commentators see an allusion to Zakir's previous status as an Aramaean in a country dominated by non-Semites, i.e. 'I was a man of humble origins, but Baalshamayn, etc.'. That Zakir was a Semitic usurper is, however, sufficiently hinted at by the absence of his father's name, and the reference of the next two lines is to his assumption of rule in Lu'ath, not in Hamath, where he was already king. The translation follows the frequent sense of 'pious' carried by Hebr. **ענו** and **עני** (e.g.

23. let Baalshamayn and Ilwer

24. and . . . . . and Shemesh and Sahar

25. and . . . . . and the gods of heaven

26. [and the gods] of earth and the Baal of

27. . . . . . [execute] the man and

28. [his son and his whole] stock.

C 1. [(But) for ever let]

2. the name of Zakir and the name [of his house endure].

Ps. cxlvii 6; Prov. iii 34); cp. the use of צדק in no. **14** Panammu 1, 19; no. **15** Barrakkab i 4. Less likely is a meaning 'oppressed, harassed'; one would expect a reason to be given why he felt so at this stage; cp. vol. I no. **16** Mesha 4–7. The same objection holds against a derivation from ʿNY = Proto-Sem. ʿNY, 'be busy, distracted, etc.'; cp. Syriac Luke x 40; i.e. 'I was a worried, anxious man when Baalshamayn, etc.'. The proposal to read a simple place-name (cp. Mesha 1–2) savours of surrender. There is room at the end of the line for three or four letters; a verbal perf. form has to be supplied; the most likely is חצל; see at 14 and note the same verbs in the context. But also possible are קראני = [qar'ánī]; לקחני; or even (omitting ל) שמע קלי; cp. Isa. xlviii 15; 2 Sam. vii 8; no. **1** Barhadad 4; no. **13** Hadad 14.

3. בעלשמין = [bʿēlšmayn]. At Byblos בעלשמם (*KAI* no. 4 Yehimilk 3) and among the Nabataeans and Palmyrenes בעלשמן was a name of the Semitic high god called El at Ugarit and in pre-Israelite Canaan. As is well known, El in his various local manifestations was fused with Yahweh in the later religion of Israel, and here the reference is therefore prob. to Hadad. This may have been the title which he was given among the Semitic inhabitants of Luʿath, and Zakir tactfully uses it in acknowledging divine assistance in obtaining the throne; Ilwer would then be the same deity's local name at Afis. Similar stelae may have been erected by Zakir to the local gods of Hadrach and the other place mentioned in B 10. קם עמי; no. **13** Hadad 2, 3; Ps. xciv 16. המלכני = [hamlkáni]; cp. no. **14** Panammu 7 (Pael). In the lacuna there is hardly room for על; for the verb with ב see Jerem. xxxvii 1.

4. חזרך = [ḥa̱drak] or [ḥa̱drēk]; the later Aram. form is חדרך = [ḥadrak], appearing in Zech. ix 1 (in pause) in conjunction with Damascus and Hamath. Several campaigns against a territory in northern Syria called Hatarikka are recorded for the second quarter of the 8 cent. in Assyrian eponym lists; *ARAB* II, 434 f.; the whole land of Luʿath, called in the

Assyrian manner after its capital city, is prob. meant. הוחד = [hawḥēd]; cp. Gen. xlix 6 (Qal). חזאל = [ḥzā'ēl], 'El has seen'. The king of Damascus at the time of the Assyrian invasion of 802 is called Mari' in Adadnirari III's annals. This must be either a title (מרא = [mari'/ē], 'lord of') or part of a longer name like מרא(י)הדד, 'Hadad is my lord', used as a throne-name by Hazael, who may still have been king (2 Kgs. xiii 22), or by Barhadad; for both this inscr. and the Bible (2 Kgs. xiii 24) make it clear that Barhadad was his father's immediate successor. If Barhadad was already king in 802, it is just possible that the inscr. should be dated a little before this (so Dupont-Sommer, *Araméens*, 47 f.), but only on the assumption that Zakir was a vassal of Adadnirari, and that the attack on Hadrach was an element in the defensive preparations of the other Syrian states prior to his expedition; and, as was pointed out in the introduction, there is no hint of such a situation in the inscr.

5. ששת עשר = [šiṯṯat 'śar]; later שתת עסר; the masc. was presumably שש = [šēṯ]; Ugar. *ṯṯ* = [ṯiṯṯu] from Proto-Sem. [šidṯu] with assimilation of the first and second consonants to the third; Arab. [sādisun], 'sixth', with assimilation of the third consonant to the first. There is room at the end of 4 for another letter, though no trace of one is visible; theoretically therefore שרין = [ṯrayn]; שלשת = [ṯlāṯat]; שבעת = [šib'at] and שמנת = [ṯmānat] also come into the reckoning, giving respectively twelve, thirteen, seventeen, and eighteen kings. See further at 8. ברגש = [bar gūš]; Akkad. *apil (al)Agusi*; not a personal name but a dynastic title of the king of Arpad, whose people called themselves בני גש and their territory בית גש; no. **7** Sefire i A 16; *KAI* no. 222 i B 3, 11; *KAI* no. 223 ii B 10; Akkad. *Bīt Gusi*, *Agusi*. This explains the omission of his territory, called Iahani in the Assyrian annals (*ANET* 276), and in the Sefire inscrs. simply Arpad. מחנתה = [maḥnātēh] or [maḥnūtēh]; the plur. is (maḥnwāt] (9); contrast Hebr. [maḥnē], masc., but plur. (maḥnōt].

6. קוה = [qwē]; 1 Kgs. x 28; a neo-Hittite state in the Cilician plain; the Karatepe inscrs. come from this region, so it was in the 8 cent. within a Phoen. rather than an Aramaean sphere of influence. עמק = ['umq], lit. 'valley, plain'; the area now known as El Amq, north of the bend in the Orontes river; the Assyrian name was Hattina. גרגם = [gurgūm]; no. **14** Panammu 15; a neo-Hittite state bordering Sam'al to the north.

7. שמאל = [śam'al], lit. 'the left, north'; no. **15** Barrakkab i 2; no. **16** ii 1; perhaps the present-day Zenjirli and therefore capital of the state of יאדי (no. **13** Hadad 1, etc.), or a Semitic name for the same territory. The Hadad inscr. is to be dated about a generation later than Zakir, so the young Panammu I or his father קרל will be the king mentioned here. מלז = [mlēḏ]; Akkad. *Melid*; the classical Melitene and modern Malatya, capital of a neo-Hittite state on the upper Euphrates, north of Commagene.

8. The restoration given for the lacuna beginning at the end of 7 fits the space neatly, and allows for two further place-names of three or four letters each. The feet of certain letters in the last word can be seen. If the rough progression from west to east is continued, we may think of the important neo-Hittite states of Commagene (Akkad. *Kummuḫi*) and Carchemish (*Gargamiš*). At the end of the line Dupont-Sommer restores מלכן, but אחרן (= ['uḥrīn] or the like) gives a better syntax; the usual Aram. for 'other' is ['uḥrān], which in the plur. would be too large for the space, but אחר occurs a few times in the Egyp. papyri (Cowley xv 32, 33; lxxxii 7).

The seven lesser kings could have included the rulers of some of the Phoen. city-states or princes from Ammon and further south, perhaps even Jehoash or the young Jeroboam of Israel; cp. the list of the twelve kings who fought at the battle of Qarqar. The lacuna is rather long, however, and other ways of filling it are possible. Thus, it is significant that to this point exactly seven kings have been mentioned, so the space could have contained some explanation of why the other five, six, nine, ten, or eleven kings (depending on our choice of numeral in 5) were unable to be present. Ignoring the doubtful ו before שבעת, and beginning a new sentence with the list of names, we could therefore supply, 'Barhadad and his army, etc., ... – only these kings came against me, in all seven kings together with their armies'. Against such a proposal, however, is the plainest reference of כל in 9 to the whole confederacy. Friedrich, in the latest treatment of the section, avoids this difficulty, reading שבעת עשר, both at the end of 4 and here, and filling out, '. . . and ten other kings; altogether they were seventeen together with their armies'. The foot of a letter is visible after ת at the end of 8, however, so ע would seem to be excluded.

9. המו = [himmō] or, if the diphthong [aw] had not reduced, so allowing ו to be used as a *mater lectionis* for a natural vowel [ō], [hốmū] or the like; cp. Arab. [humu]. מחנות׳הם = [maḥnwāthōm]; for the separate writing of the suffix see also no. **16** Barrakkab ii 7 and after a verb vol. I no. **16** Mesha 18; see also the note to no. **9** Sefire iii 2. מלכיא = [malkayya'/ā]. אל = ['ēl]; no. **13** Hadad 29; Ezra v 15 (Qere); contrast אלן in the Sefire (no. **7** i A 7, etc.) and later dialects. מצר = [mṣār]; Hebr. מצור (Mic. iv 14).

10. הרמו = [hrímū]. שר = [šūr]. העמקו = [haʿmḗqū]; cp. Hos. v 2 (reading שחת, 'pit'?). חרץ = [ḥrīṣ]; so Palest. Aram.

11. ואשא = [w'iśśa'/ā]. There are a few cases of so-called imperfs. with past meaning in biblical Aram.; יחיטו (Ezra iv 12); יהך (v 5); ידחלנני (Dan. iv 2); יתוב (iv 31). These along with the examples in this inscr. may be regarded as rare survivals in Aram. of the Proto-Sem. verbal theme [yaktub] with past meaning, which is found much more frequently in Hebr. and Moabite, although in these dialects it is restricted to the place immediately following ו in consecutive prose. The two south Canaanite dialects delimited the usage formally by retaining a full [wa] before it; this they achieved as in the case of the article [ha] by secondary gemination of the following consonant (or what comes to the same thing, by lengthening [a] before a pharyngal or laryngal). The biblical Aram. examples suggest that Aram. did not so confine its use (note simple [w] in Dan. iv 2), which may be a reason why it disappeared more quickly from its dialects. The same theme [yaktub] is, of course, found in all the Syrian Sem. dialects with a jussive meaning; it has a similar double semantic role in Ugar. See further on these matters Gibson, *Journal of Linguistics* 2 (1966), 48 f. ידי = [yday]; dual with suffix. ויענני = [wyiʿnḗnī] with lapsed diphthong; cp. תרקהם (no. **9** Sefire iii 6). וימלל = [waymallēl]; no. **9** Sefire iii 2.

12. אלי = ['lay]. ביד; Driver xiii 2; vol. I no. **12** Lachish ix 7. חזין = [ḥāzayn]; plur. עדדן = [ʿād(ᵉ)dīn]; cp. the name in 2 Chron. xxviii 9; Ugar. *ʿdd*, 'herald' (II AB vii 46). ויאמר = [wyi'mar].

13. תזחל; base ḎḤL, later DḤL; Hebr. ZḤL. כי; no. **9** Sefire iii 22 and Ahiqar, *passim*, though not elsewhere in Aram. המלכתך = [hamlaktāk].

14. אחצלך; the base occurs again in no. **21** Adon 7; it may come by metathesis

from חליץ, i.e. [’ḥaṣṣlāk], although only Hebr. (Piel) and Phoen. have the required meaning; Syriac Pael, ‘to despoil’. Note the omission of [inn] before the suffix; cp. יענני (11) and contrast יהנסנה (B 20). See further in the introduction to Sefire (grammar). The restoration at the end scarcely fills the space, but the parallel with 9 f., 16 demands it.

15. מחאו = [mḥá’ū], lit. ‘they beat’; no. **7** Sefire i A 42; cp. Syriac with [qrābā], ‘to conduct war’; Hebr. מחה is prob. not connected. עליך = [ʿlayk].

16–17. The brackets in the translation fill out the obvious sense, but the lacunas are too large for restoring exact wording. שורא; note the internal *mater lectionis*. זנה = [d̲nā]; later דנה.

B 1–3. These lines prob. contained a summary of Zakir's victory at Hadrach and his safe resumption of the throne of Luʿath. With the phrase in 2 cp. Exod. xv 21, i.e. רכב = [rākēb]; פרש = [pārāš]. Alternatively רכב = [rkēb], collect., ‘chariots’, and פרש is ‘cavalry’, but though it means ‘horseman’ as well as ‘horse’, the latter is never a collective in Hebr. מלכה = [malkah]. גוה = [gawwah].

4. בנית prob. = [bnayt]; later in biblical Aram. the diphthong is reduced in free forms but retained before suffixes. The meaning is prob. ‘rebuild’, as often in vol. I no. **16.** Mesha; on their way to besiege Hadrach, the allies doubtless laid waste much of Zakir's new kingdom. הוספת = [hawspēt]; cp. vol. I no. **16** Mesha 21, 29 (Qal).

5. אית = [’iyyāt]; cp. Phoen. אית; Arab. [’iyyā] (before suffixes); later Aram. [yāt]; contrast Hebr. [’ēt], [’ōt]; Phoen. את (Poenulus *yth*]; Zenjirli ות; Syriac (lwāt], ‘towards’. מחגת = [mḥūgat]; constr. sing.; contrast Hebr. מחוגה, ‘compass’ (Isa. xliv 13). With the emph. state cp. the use of the article in Exod. xvii 14 (‘in a book’), etc.; Zakir strengthens his defences against any future attack.

6. חסניא = [ḥusnayya’/ā]; so Palest. Aram.; cp. 8 and *KAI* no. 26 Karatepe i 13 f. (a different word). שמתה = [śāmtah]; cp. Ps. lxxxix 30. מלכתי = [malkūtī]; there may just be room for three letters.

7. ארקי = [’arġī]; later ארע = [’raʿ]; Hebr. ארץ.

8. אית could be restored instead of כל, though there is scarcely space.

9. בתי אלהן = [bātay ’lāhīn].

10. The lacuna prob. contained the name of some other place in Luʿath that suffered in the invasion.

11. אפש = [’āpēš]; the modern Arab. name is [’āfis]. הושבת; no. **13** Hadad 19; *KAI* no. 26 Karatepe ii 18; *CIS* i 3 = *KAI* no. 14 Eshmunazar 16.

12. For the omission of ב before בית in the constr. see vol. I no. **13** Tell Arad C 9; Gen. xxiv 23, etc.; also in Ugar. (Gordon, *Textbook* (1965), 95.)

13. קדם = [qdām]. שמת = [śāmit]; Ezra vi 12.

15. אשר ידי = [’t̲ar yday], lit. ‘the tradition of my hands’; Arab. [’at̲arun]; later Aram. אתר only with the meanings ‘trace’ or ‘place’. The word may occur in 21 with the latter meaning.

16. כל מן = [kul man]; so Nabat., Palest. Aram. With the imprecations in the following lines cp. no. **7** Sefire i C 17 f.; no. **8** ii C 1 f.; no. **18** Nerab i 5 f., etc. יהגע = [yihgaʿ]; Peal, possibly also in no. **36** Bahadirli 5. The derivations proposed, Haph. from GWʿ, ‘make to perish’ (this base does not occur in Aram.), or from NGʿ, ‘make to strike, fall’, carry no conviction.

20. יהנסנה = [yihnsinnēh]; only elsewhere in the Nerab inscrs.; perhaps connected with אנס, Palest. Aram., ‘to demolish, rob, compel’. The ending

[inn] is regular in later Aram. with suffixes to the imperf.; it is not used with יענני (A 11) or אחצלך (A 14). For the restoration see no. **18** Nerab. i 8.

21. ב could be the prepos. with יד omitted (2 Sam. vi 6); but cp. 27–8; no. **8** Sefire ii C 11 f. If the prepos. is read, the next line may contain a reference to the killing of Zakir and his house, but there is not much room.

23. יקתלו with ת as at Sefire; cp. no. **18** Nerab i 11; for another suitable verb see no. **7** Sefire i C 21; the form (lacking [n]) is jussive.

24. רשף is possible in the lacuna (no. **13** Hadad 2). שהר = [śhar], the Aramaean moon-god; Syriac (sahrā], 'moon'.

25. Restore perhaps עלין = [ʿilyān] (no. **7** Sefire i A 11); Hebr. [ʿilyōn]; Ps. ix 3, etc. שמין = [šmayn]; no. **7** Sefire i A 11; Deut. iv 26.

26. בעל; in this position perhaps a patron god of the royal family; cp. בעל ב(י)ת; *KAI* no. 24 Kilamuwa i 16; no. **14** Panammu 22; read ב for ע?

28. שרשה = [šuršēh] or [širšēh] (Syriac); no. **7** Sefire i C 24; Isa. xi 10.

C. For the restoration see *KAI* no. 26 Karatepe lion 1, 2; Ps. lxxii 17. יהוי = [yihway]; jussive; no. **7** Sefire i A 25. For עד with [ʿālam] see no. **9** Sefire iii 25; ל is also possible (Dan. ii 4, etc.). One is tempted to preface אפס, 'nevertheless', as in Karatepe lion 1, but this particle is only attested for Hebr. and Phoen.

6. Hamath: Graffiti

Fig. 7 (i)

Eleven inscribed bricks were unearthed in a Danish expedition to Hamath in 1932–8, and are dated archaeologically to the 9–8 cents. The longest inscr. (i below) has the name and title of a high official to the royal court; all the other bricks except one also contain personal names, presumably of lesser officials in charge of building operations; the exception has only the place-name Hamath written on it. Four of the bricks have before the personal name the word צבה, which some understand as a place-name, others as a title. Linguistically, the ה in מלכה (i) is significant, indicating a tendency for final ['] to lapse, at least in the emph. ending of nouns.

The inscrs. are published in H. Ingholt, *Rapport préliminaire . . . fouilles à Hama* (Copenhagen, 1940), 115 f., but with photographs of only five; these are given below. On the basis of the א in iii and iv (cp. no. **3** Ein Gev), the כ in i (cp. no. **1** Barhadad) and the צ in iii (cp. *CIS* i 144 = *KAI* no. 46 Nora), I am inclined to date them early rather than late in the 8 cent. The ח, ס, and ת seem much later, but are probably due to the influence of a developing cursive style, of which no pure examples are extant till the end of the cent.; see the introduction to no. **20** Ashur ostracon. See further Naveh, 'Script' 12.

אדנלרם . סכן̊ [. ב]ית . מלכה i

ללעבד̊בעלת ii

צבה אנן iii

iv אחמה

v חנן

NOTES

Most of the personal names are Semitic, including that of the high official in i, strongly suggesting that the majority of the population was Aramaean; a similar situation probably obtained in 8-cent. Zenjirli. אדנלרם = ['dān lū rām], 'the lord (god) is indeed exalted'; cp. in Hebr. אברם; אדנירם; and the shorter form אדרם = ['dōrām] (1 Kgs. iv 6; xii 18; 2 Sam. xx 24); with the particle cp. לו in Gen. xxx 34. ללעבדבעלת; the first ל is the prepos.; hardly 'belonging to', but perhaps 'authorized by' as in the case of the למלך stamps in Hebr. (vol. I 64 f.). The second ל seems to be the particle [lū] as in the previous name, though it stands rather awkwardly before a constr. relation. בעלת (with the [t] retained as in Phoen.) is doubtless the Canaanite mother-goddess Astarte. אנן is not obviously Semitic and may be Anatolian. אחמה = ['ḥimmēh], contracted from ['ḥī 'immēh], lit. 'brother of his mother', a strange structure, but not unparalleled; cp. the female name אחתבו (no. **23**, 2) and Akkad. *Aḫi-ummišu* (Tallqvist, *Names*, 18). חנן; cp. Hebr. [ḥanān] (1 Chron. xi 43); [ḥanūn] (2 Sam. x 1).

The title סכן is found in Ugar. (Gordon, *Textbook* (1965), text 113, 63), in the Canaanite of Tell el Amarna (*zu-ki-ni*; *EA* no. 256, 9), in Phoen. (*KAI* no. 1 Ahiram 2) and in Hebr. (Isa. xxii 15); in the last example it is followed by the phrase אשר על הבית; see further on this at Silwan 1 (vol. I no. **8**). Translate 'steward of the king's house', i.e. overseer of the royal property. There is an etymological connection with Akkad. *šaknu*, which, however, appears in Syrian Sem. as סגן when used in its technical Mesopotamian meaning of prefect or governor; Isa. xli 25; Dan. iii 2; Cowley viii 13.

צבה (iii) may preserve, as at a later date did the Assyrian province of Ṣubiti, the name of the powerful 10-cent.-Aramaean state of Zobah (2 Sam. viii 3, etc.), which disappeared as an independent entity after the rise of Damascus; it lay immediately south of Hamath; we may assume some part of it was taken over by Hamath at its collapse or was subsequently captured from Damascus. If this is so, the bricks inscribed צבה and that inscribed חמת could either have been manufactured in these places or belong to assignments for building-works there. Ingholt thinks rather of a title of Hittite or Phrygian origin, in which case the inscr. here reads 'the official 'NN', and is in line with that on i; the latter language comes into the reckoning, since two bricks in Phrygian script were unearthed in the excavations.

7–9. Arpad: Sefire i–iii Fig. 3 (i A 1–16); Pl. II (i A 20–42); Fig. 4 (iii)

Stelae i (no. **7**) and ii (no. **8**) were reconstructed from fragments acquired at Sefire in 1930 by a dealer from Aleppo; they have been housed in the national museum at Damascus since 1948. The precise site is uncertain; according to the first editor (Ronzevalle) it was 1·3 km. NE. of Sefire at the village now called Sūjīn, where an excavation was being conducted at the time. Stele iii (no. **9**) was known to Ronzevalle, but no publication was made until it came into the possession of the museum of Beirut in 1956. The three stelae together comprise the most substantial stretch of text in Syrian Sem. epigraphy.

Note: in the introduction and notes citations are sometimes made from portions not included in this textbook; references are given to *KAI* in these cases; the full text is also available in the edition of Fitzmyer (see bibliography below).

Writing and date

Stele i was carved in the shape of a truncated pyramid, the height being 1·31 m. The width of face A, on which the inscr. begins, varies from 0·52 m. at the top to 0·66 m. at the bottom, that of face B from 0·50 to 0·69 m. The left side C, on which the inscr. finishes, is 0·34 m. broad. The right side has been cut or broken off along with a section containing the ends of the lines on face A and the beginning of those on face B; it was prob. inscribed and came between A and B. Faces A and B were carved by the same mason, but side C shows a different hand; cp. א with higher cross-bars; the broader ה; ח with protruding sides; the sharper ל; ט with no projection of the middle line at the top. The lettering on face B is very faded. Stele ii was similar in shape and contents to i, but survives in a very imperfect condition, side C alone having a continuous text. The script has one or two letters peculiar to itself, notably ו and פ. Of stele iii only one face, prob. the reverse, has been recovered; it measures 0·82 m. in height, 1·25 m. in width. This stele shares the ו and ח of i A, B, but the pronounced curves on the downward strokes of כ and ת, which perhaps betray cursive influence, and the very short leg of ד show that it was carved by yet another mason.

The writing belongs to the mid 8 cent. B.C. but, due to the distribution of features among the four hands, an exact dating is difficult to arrive at. The parallels are early for the squatter ח of i A, B, and iii (no. **5** Zakir); the י with sharp bottom corner and the כ with the tittle dropped from the cross-bar (Zakir and *KAI* no. 25 Kilamuwa ii); the ד of iii and the ט of i A, B with the middle stroke projecting at the top (*KAI* no. 24 Kilamuwa i). The ח of i C and ii (no. **13** Hadad and no. **14** Panammu) points, however, in the opposite direction. I suggest a date for stelae i and iii around 760 B.C., and place stele ii a decade or so later, about the same time as the Hadad inscr. (q.v. no. **13** introduction); unless it were added many years later, i C prevents us from making this gap larger.

Scripta continua is the rule throughout, making in several difficult passages for divergence of opinion about where words should be divided; cp. no. **18** Nerab and in Hebr. the Ophel ostracon (vol. I no. **9**). Larger spaces are found now and again, particularly on stele iii, where I have counted 28 as against, for example, only 9 on face i A. Of these 28, 2 occur at the ends of lines (5, 15), 10 within words, and the other 16 between words; e.g. after הסכר (2); סחרתי (8); תפוה, פקדי, and עמא (13); רקה (18); שבת (25). That these 16 are statistically significant may be doubted, but it is interesting that of the 9 on i A all except 1 (after יגזר; 40) come inside a word.

Internal *matres lectionis* are found as follows: תואם (i A 34; a place-name); שעותא (i A 35; ?); יעורן (*KAI* no. 223 ii B 4; see note to i A 39); כים (iii 1; a loan-word ?); רוח (iii 2); ימות (iii 16); שיבת (iii 24). The inscr. shows a marked advance upon Zakir in this respect, although there are not so many as on Hadad and Panammu (see no. **13** introd.).

There are several mistakes, certain or probable, by the stone-cutters. The three at *KAI* no. 223 ii B 16 (יהונה; omission of נ); ii C 5 (אהבד; omission of א); and iii 3 (יסכר; omission of ה) are suggested by fuller forms in the immediate context. There are others at iii 13 (תפוה with פ for כ; איה for איתה) and iii 22 (מך for מנך). Add possibly the ה in דבהה (i A 31) as a case of dittography. A demonstrative pronoun should probably be inserted after קשתא (i A 38) and גבר שעותא (39). See also the notes to i A 5; i A 16; i A 24 (end); i C 8; iii 6. Cp. no. **13** Hadad, which has an equally larger number of errors.

Historical circumstances

Stelae i and ii record two treaties between Barga'yah, king of an unknown city or territory called KTK, and Matiʿel, king of Arpad. The first named seems on the surface to be the dominant partner, but there is nothing specific to suggest that the relationship was one of suzerain and vassal, no statement, for instance, that Matiʿel owed his throne to Barga'yah. For all we know, parallel stelae, in which the partners' names were reversed, had been set up in KTK. The contents can be briefly summarized as follows:

i A 1–7. The title, introducing the contracting parties. If, as proposed by Dupont-Sommer, the name Urartu is restored in the lacuna at the end of 4, KTK was a dependency or ally of this northern power, as was Arpad a member of a larger Aramaean confederacy referred to in 5–6.

i A 7–14. The list of gods who are called upon to witness the treaty. Barga'yah's gods come first, and are mostly, though not entirely, Babylonian.

i A 14–35. Curses against Matiʿel if he violates the treaty. The few legible lines of *KAI* no. 223 ii A contain similar curses.

i A 35– . Magical rites with wax models, to be made effective should Matiʿel break the treaty. This section was presumably continued on the lost left side, and the next begins there.

–i B 12 (*KAI* no. 222). The heading with the names of the contracting parties, including this time the gods of KTK and Arpad, is repeated, apparently to underline the sacred nature of the treaty. This section ends and the next begins in the large lacuna between 13 and 20.

i B 21–end (*KAI* no. 222). The stipulations of the treaty. This section is very poorly preserved, but fortunately the surviving face of stele iii is of an equivalent section, and gives a good idea of the kind of detailed demands made upon Matiʿel. The readable lines of *KAI* no. 223 ii B list a few similar clauses.

i C. A warning to Matiʿel's successors to observe the treaty. This section, with its different script, may have been written later. The parallel section in ii is also C.

From no. **5** Zakir A 5 (q.v.) we know that a former ruler of the kingdom of Bayt Gush, of which Arpad was the capital, had been involved in the coalition against Hamath in *c.* 780. He is mentioned second in the list of kings immediately after Barhadad of Damascus, which implies a position of some weight in the Syrian world. That this did not diminish in the next generation is shown by the long siege of three years it took before Tiglathpileser III captured and destroyed Arpad around 740; *ARAB* II, 436. Significantly, the immediate cause of Assyria's move westwards on that occasion was the arrival of Sardur III of Urartu at Arpad with an army; he was quickly defeated and forced to retreat to his own territory; ibid. I, 272 f. It was during this campaign that Tiglathpileser overcame the alliance of Syrian states led by Azariah of Judah, which was perhaps organized in response to treaties which some of them had with Urartu; see further at no. **13** Hadad 1. Such alliances formed an important element in Sardur's policy of active interference west of the Euphrates, which began in 749 with his collection of tribute from Melitene and Commagene and the capture of Aleppo. Previous to this Arpad had in 754 made submission to Assyria, a treaty being concluded between Ashurnirari V and Matiʿel; part of the Akkad. version survives, and is translated in *ANET*, 532 f. In the light of this historical background I am inclined to accept the restoration of Urartu in i A 4. I would place the treaty of stele i in the period before 754, regarding it as one among a number of diplomatic marriages arranged by Urartu between its dependent states and the various Aramaean kingdoms. If therefore Matiʿel was a vassal of anyone at this time, it was of the king of Urartu and not of the lesser king of KTK. Ashurnirari's invasion in 754 would put a temporary end to such arrangements, but they were likely to have been renegotiated soon after his return to Assyria, now being backed up by a physical Urartian presence in Syria. Stele ii probably belongs to this period, and represents a revision of the treaty with KTK drawn up in the interval before Tiglathpileser's accession.

Dupont-Sommer (see bibliography for references to authorities in the following paragraphs) connects stele iii with i and ii, restoring Barga'yah's name in the lacuna in 25; but the letter he reads as the final ה of the name is very unclear and looks more like ע. I prefer to regard this stele as part of a treaty concluded between Arpad and another Urartian vassal state, situated, as the references to תלאים in 23 f. suggest (see the note), east of the Euphrates near the source of the river Balih. I believe KTK, with its Babylonian or partly Babylonian pantheon, was a small state or the capital of a small state in the same general region, which had from earliest times been more directly influenced by Akkadian culture than the areas west of the Euphrates. At the same time, however, it is difficult to deny a link between the name KTK and the Kasku or Kaskaean people, who in the late 2 millennium B.C. lived in the extreme north of Asia Minor, caused constant trouble to the Hittite rulers, and after the empire's collapse moved south to occupy the Hittite heartland on the Halys river; for a full study of their history see von Schuler. The state the Kaskaeans established is referred to several times under the name (*uru*) or (*māt*) *Kasku/a* in the Assyrian annals, in Tiglathpileser III's reign as paying tribute along with Melitene and Tabal (*ANET*, 283; *DOTT*, 54) and in Sargon's reign in lists of his conquests along with Tabal and Cilicia (*ARAB* II, 41, 46, 51) or Tabal and Urartu (61). Dupont-Sommer was at first (*Araméens*, 59 f.) attracted to the equation of KTK with this Kaska, but later abandoned it. Von Schuler (op. cit., 65 f.) has more recently returned to it, but believes that the Phrygians (Akkad. *Mushki* or *Muski*) are meant and that KTK was used to describe them because at the time Kaska was under Phrygian overlordship. But these identifications can only be sustained if Barga'yah is taken to be an Aram. translation of an Anatolian title and not a personal name, and if similarly the names of Babylonian deities were employed to represent their equivalents in an Anatolian pantheon; I can think of no reason why the people of Arpad should so wish to obscure the identity of their ally and his gods. There is, however, one earlier allusion in the annals of Tiglathpileser I (1117–1078), which brings us nearer the Upper Mesopotamian area (*ARAB* I, 77); this shows the presence of marauding Kaskaeans in the region of Tur Abdin and it refers explicitly to the capture of some thousands of them and to their settling down. I therefore propose to locate the KTK of stelae i and ii here, astride the boundary between Assyrian territory and Urartu, and to regard it as a small client state of Urartu, whose king was an Aramaean but whose population included elements of Kaskaean extraction and which (or whose capital) in fact derived its name from these; for evidence of the penetration of Aramaeans into the same area see the introduction to no. **10** Tell Halaf. The name should be vocalized (ktak] or the like from an earlier [kṯak]; the Anatolian consonant, which was heard as [ṯ] by the Aramaeans, was heard as [š] in 2-millennium Mesopotamia and consequently by the 1-millennium Assyrians as [s].

The objections I have raised against Dupont-Sommer's earlier suggestion and von Schuler's theory also weaken Dupont-Sommer's subsequent attempt (1956, 38 f.; 1958, 22) to equate Barga'yah directly with Sardur III; he thinks Barga'yah was a Semitic title which Sardur used in his dealings with Aram, and KTK not a dependent state, but a town in actual Urartian territory; as far as we know, Urartu's gods were Hurrian in origin. They (or some of them) hold equally against attempts to locate KTK in central Syria (Alt, 237; Landsberger, 59), where as at Arpad the pantheon would be native Aramaean, or in Gurgum in northern Syria (so tentatively Fitzmyer, 1967, 132 f.), where on the evidence of the name Tarhulara borne by its king in Tiglathpileser's annals (*ANET* and *DOTT*, loc. cit.) it would at this period still be Hittite. Noth's equation (166 f.) between KTK and an obscure city called Kisik in southern Babylonia cannot be seriously entertained. More details about these theories, which seem to me to be outdated by von Schuler's book, may be found in Fitzmyer, op. cit. 127 f. See also, however, Degen (1967), who regards the question as still open.

Parallels with similar texts

There are frequent parallels in format and phraseology between the Sefire stelae and Hittite and Assyrian treaties of the late 2 and the 1 millennia B.C., and between all of these and a number of biblical passages in which the themes of covenant or of blessing and curse are prominent. Attention is drawn to the more relevant of these in the notes, ad locc.; see further the studies listed in the bibliography under Fensham ('Malediction'; 'Common trends'); Moran; McCarthy; Hillers; Fitzmyer (1967), 121 f. How the biblical parallels should be explained is a matter of strenuous argument among critics, but in my opinion much of it is misplaced. There was not necessarily any direct influence from Asia Minor or elsewhere upon those responsible for preserving Israel's traditions. It is much more likely that common formulas for the making of agreements were current throughout the ancient Near East, and that the kings of whose treaties we have knowledge and the biblical writers both drew upon these in their different ways and for their different purposes.

Language

The inscrs. are long enough to enable us to study the dialect in some depth. It seems to me to have fewer points of contact with the Canaanite dialects than no. **5** Zakir, and prob. did not differ to any great extent from that of Damascus which, due to the leading role played by its kings in the politics of Syria in the 8 and 7 cents., is the most likely candidate for ancestor of the later imperial dialect. Due to the paucity of texts from Damascus, it must therefore figure centrally in attempts to trace the origin and development of that dialect. See further in the introduction to no. **15** Barrakkab.

In *phonology*, there seems (excluding the special case of KTK above) to be a case of the shift [ṯ] to [t] in ירת (i C 24), the earliest recorded for an Aram. dialect; but another explanation of the ת can be found (see the note). If words are differently divided than in the transcription, there is a further example in i A 32 (q.v. note; בתן). The צ in חצר (i A 28) is anomalous, ק = [ġ] (Proto-Sem. [ḏ]) being expected. The occasional substitution of [b] for [p] is a feature shared with the inscrs. from Zenjirli; thus נבש (*passim*) and possibly חבזו (iii 24); see also the notes to i A 32 (בתן) and iii 2 (יבעה). There is in contrast with Zakir no evidence of the suppression of ['] in final position; thus א appears consistently as the emph. ending and ה as the fem. abs. In internal position ['] is suppressed in שאת (i A 21; q.v.) and in the negative ל (from לא), which is always joined to a following verb but, since these are special cases, prob. not elsewhere. On the א in נבא see the note to i A 8. Prosthetic ['] occurs in אשם (i C 25). Diphthongal reduction is evidenced by בניהם and בני (iii 18, 21) and frequently by forms from bases final weak; thus יתחזה (i A 28) and similar imperfs.; ארבה (i A 27) and similar nouns. The reduction in בניהם and בני may have to do with the conjunction of two syllables containing [ay], and need therefore yield only one historical spelling; עיניכם (i A 13). The nominal form צבי (i A 33) is another possible case, but elsewhere diphthongs should probably be vocalized as such where ו and י are written. On the readings תהוי (i A 25) and יהוה (*KAI* no. 223 ii A 4)—a jussive meaning is required for both—see the next paragraph. Metathesis of [t] and [š] occurs in ישתחט (i A 32), but not in יתשמע (i A 29).

In *grammar*, the fem. plur. participle ends in ן (abs.), but nouns and adjectives have ת as in the Canaanite and Zenjirli dialects; מהינקן (i A 21); לחית (i C 20; iii 2); מרמת (iii 22). There is a Peil verbal theme (imperf. [yuktab]) as well as a Hithpeel, both with passive meaning. Instead of the later Ittaphal, the dialect has a Huphal, formed as in biblical Aram.; יער (i A 39). This example shows elision of [h] in the imperf., a feature also found with the Hithpeel and Haphel, i.e. Ithpeel and Aphel. The 1 plur. ending in perfs. is ן as in Egyp. Aram. and Syriac against the [nā] of later western dialects. Imperfs. (Proto-Sem. [yaktubu]) and jussives (Proto-Sem. [yaktub]) are distinguished in the 3 and 2 masc. plur. of all verbs, and in the 3 masc. and fem. sing. of verbs final weak; thus ישחדן = [yišḥdūn] (iii 28) against יצרו = [yiṯṯárū] (i C 15); תפנו = [tipnaw] (iii 7); יבעה = [yibʿē] (iii 2) against תהרי = [tihray] (i A 21); cp. יתקרי (Dan. v 12). Occasionally an imperf. is used where a jussive is expected; e.g. ישלחן (i A 30); this would explain the form יהוה in *KAI* no. 223 ii A 4. The infin. of the Peal theme is attested both with and without a prefixed מ; שט (i A 24); שגב (*KAI* no. 222 i B 32); משלח (i B 34); so biblical Aram. with לבנא (Ezra v 3) but —מ elsewhere. Infins. of the derived themes end, as in later Aram., with ה = [ā]; constr. [ūt]; חזיה (i A 13; Pael); הלדת (ii C 2; Haph.). The dialect has also an infin. absolute, construed with a following verb as in Hebr.; the form is distinguished from that of the ordinary infin.; נכה (iii 12, 13; Peal); רקה (iii 6; Pael); הסכר (iii 2; Haph.). This feature may be regarded as a survival from the common Syrian Sem. stock of the 2 millennium B.C.; it is found in no. **20** Ashur ostracon 9, but not in later Aram. dialects. The 3 masc. plur. suffix with verbs is הם, joined to the verb; תהסכרהם (iii 2); תרקהם (iii 6); contrast vol. I no. **16** Mesha 18 and the later Aram. dialects, where this suffix is written separately. In later Aram. other suffixes with the imperf. are preceded by [inn]; in biblical Aram., where a jussive is distinguished, [inn] is omitted; thus ידחלנני (Dan. iv 2); יתננה (iv 14); יבהלך (iv 16). At Sefire, this system does not operate with 1 pers. suffixes, which are always ני; thus יסבני (*KAI* no. 222 i B 28; imperf.); תעשקני (iii 20; jussive). With 3 pers. suffixes it generally seems to work; thus יעברנה (iii 17; imperf.); תשריה (iii 18; jussive). The only exception I can find is תכוה (iii 13; correction), where the meaning is imperf. There is another possible case in *KAI* no. 223 ii B 16 (יהונה), but the form יהוננה in the same line suggests that it is a scribal error. Cp. no. **5** Zakir, where out of 3 examples one (a 3 pers. suffix) has [inn] (B 20), and two (a 1 pers. and a 2 pers.) lack it (A 11, 14). The object-marker is אית as at Hamath and in Phoen.

In *syntax*, the examples of *casus pendens* in ii C 1 f (see at 10) and iii 7, 19 are noteworthy; in the first it is linked to the main clause by ו. There is occasional confusion between sing. and plur. verbs and suffixes; see the notes at ii C 15 and iii 4, 6.

The *vocabulary* is almost entirely Aram.; the only words attested in Canaanite but not in other Aram. dialects are אדמה, 'ground' (i A 10; this may be a place-name); אש, 'fire' (i A 25, 35; masc. form); המן (i A 29); the bases MLL (i A 25) and MŠL (iii 9); the adverb שם (also in no. **13** Hadad 8); גבל (iii 23). The base LWD (i C 18, etc.) is not otherwise known. The preposition כים (iii 1) has to be illustrated from Akkad. The [t] in QTL is paralleled at Zenjirli; cp. Arab. and contrast Hebr. and later Aram. ([ṭ]). The intrusive ה in דבהה (i A 31) and כהסאי (iii 17) is peculiar; see the notes for possible explanations.

Bibliography

Primary and standard publications with plates and sketches:

S. Ronzevalle, 'Fragments d'inscriptions araméennes des environs d'Alep', *Mélanges de l'Université Saint Joseph* 15 (1930–1), 237–60 (i).

A. Dupont-Sommer and J. Starcky, 'Les inscriptions araméennes de Sfiré', *Mémoires présentées par divers savants à l'Académie des inscriptions et belles-lettres*, Tome XV (Paris, 1958), 197–351 (i and ii).

A. Dupont-Sommer and J. Starcky, 'Une inscription araméenne inédite de Sfiré', *Bulletin du Musée de Beyrouth* 13 (1956), 23–41 (iii).
(both cited below as Dupont-Sommer).

J. A. Fitzmyer, *The Aramaic Inscriptions of Sefîre* (Rome, 1967) (all; cited below as Fitzmyer).

Other studies:

R. Dussaud, 'Nouvelles inscriptions araméennes de Séfiré, près Alep', *CRAIBL*, 1931, 312–21.

H. Bauer, 'Ein aramäischer Staatsvertrag aus dem 8 Jh. v. Chr.', *AfO* 8 (1932–3), 1–16.

J. Friedrich and B. Landsberger, 'Zu der altaramäischen Stele von Sudschin', *ZA* 7 (1933), 313–18.

A. Alt, 'Die syrische Staatenwelt vor dem Einbruch der Assyrer', *ZDMG* 13 (1934), 233–58. Reprinted in *Kleine Schriften* (1959), III, 214 f.

EHO, 27 f. (on i).

Garbini, 'Antico', 264 f. (on i).

H. Donner, 'Zur Inschrift von Sūdschīn Aa 9', *AfO* 18 (1957–8), 390–2.

J. A. Fitzmyer, 'The Aramaic suzerainty treaty from Sefîre in the Museum of Beirut', *Catholic Biblical Quarterly* 20 (1958), 444–76 (on iii).

G. Garbini, 'Nuovo materiale per la grammatica del'aramaico antico', *RSO* 34 (1959), 41–54 (on iii).

F. Rosenthal, 'Notes on the third Aramaic inscription from Sefîre-Sûjîn', *BASOR* 158 (1960), 28–31.

J. A. Fitzmyer, 'The Aramaic inscriptions of Sefîre I and II', *JAOS* 81 (1961), 178–222.

G. Garbini, 'Sefīre I A, 28', *RSO* 36 (1961), 9–11.

Gevirtz, 'Curses', 144.

M. Noth, 'Die historische Hintergrund der Inschriften von Sefīre', *ZDPV* 77 (1961), 118–72.

F. C. Fensham, 'Malediction and benediction in ancient Near Eastern vassal-treaties and the Old Testament', *ZAW* 74 (1962), 1–9.

F. C. Fensham, 'Salt as curse in the Old Testament and the ancient Near East', *BA* 25 (1962), 48–50.

Koopmans, *Chrest.*, no. 10.

KAI nos. 222–4.

C. Brekelmans, 'Sefire I A 29–30', *VT* 13 (1963), 225–8.

F. C. Fensham, 'Common trends in curses of the Near Eastern treaties etc.', *ZAW* 75 (1963), 155–75.

F. C. Fensham, 'The wild ass in the Aramaic treaty between Bar-Ga'ayah and Mati'el', *JNES* 22 (1963), 185–6.

D. J. McCarthy, *Treaty and Covenant: A study in form in the ancient oriental documents and in the Old Testament* (Rome, 1963).

W. L. Moran, 'A note on the treaty terminology of the Sefîre stelas', *JNES* 22 (1963), 173–6.

D. R. Hillers, *Treaty Curses and the Old Testament Prophets* (Rome, 1964).

S. Segert, 'Zur Schrift und Orthographie der altaramäischen Stelen von Sfire', *Archiv Orientální* 32 (1964), 110–26.

J. C. Greenfield, 'Stylistic aspects of the Sefire treaty inscriptions', *Acta Orientalia* 29 (1965), 1–18.

E. von Schuler, *Die Kaškäer: Ein Beitrag zur Ethnographie des alten Kleinasiens* (Berlin, 1965).
J. C. Greenfield, 'Three notes on the Sefire inscription', *JSS* 11 (1966), 98–105.
R. Degen, 'Zur Schreibung des Kaška-Namens', *Welt des Orients* 4 (1967), 48–60.
Rosenthal, *Handbook*, sect. I, 2 (i A, C; iii).
Degen, *Grammatik*, 9–23 and index.
J. A. Fitzmyer, 'A further note on the Aramaic inscription Sefîre III 22', *JSS* 14 (1969), 197–200.

Translation

ANET, 659 f. (by Rosenthal; i A, C; ii C; iii).

Plates and figures

Primary publications; *KAI* Taf. XV–XXIII.

Note: In the transcriptions below, which have been made from the plates and figures (by Starcky) in Dupont-Sommer (1958, 1956), the faded and fragmentary portions i B and ii A and B are not included. Only in a few places do they offer additional unambiguous information on the content of the treaties or on features of the dialect, and these have already been mentioned in this introduction, or will be referred to in the notes.

No. 7

i A

1 ע֯די בר ג֯איה [מ]לך כתך עם מתעאל בר עתרסמך מלך֯
[ארפד וע]

2 [ד]י בני בר ג֯איה עם בני מתעאל ו֯עדי בני בני בר ג֯א[יה
ועקר]

3 ה עם עקר מתעאל בר עתרסמך מלך א֯רפד ועדי כתך
עם [עדי]

4 ארפד֯ ועדי בעלי כתך עם עדי֯ בעלי ארפד ועדי חב[ר
אררט]

5 ו֯ עם ארם כלה ועם מצר ועם בנ֯וה זי יסקן באשר֯[ה] ו֯[עם
מלכי]

6 כל עלי ארם ותחתה ועם כל עלל בית מלך וע֯[ם כל זי
נצבא ז]

7 נה שם ועדיא אלן זי֯ ג֯זר בר ג֯א[יה שם קדם - - - -]

8 ומלש וקדם מרדך וזרפנת וקדם נבא ות[שמת וקדם ארא ונש]

9 ך וקדם נרגל ולץ וקדם שמש ונר וקדם ס[ן ונכל - - - - - וק]

10 דם נכר וכדאה וקדם כל אלהי רחבה ואדמ[ה וקדם הדד זי ח]

11 לב וקדם ס֯בת וקדם אל ועלי֯ן וקדם שמי[ן וארק וקדם מצ]

12 ל֯ה ומעינן וקדם יום ולילה שהדן כל א[להי כתך ואלהי אר]

13 [פ]ד֯ פ֯קחו עיניכם לחזיה עדי בר גאי[ה עם מתעאל מלך]

14 [ארפד] ו֯הן ישקר מתעאל בר עתרסמך מל[ך ארפד לבר גאי]

15 [ה מלך כתך וה]ן י֯שקר עקר מתעאל [לעקר בר גאיה מלך

16 כתך והן ישקרן בני] גש כ - .... *c.* 19 letters missing ....

17–19 missing

20 .... *c.* 33 .... מ֯ן ימ .... *c.* 8 ....

21 .... *c.* 14 .... שאת ואל תהרי ושב֯[ע מהי]נ֯קן ימשח[ן
שדיהן ו]

i A

1. Treaty of Barga'yah, king of KTK, with Matiʿel, son of Attarsamak, king of [Arpad]; treaty
2. of the sons of Barga'yah with the sons of Matiʿel; treaty of the grandsons [and descendants] of Barga'yah
3. with the descendants of Matiʿel, son of Attarsamak, king of Arpad. Stipulations applying to KTK along with stipulations applying to
4. Arpad; stipulations applying to the citizens of KTK along with stipulations applying to the citizens of Arpad. Treaty of the confederacy of [Urartu]
5. with all Aram, with (the king of) Musr and with his sons who come after him, [with the kings of]
6. all upper and lower Aram, with all who pay court at the king's palace and with [all who] have set up [this stele]
7. and this treaty. This treaty, which Barga'yah has concluded, [he has set up in the presence of . . . . . .]
8. and MLŠ, in the presence of Marduk and Zarpanit, in the presence of Nabu and [Tashmet, in the presence of Irra and Nus]k,
9. in the presence of Nergal and Laṣ, in the presence of Shamash and Nur, in the presence of Sin [and Nikkal . . . . . .],
10. in the presence of NKR and KD'H, in the presence of all the gods of the open country and the cultivated ground, [in the presence of Hadad of]
11. Aleppo, in the presence of the Seven, in the presence of El and Elyon, in the presence of Heaven [and Earth, in the presence of Abyss]
12. and Springs, in the presence of Day and Night. Witnesses (be) all [you gods of KTK and all you gods of Arpad!]
13. Open your eyes to behold the treaty of Barga'yah [with Matiʿel, king of
14. Arpad]! If Matiʿel, son of Attarsamak, king of [Arpad] deals falsely [with Barga'yah,
15. king of KTK], or if the descendants of Matiʿel deal falsely [with the descendants of Barga'yah, king of
16. KTK, or if the Bene] Gush [deal falsely] . . . .

17–20 are missing or faded

21. . . . . . . (seven rams shall tup) a ewe, but let her not conceive; seven nurses shall anoint [their breasts, and]

22 [יה]י֯נקן עלים ואל ישבע ושבע ס֯סיה יהינקן על ואל יש[ב]ע֯ [ושבע]

23 שורה יהינקן עגל ואל ישבע ושבע שאן יהינקן אמר ו[אל יש]

24 בע ושבע בנ֯תה יהכן בשט לחם ואל יה֯רגן והן ישקר מתע֯[אל ול]

25 ברה ולעקרה תהוי֯ מלכתה כמלכת חל מלכת חלם זי ימל כאש [ויסך ה]

26 דד כל מה לחיה בארק ובשמין וכ֯ל מה֯ עמל ויסך על ארפד֯ [אבני ב]

27 רד ושבע שנ֯ן יאכל ארבה ושבע שנן תאכל תולעה ושבע [שנן יס]

28 ק תוי על א֯פי ארקה וא֯ל י֯פק חצר ולית֯חזה ירק ולי֯[תחזה]

29 אחוה֯ ואל יתשמע קל כ֯נר [ב]א֯רפד ובעמה֯ הן למרק וה֯[מן וזע]

30 קה֯ ויללה וישלח֯ן אלהן מנ֯ כל מה֯ אכל בארפד ובעמה֯ [יאכל פ]

31 ם חוה ופם עקרב ופם דבהה ופם נמ֯ר֯ה֯ וסס֯ וקמל וא֯[ל יתחזי]

32 עלה֯ קקבת֯ן י֯[ש]תחט לישמ֯ן אח֯וה֯ ותהוי ארפד תל ל[רבק ו- - -]

33 צבי ושע֯ל וארנב ושרן וצדה֯ ו֯- - ו֯עקה ואל תאמר קר֯[יתא זך ו]

34 מ֯דרא ומרבה ומזה ומ֯בלה ושרן ותואם וביתאל ובינן ו[- - - - וא]

35 רנה וחזז ואדם איך זי תקד֯ שעותא זא באש כן תקד ארפד ו[בנתה ר]

36 ב֯ת ויזרע בהן ה֯דד מלח ושחלין ואל תאמר גנ֯בא זנה ו[נבשא זא]

22. suckle a child, but let him not be satisfied; seven mares shall suckle a colt, but let it not be satisfied; [seven]

23. cows shall suckle a calf, but let it not be satisfied; seven sheep shall suckle a lamb, but [let it not be]

24. satisfied; his seven daughters shall go walking while the bread gets burnt, but let them show no concern! If Mati'el deals falsely (with Barga'yah or)

25. his son or his descendants, let his kingdom become as a kingdom of sand, a kingdom of dream(s) that fade away like fire; [let] Hadad [pour out]

26. all manner of evil in earth and heaven and all manner of trouble; let him pour out upon Arpad hail[stones];

27. seven years let the locust devour; seven years let the worm devour; seven [years] let blight [come up]

28. over the face of its land; let no grass sprout, nor let anything green be seen, nor

29. let its pasture be [seen]; let not the sound of the lyre be heard in Arpad and among its people, but (the sound) of affliction and [confusion and]

30. crying and lamentation; let the gods send all manner of devourer against Arpad and its people; [let the mouth]

31. of the snake [devour], and the mouth of the scorpion, and the mouth of the bear, and the mouth of the leopard, and the moth and the louse; [let not]

32. a leaf [appear]; lopped off, let it perish; its pasture shall not ripen, but let Arpad become a mound, [a home for . . . . . . and]

33. gazelle and fox and hare and wild cat and owl and . . . . . . and magpie; let not [that city] be spoken of, [nor]

34. MDR' nor MRBH nor MZH nor MBLH nor Sharun nor Tu'im nor Bethel nor BYNN nor . . . . . . [nor]

35. Arneh nor Hazaz nor 'DM! Just as this piece of wax is burned with fire, so shall Arpad and [her daughter-cities] be

36. utterly burned; let Hadad sow in them salt and cress; and let it not be spoken of! This bandit and [this life]

37 מתעאל ונב֯שה הא איכה֯ זי תקד שעות[א] זא באש כן יקד מ[תעאל בא]

38 ש ואיך זי תשבר קשתא וחציא אלן כן ישבר אנר֯ת והדד [קשת מתעאל]

39 [ו]קשת ר֯בוה ואיך זי יער גבר שעותא כן יער מתעא[ל ואיך ז]

40 [י] יגזר עגלא זנה כן יגזר מתעאל ויגזרן רבוה֯ ו[איך זי יע]

41 [רר ז]נ֯[ה] כ֯ן֯ י֯ער֯ר֯ן נשי מתעאל ונשי עקרה ונשי ר[בוה ואיך ז]

42 [י תקח גברת שעותא זא] וימחא על אפיה כן יק֯ח֯ן [נשי מתעאל ו]

i C

1 כה אמרן֯ [וכה כ]ת֯בן֯ מה

2 כתבת א[נה מתע]אל לזכ

3 רן לברי [ולבר] ברי ז

4 י יסקן ב[אשר]י לטבת֯

5 [א] יעבד[ו תחת] שמשא

6 [לב]י֯ת מ[לכתי ז]י כל'לח

7 [יה לתתעבד על] ב֯ית מ

8 [תעאל וברה ובר] ב֯רה ע[ד]

9 [עלם] .... *c.* 8 .... ו- [--]

10–13 missing

14 ..... *c.* 10 ..... מ---

15 י֯צרו אלהן מן יו

16 מה ומן ביתה ומן

17 ל֯יצר מלי ספרא זי בנצבא זנה

18 ו֯יאמר אהלד מן מלו

37. are Matiʿel and his life; just as this piece of wax is burned with fire, so shall [Matiʿel] be burned [with] fire.

38. Just as (this) bow and these arrows are broken, so shall Inurta and Hadad break [the bow of Matiʿel]

39. and the bow of his nobles. Just as (this) man of wax is blinded, so shall Matiʿel be blinded. [Just as]

40. this calf is cut up, so shall Matiʿel be cut up, and his nobles shall be cut up. [Just as]

41. this thing [is stripped naked], so shall the wives of Matiʿel be stripped naked, and the wives of his descendants, and the wives of [his] nobles. [Just as

42. this woman of wax is taken] and is struck on her face, so shall [the wives of Matiʿel] be taken [and]

. . . .

i C

1. Thus we have spoken [and thus] we have written. What
2. [I, Matiʿel,] have written will serve as a
3. reminder to my son and my [grand]son who
4. come [after] me.
5. Let their labour [beneath] the sun be
6. for the welfare of my [royal] house, so that no
7. evil [may be done against] the house of
8. [Matiʿel and his son and his grand]son for
9. [ever] . . . . . .

9–14 are missing or faded

(whoever keeps . . . . . .)

15. may the gods keep (him) all
16. his days and his house as long as it lasts! But whoever
17. does not keep the words of the inscription which is on this stele,
18. but says, I shall efface some of its words,

19 ה̊ או אהפך טבתא ואשם

20 [ל]לחית ביום זי יעב

21 [ד] כן יהפכו אלהן אש̊

22 [א ה]א וביתה וכל זי [ב]

23 ה̊ וישמו תחתיתה [ל]

24 [ע]ליתה ואל ירת ש[ר]

25 [ש]ה̊ אשם

NOTES

1. עדי; constr. plur.; the abs. is עדן, the emph. עדיא. There is an undoubted semantic link with Akkad. (*w*)*adū*, the plur. of which (*adē*) is used in identical contexts in vassal-treaties like those of Esarhaddon (*ANET*, 534 f.); *adē* is usually translated 'treaty', but the precise sense is 'terms' or 'stipulations' imposed by Esarhaddon on his subject princes; none of the clauses applies to the suzerain. This is generally true of עדי also; only in two cases (*KAI* no. 222 i B 24–5 = *KAI* no. 223 ii B 6–7; iii 19–20) does Barga'yah put himself under an obligation. The cognate Akkad. verb is *adū*, 'to decide, fix, appoint', which presumably comes through metathesis (WDʿ) from the Proto-Sem. base WʿD; Arab. 'promise, threaten'; III, 'appoint a time or place'; Hebr. and Aram. YʿD. It is not possible, however, to derive עדי from YʿD, since in Syrian Sem. only fem. nouns from Proto-Sem. bases beginning with [w] drop the first radical; thus e.g. Hebr. [ʿēṣā]; Aram. [ʿēṭā], 'counsel'. Etymologically, therefore, עדי should be connected with Hebr. [ʿēdōt), 'testimonies', in the Bible restricted to statutes of the divine law (Deut. iv 45; Ps. cxix 14; cxxxii 12), but perhaps having had a wider usage in the language in general; cp. the range of meaning of the verb ʿWD. We have, it would seem, a case of two words which are etymologically distinct, but whose semantic fields intersect in one particular context. Vocalize abs. [ʿēdīn]; constr. [ʿēday], with unchangeable first vowel. A masc. plur. form perhaps occurs in Num. xxiii 18, transferred into Hebr. from the Aram. tongue of Balaam; *NEB*, 'hear what I am charged to say'. See further on this difficult word J. A. Thompson, *JSS* 10 (1965), 222 f.; F. O. Carcia-Treto, *ZAW* 79 (1967), 13 f. גאיה = [ga'yā], 'majesty'; cp. Syriac [ga'yūtā]; Hebr. [ga'wā]. The structure of the name is not a common one, which is no doubt why some commentators argue that it is a title, but cp. Hebr. בן חיל (2 Chron. xvii 7). Since his father's name is not given, Barga'yah may have been a usurper or founder of a new dynasty like Zakir of Hamath and QRL of Zenjirli. מתעאל = [mtīʿ 'ēl], 'protégé of El'; the base occurs in South Arabian and in the Nabat. name מתיעאל (*Syria* 35 (1958), 238); the Akkad. form in the treaty of Ashurnirari is *ma-ti-'-AN*. עתרסמך = [ʿattar smak], 'Athtar has supported', with [ṯ] assimilated to [t]; like Moabite עשתר, Athtar is the male counterpart of the Canaanite goddess Astarte; cp. Ugar. *ʿṯtr* and *ʿṯtrt*; Phoen. and Hebr. עשתרת = [ʿaštart].

3. עקר = [ʿiqqār], lit. 'root'; with the meaning here cp. Hebr. [ʿēqr], Levit.

19. or, I shall change the good things and turn them
20. into evil, on a day when he does
21. so, may the gods overturn that man
22. and his house and all who are [in]
23. it, and make its lower part
24. its upper part; and may his stock inherit
25. no name!

xxv 47. The lacuna at the end of the line should on the pattern of 1, 2 contain five or six letters, but comparison with the following phrases only allows for the restoration of three letters. The repetition of עדי in these two phrases is significant; the literal meaning can only be 'regulations for KTK along with regulations for Arpad'. This shows that עדי may refer to a treaty between equals, a meaning not attested for Akkad. *adē*. In *KAI* no. 222 i B 5 עדי אלהי כתך will mean 'regulations imposed by the gods of KTK, etc.'.

4. בעלי; either 'citizens' (Josh. xxiv 11) or 'rulers, commanders, nobility' (Isa. xvi 8); if the first, understand 'property-owners, burgesses', since they are in *KAI* no. 222 i B 4–5 distinguished from עם, the populace in general; cp. the Hurrian Maryannu (see Wiseman in Winton Thomas (ed.), *Archaeology and Old Testament Study*, Oxford, 1967, 125 f.); no. **14** Panammu 10. חבר = [ḥbar] (Hos. vi 9) or [ḥbōr] (CD xii 8); cp. the use of the verb in Gen. xiv 3 (Qal); 2 Chron. xx 35 and Dan. xi 6 (Hithpa.) אררטו is the biblical Ararat. The reference is to a confederacy of smaller states allied or subject to Urartu, one of which was KTK. By this and presumably other similar treaties the Urartian league is brought into association with a wider Aramaean confederacy. The statement in Tiglathpileser's annals about Sardur joining Matiʿel in revolt makes it likely that Arpad was a prime mover in setting up the coalition, but it would be wrong to conclude that it exercised any hegemony over the other Aramaean states; the title 'king of Aram' was prob. still held by the rulers of Damascus (no. **1** Barhadad 3; no. **5** Zakir A 4). The locations listed in *KAI* no. 222 i B 8 f., which perhaps include יאדי and Damascus, will therefore refer to the boundaries of the whole Aramaean coalition, not of territory controlled by Matiʿel.

5. ארם כלה = ['ram kullēh]. מצר; no doubt the Muṣru mentioned after Kue among the allies of Hadadezer at the battle of Qarqar in 853 (*ANET*, 279; *DOTT*, 47); this suggests it was a neo-Hittite state adjacent to Cilicia. Since it is specifically mentioned, it seems not to have been included in Aram. This Anatolian country may originally have stood in the text of 1 Kgs. x 28; 2 Kgs. vii 6; the Hebr. now has מצרים, Egypt. The place-name is used for the king's, unless the word מלך has dropped out. בנוה = [bnawh]. יסקן = [yissqūn]; the base is SLQ. באשרה = [b'aṯrēh]; no. **13** Hadad 27. There is just room at the end for six letters.

6. עלי ארם = [ʿillāy 'rām], lit. 'the upper (part) of Aram'. תחתה = [taḥtēh] or more prob. [tḥōtēh]; cp. תחתכם (iii 7); the prepos. is used as a noun and

the suffix is apparently added to the sing. as in Phoen. (Friedrich, *Phön.-Pun. Grammatik*, 1951, 117) and against the practice in later Aram. and Hebr. The precise reference of the terms upper and lower is unknown; possibly it is to the northern states around Arpad and the southern around Damascus (cp. the usage of עליה and תחתיה in Egyp. Aram.; Cowley viii 4; xiii 13), although some, looking at the geography from an Assyrian vantage-point, understand it the other way round. עלל = [ʿālēl]; prob. constr. before בית, which explains the absence of a prepos.; cp. in Hebr. באי מועד (Lament. i 4) and with the nuance Jerem. vii 2. בית מלך; note the abs.; cp. Hebr. אהל מועד, 'the tent of meeting', always without the article; בית כלא (2 Kgs. xxv 27). The reference is prob. to neighbouring princelings subject to Matiʿel, perhaps the rulers of the territories mentioned in 34–5; it hardly implies that all the Aramaean nations acknowledged the sovereignty of Barga'yah. At the end there is space for about eleven letters. On the basis of i C 17 Dupont-Sommer restores: ונצבא עם ספרא זנה, 'the stele with this inscription he has set up, as well as this treaty'. The restoration in the text is more suitable, since it allows a new section to begin in the next line with the repetition of Barga'yah's name.

7. עדיא אלן = [ʿēdayya' 'illēn]. גזר; lit. 'cut, decreed'.

8. The names of Barga'yah's gods come first, Matiʿel's beginning at the end of 10 (Hadad). מלש perhaps = [mullēš]; see Friedrich and Landsberger (1933), 315, who compare the name *Ardi (il)Mullēšu* on a Babylonian tablet from the Persian period; he is otherwise unknown. If the two deities mentioned in i A 38 are the chief gods of the respective partners, we may restore אנרת in the previous lacuna. אנרת is a form of the name Ninurta, the son of Enlil and god of battle; it is paralleled on an Aram. or Ammonite seal found in Babylonia (see Avigad, *IEJ* 15, 1965, 224). In view of the pairing of male and female deities in the following lines, however, we should expect Ninurta to have been accompanied by his consort Gula (*ANET*, 533). The first two deities may therefore be indigenous gods of the Kaskaeans. Marduk, the deity of Babylon, with his consort Ṣarpanitu and Nabu, the god of writing, with his consort Tashmetu are found together in Ashurnirari's treaty. Note the ז in זרפנת, an unusual equivalent of Akkad. [ṣ] (Ṣarpanitu). The א in נבא is also strange; Akkad. Nabū; the usual Syrian Sem. spelling is נבו (Isa. xlvi 1). Could it reflect the base NB', with which the Akkad. verb *nabū*, 'to call, proclaim' is possibly connected? Irra or Girra (*ANET*, 533), the god of pestilence, and Nusku, the god of fire, also appear on Ashurnirari's treaty, as do the next pair (9), Nergal, the underworld god and his consort Laṣ.

9. In Ashurnirari's treaty Shamash (the Akkad. pronunciation) is accompanied by his consort Aya, presumably meant here by נר. Donner (1957–8) has collected cuneiform evidence to suggest that the Akkad. word *nūru*, 'light', which occurs frequently in epithets of gods like Shamash, Aya, and Nusku, could sometimes be used as an alternative name for them; the most instructive text is one in which *(il)Nūru* clearly stands for Nusku. Sin, the Mesopotamian moon-god, and his consort Ningal precede Shamash and Aya on Ashurnirari's treaty. Ningal appears in the contracted form Nikkal in no. **18** Nerab i 9, and this should prob. be restored here. The lacuna has room for about thirteen letters, so a third deity or an epithet qualifying Sin or Nikkal must be assumed.

10. The last pair of named deities in the first list is so far unidentified; they were possibly (like מלש, 8?) members of KTK's native pantheon. רחבה; a fem.

noun from the base RḤB, 'be wide'; cp. Job xxxviii 18. אדמה; cp. Gen. iv 2; 2 Sam. ix 10; this word is not otherwise attested outside Hebr. Alternatively, we may simply have two place-names; cp. אדם in 35; in that case, Matiʿel's deities begin here. Dussaud (1931), 321 mentions a place called Ruḥba on the Euphrates, the modern Medayin. There is not room for another noun or place-name at the beginning of the lacuna, although the restoration gives only eleven letters where twelve or thirteen are expected. Hadad, the chief Aramaean deity, is frequently associated with Aleppo in Assyrian texts.

11. סבת is clearly connected with Akkad. *Sibit ilāni*, 'the seven gods', in incantation texts an inclusive name for the demonic host, seven being used to suggest an uncertain but considerable number. The form Sibitti, qualified by the phrase *ilāni qardūti*, 'the warrior gods', appears in the treaty of Ashurnirari with Matiʿel, where as here it follows Hadad, and in the treaty of Esarhaddon with Baal, king of Tyre (*ANET*, 534). It is worth noting that in the latter text the phrase (*ilu*)*Sibitti ilāni qardūti* is construed with a sing. verb (*liškun*, 'may he cause'), an interesting example of what Johnson, *The One and the Many*, etc. (Cardiff, 1961), 26, calls 'fluidity of reference as between the one and the many'; cp. Hebr. אלהים, both 'God' and 'gods'; Deut. vii 16 ('for he (?) is a snare to you'); Gen. i 26, 27; Mark v 9. Mesopotamian influence on Canaanite and so on Hebrew demonology (to be distinguished from the worship of full Mesopotamian deities) is early and extensive; cp. the biblical Cherubim with Akkad. *kuribu*, 'tutelary spirit'; Hebr. [šēdīm] (plur. only, unless the sing. occurs in Job v 21) with Akkad. *šēdu*, 'demon'; לילית (Isa. xxxiv 14), con-connected in tradition with לילה, 'night', but doubtless in origin identical with the Mesopotamian storm-demon Lilitu. We have evidence in this and the treaty of Ashurnirari of a similar influence in the Aramaean area. עלין = [ʿilyān]. El Elyon (Gen. xiv 19) was the god of pre-Israelite Jerusalem, prob. a fusion of two distinct Canaanite deities; cp. עשתר כמש (vol. I no. **16** Mesha 17); this fusion of two gods may be regarded as a special application of Johnson's 'fluidity of reference'. Both names occur frequently as epithets or alternates of Yahweh, and once (Ps. lxxviii 35) the two come together. In the present context it seems they are distinct, but it is not impossible that one deity is meant; cp. the common juxtaposition in Ugar. of two names of one god by means of the copula; e.g. *kṯr wḫss*, the divine craftsman (IID v 23); in lines 25, 26 sing. verbs are used, but in lines 10 and 11 of the same tablet the two names occur separately. שמין = [šmayn]; ארק = ['raġ]; cp. Job xvi 19, and in a covenant context Deut. iv 26; xxx 19; and outside the Bible no. **5** Zakir B 25–6, and a Hittite–Hurrian treaty (*ANET*, 206), where in the Hittite section the winds and clouds and in the Hurrian section the mountains and rivers are also invoked as witnesses. In a treaty between the Hittite king and the king of Amurru (*ANET*, 205) the springs and the great sea are mentioned; cp. also רחבה and אדמה (10).

12. מצלה = [mṣūlā]; Ps. cvii 24; Job xli 23; cp. Isa. xliv 27, where the related word צולה is personified. מעינן = [maʿyānīn]; Ps. civ 10; the sing. may occur in vol. I no. **16** Mesha 23. לילה = [laylā] or possibly still [laylah]; on the ending see at Mesha 15. שהדן = [śāhdīn]; later סהד. The restoration is plausible; cp. no. **14** Panammu 22; a corner of the final ד in 13 can be seen. With 12, 13 cp. the similar phrases following the invocations in the two Hittite treaties mentioned in the previous note; cp. also Gen. xxxi 44 f.

13. פקחו = [pqáḥū]; imper.; cp. 2 Kgs. xix 16; Dan. ix 18; vol. I no. **12** Lachish iii 4 (הפקח). עיניכם = [ʿaynaykōm] or possibly [ʿēnaykōm]; cp. בניהם

(iii 18). לחזיה = [lḥazzāyā]; Pael as in no **19** Nerab ii 5 (partic.); elsewhere in Aram. the Peal is used, but if this is a Peal infin., the ה is not easy to account for; there is no evidence for an ending [ā] with the few Old Aram. examples of such a form.

14. ישקר. In the Bible this verb occurs twice in the Piel with ב in the sense 'be false to' a covenant (Ps. xliv 18; lxxxix 34), and once (Levit. xix 11) with ב in the sense 'deal falsely with' a person; it also occurs once in the Qal with ל in the latter sense (Gen. xxi 23; the context is an agreement between Abimelech of Gerar and Abraham); vocalize here therefore [yišqu/ōr]; cp. *KAI* no. 223 ii A 3; iii 4, etc. In Josh. xxiv 27 (the covenant at Shechem) the verb כחש (Piel) is used.

16. בני גש; cp. *KAI* no. 222 i B 3. Thereafter כתך with ל carelessly omitted?

21. For similar lists of curses see *ANET*, 206, 533 f.; for a case in which such curses were held to have been fulfilled see the statement in Ashurbanipal's annals, ibid. 300(a); in the Bible cp. particularly Deut. xxvii, xxviii; Levit. xxvi. שאת = [ṯāt] with suppressed ['], explaining the retention of [t]; Ugar. *ṯ'at*; Egyp. Aram. תאתא; the plur. שאן occurs in 23. Etymologically, it is difficult to connect this word with Arab. [šātun] and Hebr. שה = [śē], which does not have a fem. form. תהרי = [tihray]; jussive; apart from 1 Q ap Gn ii 1, 15 this verb is not found elsewhere in Aram. מהינקן = [mhaynqān] and יהינקן (22) = [yhaynqān]. שדיהן = [ṯdayhēn]; Hebr. שדים (dual); later Aram. תדיא; Arab. [ṯadyun] (sing.); cp. Hos. ix 14. For the use of משה see Amos vi 6.

22. עלים = [ʿlaym] (Syriac). ישבע = [yiśbaʿ]; later סבע. סוסיה = [sūsyā] with the [y] characteristic of Aram.; Hebr. סוסה; presumably collect. like שורה (= [ṯawrā]) in 23, since the other nouns in these lines are plur. על = [ʿīl] (Syriac).

23. שאן = [ṯ'īn]; plur. abs.; the gender is fem. (21), but the form is prob. masc., since elsewhere with nouns the fem. abs. ending is ת; לחית (i C 20); מרמת (iii 22). אמר = ['immar].

24. יהכן = [yhākān]; imperf. בנתה = [bnātēh]; the reading is uncertain, as is the interpretation of the whole phrase. Dupont-Sommer prefers בכתה and compares Syriac emph. [bakktā], 'hen'; thus, 'Seven hens shall go in search of food, but let them not kill (anything)'. This gives a domestic picture in keeping with the context, but the emph. form is unacceptable, as is the meaning 'search' for שט (= [šūṭ]; infin.); Hebr. and Palest. Aram. ŠWṬ, 'move about, rove; swim; row'; Arab. [sāṭa], 'whip (a beast); mix up (liquids, affairs)'; Akkad. *šâṭu*, 'drag'; Syriac only [šawṭā], 'whip'. Also difficult are the prepos. [b], and the verb הרג applied to hens, particularly when the sense 'slay, kill' is not attested elsewhere for Aram. (though it occurs in the Zenjirli dialect; no. **13** Hadad 33; no. **14** Panammu 3). Garbini, *AION* 17 (1967), 89 f. connects לחם with the base LḤM, 'to fight' (not found in Aram.), and proposes, 'His seven daughters shall go in search of war, but let them not slay (anyone)'. Beyond some vague remarks about a Tammuz liturgy, he is unable to be precise about the purpose of such a curse. In the translation שט is taken as the infin. of ŚWṬ; Syriac [sāṭ], 'burn, be consumed'; cp. Arab. [šāṭa], 'cook (meat); blast a plant (cold)'; Hebr. cognate שטה, 'swerve, fall away'. Jean-Hoftijzer, *Dictionnaire*, citing these verbs, suggests a meaning 'when food is lacking', illegitimately, I think. יהרגן = [yihrgān] or the like; imperf. for jussive? With the sense given here cp. Syriac, 'muse upon, apply one's mind to'; Arab. 'exert oneself'. With the thought cp. Levit. xxvi 26;

Isa. lvii 1; Jerem. xii 11. Hillers (1964), 71 f., explains יהרגן as Haph. from RGG (Syriac, 'desire, covet') and translates, 'May his seven daughters go looking for food, but not seduce (anyone)', i.e. times will be so bad that Matiʿel's daughters will be forced to turn to prostitution, but there will not be enough men to make it worth while; cp. 1 Sam. ii 5; Deut. xxviii 68; Isa. iv 1. Against this view is the fact that in Syriac the Aphel has the same intransitive meaning as the Peal. A final suggestion (with שט = [šūṭ]); 'His seven daughters shall go walking while the battle waxes and wanes, but let them show no concern!' At the end of the line the name ברגאיה has evidently dropped out through haplography of בר.

25. תהוי = [tihway]; jussive; cp. יהוה (*KAI* no. 223 ii A 4; imperf. for jussive). מלכת = [malkūt]. חל = [ḥāl]; cp. Matt. vii 26. חלם = [ḥlēm]; sing. ימל = [yimmal]; cp. Job xx 8 with xviii 16; xxiv 24; cp. also Ps. lxxiii 20. אש occurs again in 35; the later Aram. form is fem. Though the base MLL is only attested for Hebr. and is rare (cp., however, 'ML), this division of words, which follows Rosenthal in *ANET*, 659, is better in the context than Fitzmyer's חל מזי ימלך אשר, i.e. '(a kingdom) of sand, as long as Ashur rules'. He cites Dan. iv 23, but מן די there means 'after', 'from the time that', not 'as long as'; moreover the coalesceing of [n] in מזי is quite anomalous. Dupont-Sommer assumes dittography of nearly two words, and reads כמלכת חלם (לכת חלם) זי ימלך אשר, i.e. 'like a kingdom of dream(s), over which Ashur rules'. *KAI* keeps both חל and חלם; thus, 'like a kingdom of sand, a kingdom of dream(s), over which . . .'. None of them offers a satisfactory explanation of the allusion to Assyria, and the letter they identify as ר is extremely faded. I prefer to restore ו, which is in any case needed to preface the next portion. יסך = [yissu/ōk]; base NSK.

26. כל מה; 30; iii 16, 28; no. **15** Barrakkab i 15. לחיה = [laḥyā], passive partic. fem., here as a noun; C 6; no. **18** Nerab i 10; Cowley xxx 7. With the restoration at the end cp. Josh. x 11; Isa. xxx 30.

27. שנן = [šnīn]. יאכל = [yi'ku/ōl]. ארבה = ['arbē] or ['irbē]; [ē] from [ay]; Ugar. *'irby*. תולעה = [tawlʿā] (Syriac). For comparable biblical passages see Gen. xli 27 f.; Exod. x 5; Deut. xxviii 38 f.; Joel i 4; ii 25; Ps. cv 31–5; Jonah iv 7. יסק = [yissaq] from SLQ; also possible is יפק = [yippu/ōq] from NPQ (28).

28. תוי is unknown; 'blight' is a guess from the context; some have compared Hebr. תהו (Gen. i 2; Deut. xxxii 10), but the metaphorical uses of this word (Isa. xli 29; xlix 4; lix 4) link it with the notion of emptiness and thus unreality or worthlessness rather than of natural disaster. אפי = ['appay]; dual constr. ארקה = ['arġah]; less likely, the suffix could be masc. referring to Matiʿel. חצר = [ḥṣīr] with an anomalous consonantal change Proto.-Sem. [ḏ̣] to Aram. [ṣ] as in the Canaanite dialects; cp. Arab. [ḫaḍira]. The juxtaposition of Hebr. חציר with ירק and דשא in Isa. xv 6 and with דשא in Prov. xxvii 25 makes it difficult to deny that the same word occurs here. Palest. Aram. חצירא for חציר in Targum Ps. cxxix 6 is hardly supporting evidence for the change, since it is likely to be a Hebraism; see Degen, *Grammatik*, 37 and cp. צרי (no. **13** Hadad 30). ליתחזה = [lā yitḥzē]; there may be a nuance of purpose or consequence as in Hebr. in Levit. x 9; but cp. 1 Kgs. xx 8; Amos v 5, where ולא follows an initial אל in normal sequence. See further on this line Garbini (1961). ירק; there is a scratch following, which may be part of ה, i.e. [yarqah].

29. אחוה = [ʾaḥwah]; also in 32; cp. Palest. Aram. emph. [ʾaḥwā] in Targum Gen. xli 2 for Hebr. אחו = [ʾaḥū]. אחו may be an Egyptian loan-word meaning '(papyrus) reeds' or 'inundated, i.e. pasture-land', but it may be genuinely Sem. and be connected with Ugar. *ʾaḫ*, used of pasture-land by a river or lake side (IV AB ii 9, 12), and Akkad. *aḫu*, 'bank (of river or canal)'; see further Lambdin, *JAOS* 73 (1953) 146. יתשמע = [yitšmaʿ] without metathesis of [t] and [š]; contrast ישתחט (32). כנר = [kinnār]; Job xxx 31; Isa. xxiv 8; Ezek. xxvi 13. הן ל; so Rosenthal in *ANET*; later Aram. [ʾillā]; this usage is not found for אם לא in Hebr. The נ is doubtful, but it is a preferable reading to מ, i.e. המל (Dupont-Sommer), since this requires the clause to begin with ובעמה, 'but among its people (sc. let there be heard) the noise of affliction'; see 30, where בארפד and בעמה are linked together. המל; Arab. [hamala], 'shed tears (eye)'; Hebr. [hmullā], 'din, noise'. מרק; lit. 'sickness'; a noun from the base MRĠ; later Aram. MRʿ; Hebr. MRṢ; Arab. MRḌ; cp. Levit. xxvi 16. The word קל should perhaps be understood before this and the following nouns. At the end Brekelmans (1963) restores המון צעקה, 'the noise of crying'; but the ו is unacceptable as a vowel letter. המן = [hmān]; Isa. xiii 4; the word is not found in any other Aram. dialect. זעקה = [zaʿqā] or the like; the base with [z] is more common in later Aram. than that with [ṣ]; cp. Isa. lxv 19. The final letter of this word is read by Dupont-Sommer as ח, the right bar being more perpendicular than is usual in the case of ה; but cp. the example in עלה (32).

30. יללה = [yil(ᵉ)lā]; emph. (ylaltā]; Isa. xv 8; Zeph. i 10. ישלחן = [yišlḥūn]; imperf., perhaps for jussive, which properly lacks the [n]; i C 15. Note the indefinite 'gods'; does this mean 'God' like אלהים in Hebr.? מן כל; for analogous constructions in Hebr. see Levit. v 24; xi 32. אכל; Mal. iii 11. פם = [pum].

31. Cp. with this line Jerem. viii 17; Deut. viii 15; 1 Kgs. xii 11; Lament. iii 10; Hos. xiii 7, 8; Isa. li 8; Targum Exod. viii 12. חוה = [ḥwē] with reduced diphthong; the later Aram. emph. form is [ḥiwyā]. עקרב = [ʿaqrab]; emph. [ʿaqrabbā]. דבהה = [dubhā]?; fem.; cp. later Aram. masc. emph. [dubbā], used like Hebr. [dōb] for both male and female. In view of the anomalous form Dupont-Sommer assumes a scribal error for דברה = [dibbōrā], 'bee'; Isa. vii 18; but could we not have simple dittography of ה? סס = [sās]. קמל; Arab. [qamlun]; later Aram. by metathesis [qalmtā]; Syriac [qalmā]. The filling of the lacuna at the end is dependent on the difficult first half of 32. Thus Dupont-Sommer . . . . . . ואף יפלן עלה קקבתן ישתחט לישמן אחוה i.e. 'and moreover, let partridges fall upon it; let its vegetation be ravaged (and turned) into a desert'. יפלן = [yipplūn]. עלה = [ʿlēh] with reduced diphthong, very unlikely in view of עליה (iii 9), 'concerning it (fem.)'; cp. אפיה, 'her face' (i A 42). קקבתן he takes as a plur. and compares Syriac [qaqbānā]; Akkad. *qaqabānu*; but he offers no explanation of the extra ת. ישתחט; (H)ithpeel; so Palest. Aram.; see further on this base and the related ŠḤT at no. **13** Hadad 27. ישמן; Hebr. [yšīmōn]; Deut. xxxii 10; but whether the base of this word is Proto-Sem. YŠM or WṮM (cp. Arab, [waṯima]), it does not occur elsewhere in Aram. Fitzmyer, noting the absence of פם before סס, suggests . . . . . . וסס וקמל וא - - יהוו עלה קק בתן . . . . . ., i.e. 'And as for the moth and the louse and the . . . . . ., let them become to it a serpent's throat'. יהוו = [yihwaw]; jussive. קק = [qōġ]; Palest. Aram. [qōʿā]. בתן = [btan]; Palest.

Aram. [pitnā]; Syriac (patnā]; Hebr. [patn]; Ugar. *bṯn*; Akkad. *bašmu*. The forms in Ugar. and Akkad. show that the middle consonant derives from Proto-Sem. [ṯ], giving for this dialect a further early instance of the shift [ṯ] to [t], and for Hebr. an anomalous instance of the same shift; see Garbini, *Rivista Biblica* 6 (1958), 263 f. The change [b] to [p] in the later Syrian Sem. forms is analogous to that of [p] to [b], which is attested for the Zenjirli dialect as well as the Arpad. Although Fitzmyer cites an interesting parallel from the Talmud (Berakot 49a), in which an opponent's throat (קועיא) is compared to a snake's (חוויא), his interpretation is far-fetched, and involves a peculiar syntax. The arrangement in the text, which largely follows Rosenthal's in *ANET*, seems to me preferable to either Dupont-Sommer's or Fitzmyer's. עלה = [ʿlē] with reduced diphthong as in חוה (31); the emph. form in Palest. Aram. is [ʿalyā]; cp. Levit. xxvi 36; Isa. i 30; Jerem. viii 13. קקבתן is an adjective with the ending [tān] formed from the base QĠB; cp. Hebr. עקלתון, 'crooked, writhing' (Isa. xxvii 1); Arab. [qaḍaba], 'cut off (branches), prune (vines)'. לישמן = [lā yišman]; imperf.; the meaning 'ripen' is common for this base in later Aram.; Hebr. only 'to be fat'.

32. רבק = [rbāġ] or [rbēġ]; Syriac [rbāʿā], 'sheepfold, stable'; Hebr. [rēbṣ]; Isa. lxv 10. The restoration is Dupont-Sommer's; alternatively an extra animal's name could be inserted, but normal usage would then demand the repetition of ל before the other names. After רבק Dupont-Sommer suggests צי = [ṣī], a desert animal; Isa. xiii 21; *NEB* 'marmot'. With this and the following line cp. also Isa. xxxiv 11 f.; Lament. v 18; Zeph. ii 13 f.

33. צבי = [ṭbay]; later Aram. emph. [ṭabyā]; Hebr. [ṣbī]; Arab. [ẓabyun]. Note also that the diphthong has not been reduced, unless the spelling is historical. שעל = [ṯʿēl]; so (with [t]) Syriac; Hebr. [šūʿāl]; Arab. [ṯuʿālun]. שרן; Akkad. *šurānu*; alternatively read שרם, 'wild ass'; Akkad. *sirrimu*; so Fensham, 'Wild ass' (1963); this word appears along with 'gazelle' in the treaties of Esarhaddon (*ANET*, 538); Isa. xxxii 14 (פרא); see also Greenfield (1966). צדה = [ṣādē]; later Aram. [ṣādyā]; Arab. [ṣadā]. עקה; Arab. [ʿaqʿaqun]. תאמר = [tuʾmar]; Peil (passive) imperf. קריתא זך = [qirytaʾ ḏāk]; fem. emph.; Ezra iv 13 (דך); also possible is הא = [hiʾ]; see C 22.

34. The place-names may be of towns in Arpad's territory or of small principalities subject to Matiʿel (or a mixture of both); see the note to 6 above. With מרבה and ביתאל cp. the biblical Meribah and Bethel. שרן is perhaps the Akkad. (*uru*)*Saruna*, mentioned in an inscr. of Tiglathpileser III as belonging to Bit Adini; it has been identified with the modern Sārīn, about 50 km. NE. of Arpad; *ARAB* I, 294. תואם may be the (*uru*)*Tuʾimmi* of the same annals; ibid. 276; the ו seems to be an internal *mater lectionis*.

35. ארנה may be the present Erin, about 20 km. SW. of Arpad, or the (*uru*)-*Ḫaurāni* of Tiglathpileser's annals, the modern Ḥawart an-Nahr, about 14 km. ENE. of Arpad; see Dussaud, *Topographie historique de la Syrie* (1927), 468, and Noth (1961), 137. חזז has been identified with Akkad. (*uru*)*Ḫazazu* and modern Aʿzaz, 13 km. NNW. of Arpad; *ARAB* I, 294. אדם; see at 10. The new set of maledictions which begin at this point were evidently accompanied by magical rites designed to render them more efficacious; similar ceremonies are described in the treaty of Ashurnirari with Matiʿel (*ANET*, 532) and in those of Esarhaddon (ibid. 539 f.); cp. also the Hittite rituals for the taking of a military oath (ibid. 353). No such rites are found in the Bible, but note the formula used in the ceremony of ordeal in Num. v 19, 22; cp. also Jerem. xxxiv 18 (see further in the note to 40). איך זי = [ayk ḏī]; a fuller

form איכה appears in 37; in the later dialects this means 'where?' תקד = [tiqqad]; Peal from YQD (intrans.). שעותא = [šʿawta'] or with internal *mater lectionis* [šʿūta']; fem. emph.; Syriac [šʿōtā]; Palest. Aram. [šʿūtā]. For a discussion of the use of such wax figurines in magic rituals see Picard, *Revue archéologique* (1961), II, 85 f. בנתה = [bnātah]; Num. xxi 25, etc. רבת = [ribbat] (Syriac); cp. Hebr. [rabbat]; Ps. lxv 10. The restoration is Dupont-Sommer's, though in spite of the absence of the emph. ending he takes רבת as an adjective.

36. בהן = [bhēn]; fem. מלח; Judg. ix 45; Deut. xxix 22; see further Fensham, 'Salt' (1962). שחלין = [t̲iḥlayn]; plur. of a noun ending in [ē] from [ay]; Mishnaic Hebr. [šḥalīm]; later Aram. [taḥlē]. In spite of the [s], Akkad. *saḫlē*, 'weeds', may be related, this word being used along with salt and the verb 'to sow' in the annals of Ashurbanipal; the country suffering is Elam; *ARAB* II, 310. Such a meaning would certainly be more suitable in the context than the garden or watercress of the later Aram. and Hebr. texts. גנבא = [gannāba']; presumably a derogatory title given to the wax model, which Matiʿel will merit if he breaks the treaty.

38. תשבר = [tušbar]. The demonstrative זא seems to have been omitted after קשתא. חציא = [ḥiṭṭayya']; Egyp. Aram. חטא; Arab. (from a related ḤẒW) [ḥuẓwatun]. ישבר; Peal; Hos. i 5; Jerem. xlix 35. אנרת; see at 8 above.

39. רבוה = [rabbawh]. יער; a difficult form, since the cognate base (ʿWR) in Hebr. and later Aram. retains consonantal [w], and is not found in the Qal or Peal. It is probably (H)uphal imperf. (Syriac has an Aphel). No imperfs. of the Huphal occur in biblical or Egyp. Aram.; and in medially weak verbs a perf. is attested only for the biblical dialect; הקימת (Dan. vii 4) and הקמת (vii 5), both vocalized by the Massoretes (h(°)qīmat] from [huqīmat]. Rosenthal, *Grammar*, 50 suggests that הקמת = [h(°)qắmat] is the original form, and that this should be read in vs. 4, and the form הקימת transferred to vs. 5 and treated as Haph., i.e. [h(ᵃ)qīmat]. Vocalize therefore [yʿār] from an original [yhuʿāra]. Contrast the Canaanite formation יומת = [yūmat]; no. **13** Hadad 26; Levit. xx 2, etc. A form written with ו occurs in *KAI* no. 223 ii B 4 (יעורן), but this seems to be from ʿWR, 'to awake, be watchful'; it is prob. Peal, i.e. [yʿūrūn], with internal *mater lectionis*; see Fitzmyer, ad loc. גבר; again the demonstrative is lacking.

40. In Gen. xv 9 f. a heifer (עגלה) and in Jerem. xxxiv 18 a calf (עגל) are cut in two as part of a ceremony of covenant-making, but in neither passage is the verb גזר used. We should therefore prob. resist seeing a parallel here, where the calf seems to be another wax model and not a real animal.

41. Dupont-Sommer proposes: . . . . . . איך זי יעבד זנה כן יעבדן, i.e. 'just as this serves as slave, so shall the wives of Matiʿel serve as slaves'; but it is difficult to see what action could accompany such a malediction. The text given reads ד as ר (cp. the example in תשבר, 38), i.e. [yuʿr(ᵉ)rān] or the like; Peil imperf. from ʿRR; Hebr. Qal and Poel; cp. Lament. iv. 21; Isa. xxxii 11. Hillers (1964), 58 f. reads תערר in the lacuna and זניה instead of זנה, i.e. [zanāyā], 'a harlot' (so Syriac); he cites Hos. ii 3–5; Nah. iii 5; Jerem. xiii 26; Ezek. xvi 37–8. But there is very little room for this restoration, and in any case we should have expected 'this harlot' (though note the omission of the demonstrative in 38, 39).

42. The restoration is suggested by the fem. suffix with אפיה (= ['appayh]). תקח = [tuqqaḥ]; the similar form in Hebr. is likewise a survival of a passive Qal, not a Hophal. גברת = [gibrat] or [gbīrat]; cp. vol. I no. **16** Mesha 16.

ימחא = [yimḥa']; impersonal subject; see at no. 5 Zakir A 15. The sentence was probably continued on the lost narrow side of the stele (B properly being the third side and C the fourth).

i C

1. כה = [kā], apparently referring against the normal usage of Hebr. [kō] to what has gone before; כן has this reference in Hebr. and below 21, though not in A 35 f. אמרן = ['marn] as in Egyp. Aram. and Syriac; the later western dialects have [nā]; the נ is not certain, but it is much clearer in כתבן.
2. כתבת = [kitbēt]. זכרן = [d̲ukrān]; cp. Exod. xvii 14; Josh. iv 7.
4. באשרי; i A 5. טבתא = [ṭābta'], lit. 'for (the) good may they work for my house, etc.'; alternatively, 'for good may they do (sc. what I have written) for my house, etc.'; Deut. vi 24. Moran (1963) compares the Akkad. phrase *ṭābūta epēšu*, 'to make a treaty of friendship'; but the ל is against a direct parallel here; it cannot indicate the object, since this dialect uses אית (ii C 5).
5. יעבדו = [ya'bědū]; jussive. תחת = [tḥōt]; cp. Eccles. i 3, etc.
6. מלכתי = [malkūtī]; there is room for 5 letters in this lacuna. Dupont-Sommer restores מלכי = [mulkī], a form which does not occur elsewhere in Aram. There is a stroke between כל and לחיה, perhaps a slip by a scribe used to dividing words this way. לחיה; fem.; i A 26.
7. עד עלם; iii 25; no. 5 Zakir C.
8. ברה. The ר seems to be written over ה.
15. יצרו = [yiṭṭárū]; jussive; later Aram. NṬR. The object will be a previous phrase beginning with מן יצר, 'whoever keeps .....'; cp. the next sentence. Note the play on the meaning of this verb and of הפך in 19 f. אלהן; i A 30. מן יומה = [min yawmēh]; cp. ii C 17 and Hebr. מימיך (1 Sam. xxv 28).
16. מן ביתה; a rather cryptic phrase, whose meaning has to be filled out on the analogy of the preceding phrase.
17. מלי = [millay]; constr.
18. יאמר = [yi'mar]. אהלד = ['hālēd](?); Haph. imperf. from LWD, otherwise unknown. The vocalization is on the analogy of יהקים (Dan. v 21), but the [ā] in this and similar forms may be due to a lapse of [h] in the spoken biblical tradition and its consequent restoration by the Massoretes; i.e. [yah(ᵉ)qēm] to [yāqēm] to [yhāqēm]; in which case vocalize ['ah(ᵉ)lēd]; cp. יהתיבון (Ezra vi 5). Peal infin. and imper. forms (לד) from the same base occur in ii C 6, 9. מלוה; the suffix may refer to Mati'el or to ספרא.
19. אהפך = ['ihpu/ōk]; the same double meaning 'turn, change' and 'overturn, pervert' is found in Hebr. and later Aram. טבתא = [ṭābāta']; this time fem. plur. אשם = ['śīm].
20. לחית = [laḥyāt]; fem. plur. abs. יום (= [yawm]) is indefinite.
21. יהפכו = [yihpú/ṓkū]; jussive.
22. הא = [hu']; personal pronoun used as demonstrative; cp. Dan. ii 32; פלגא הו (Cowley ix 12).
23. תחתיתה = [taḥtāytēh]; fem. adjective as noun. So עליתה (24) = ['illāytēh]; cp. עלי (A 6).
24. ירת = [yērat] from [yirrat], an early instance of the change [t̲] to [t], which did not take place generally in Aram. till the Persian period; Hebr. ירש. Degen, *Grammatik*, 43 avoids this conclusion by supposing a case of dissimilation, of [t̲] to [t] before the [š] of the following word. שרשה; no. 5 Zakir B 28; cp. עקר (A 3, etc.).
25. אשם = ['ušm] with prosthetic [']; no. 13 Hadad 16.

No. **8**

ii C

1 [ומן י]א . . . . *c.* 15 . . . .

2 מר להלדת ספרי[א א]לן מן ב

3 תי אלהיא אן זי י[ר]שמן ו

4 [י]אמר אהאבד ספר[י]א ולמ[ח]

5 [ר] אהבד אית כתך ואית מלכ

6 ה ויזחל הא מן לד ספר

7 [י]א מן בתי אלהיא ויאמר ל

8 זי לידע אנה אגר אגר ו[י]

9 אמר לד [ספ]ריא אלן מן ב[ת]

10 י [א]להיא ובלחץ עלב י[מת הא]

11 וברה

12 . . *c.* 4 . . את . . . *c.* 7 . . . . מ - - - [י]

13 [צר]ן כל אלה[י עדי]א זי בספרא

14 [זנ]ה אית מתעאל וברה ובר ברה

15 ועקרה וכל מלכי ארפד וכל רב

16 וה ועמהם מן בתיהם ומן

17 יומיהם

1. . . . . [whoever]
2. has it in mind to efface these inscriptions from
3. the sacred stones where they are written, and
4. says, I shall destroy the inscriptions, and [tomorrow]
5. I shall destroy KTK and its king,
6. or he is afraid to efface the inscriptions
7. from the sacred stones, and says to
8. someone who does not know, I (wish to) hire a workman, and
9. says, Efface these inscriptions from
10. the sacred stones, then by crushing torment [let him]
11. and his son [die]!
12. . . . .

13. all the gods of the [treaty], which is in this inscription,
14. [shall keep] Mati'el and his son and his grandson
15. and his descendants and all the kings of Arpad and all his
16. nobles and their people as long as their houses last and
17. all their days.

NOTES

1. יאמר has prob. here the sense 'think, purpose' as in Hebr. in Gen. xx 11, etc. להלדת; constr. infin. Haph.; vocalize [hlādūt] as in Ezra v 10 (להודעותך) or possibly [hlādat] as in Ezra iv 22 (להנזקת).
3. בתי אלהיא = [bātay 'lāhayya'], lit. 'houses of the gods', apparently referring to the stele, or since the plur. is used, perhaps to a number of stelae containing treaties drawn up between Arpad and members of the Urartian confederacy. The origin of the term can be traced in Gen. xxviii 22, where a sacred pillar (מצבה; from the same base as נצבא) is called a house of god, and was clearly thought of as a symbol of the deity's presence, if not as actually indwelt by the deity; cp. the name אל ביתאל in Gen. xxxi 13. The Greeks later saw these standing stones in Phoenicia and Syria and called them *βαιτύλια*, a word that recalls the Sem. name. Dupont-Sommer cites an interesting passage from Philo Byblius, in which these *βαιτύλια* are described as 'animate stones' *λίθους ἐμψύχους*; Eusebius, *Praep. Ev.* i 10, 23. In Israel they were not unexpectedly condemned by the prophets; Hos. x 1; Mic. v 12; Deut. vii 5, etc.; but even in pious circles the conception behind them lingered on; see 1 Kgs. vii 15 f., where suggestive names are given to the two bronze pillars at the entrance of the Temple. In the present context the use of the term 'bethel' is no doubt also figurative, since there is no suggestion that worship was directed at the stelae. אן זי = ['ān d̲ī]; Cowley xv 25, 29. ירשמן (Dupont-Sommer) = [yuršmūn]; Peil imperf.; for the verb see Dan. v 24. Perhaps better, since it would be construed with the nearer noun, is יתשמן = [yittśāmūn] (Dan. ii 5), i.e. 'where they are set up'; so Rosenthal in *ANET*, 660.
4. אהאבד = ['ha'bēd]; Haph. with the ['] retained as in Hebr. Hiph. In the next line אהבד is prob. a scribal error; there is in biblical Aram. an alternative Haph. formed on the analogy of verbs initial [y, w], i.e. ['hōbēd]; cp. Dan. ii 24; but the reduction of the diphthong [aw] being involved, that solution is unlikely here. למחר = [limḥar]; so Palest. Aram.; the restoration is Rosenthal's. Dupont-Sommer finds a trace of the leg of נ at the beginning of 5 (which could, however, be simply a score on the stone), and proposes למלן = (lmillīn], lit. 'for words'; he compares לבקרים, 'every morning' (Ps. lxxiii 14) and similar distributive usages in Hebr., and translates, 'and word by word I shall destroy KTK, etc.'. This is less satisfactory, though it brings into prominence, if rather cryptically, the notion of sympathetic magic that motivated such acts of desecration.
5. אית = ['iyyāt]; see at no. 5 Zakir B 5.
6. יזחל = [yid̲ḥal]; no. 5 Zakir A 13. לד = [lūd]; infin. Peal, with the same meaning as the Haph. (i C 18).
8. לידע = [lā yidda']. אגר; I take the first occurrence as an active partic. (['āgēr]), the second as a passive (['gīr]), lit. 'I am hiring a hireling'; cp. Matt.

xx 1 (Syriac). This seems preferable to Fitzmyer's suggestion, 'I shall reward (you) indeed', in which both the apparent infin. abs. and the absence of the suffix are awkward.

9. לד = [lūd]; imper.

10. The ו does not strictly speaking link a subordinate and a main clause, but picks up the reference earlier to מן, i.e. 'as for him who has it in mind, etc. . . . . . , then by crushing torment . . . . .'; cp. *KAI* no. 24 Kilamuwa i 12 f. (after a clause beginning with מי); vol. I no. **16** Mesha 5 (after a proper name); and in Aram. Driver xii 9 (after אנת). לחץ עלב, lit. 'with affliction of oppression'; the first base is attested in the Christian Palest. dialect; with the second cp. Syriac [ʿlīb], 'oppressed' and particularly 'snatched away' by death. The

---

No. **9**

iii

1 או אל ברך או אל עקרך֯ או אל חד מלכי ארפד וי[מל]ל [ע]ל֯י֯ או על ברי או על בר ברי או על עקרי כים כל גב

2 ר זי יבעה רוח אפוה וימלל מלן לחית לעלי֯ - - - - - תקח מליא מן ידה הסכר֯ תהסכרהם בידי וב

3 רך יהסכר לברי ועקרך יסכר לעקרי֯ ועקר [חד מל]כי ארפ֯ד יהסכרן לי מה טב בעיני אעבד להם ו

4 הן להן שקרתם לכל אלהי עדיא זי בספרא [זנה] והן יק֯רק מני קר[ק] ח֯ד פ֯ק֯די או חד אחי או חד

5 סרסי או חד עמא זי בידי ויהכן חלב לתס[ך לה]ם לחם ולתאמר להם של֯ו על א֯שרכם ולתהרם נ

6 בשהם מני רקה תרקהם ותהשבהם לי והן לי֯[שבן] ב֯אר֯קך רקו שם עד אהך אנ֯ה וארקהם והן תהרם נבשה

7 ם מני֯ ותסך להם לחם ותאמר להם שבו לתחתכ[ם] ו֯אל ת֯פנ֯ו באשרה שקרתם בעדיא אלן וכל מלכ֯יא זי ס

8 חרתי או כל זי רחם הא לי ואשלח מלאכי א[ל]וה לשלם֯ או לכל חפצי או ישלח מלאכה אלי פתח

restoration at the end is Dupont-Sommer's, although he prefers, ignoring a reduced diphthong, to read בנה = [bnōh], 'his sons' in 11.

12. With the last section cp. i C 15 f. The letter מ perhaps begins מלוה, 'its words', with a part of the verb NṮR preceding.

13. יצרן = [yiṭṭrūn]; imperf., not jussive as in i C 15, unless it stands for the latter; cp. i A 30.

15. מלכי; future occupants of the throne; cp. iii 1. רבוה; i A 39; Arpad cannot be meant, since the suffix is masc.; it probably refers to both Matiʿel and his successors; there are several comparable examples of confusion between sing. and plur. in iii (see at 4, 22).

16. עמהם = [ʿammhōm]; iii 5, 21. On the final phrases see at i C 15, 16.

---

iii

(. . . . . . . If any . . . . . . comes to you)

1. or to your son or to a descendant of yours or to any of the kings of Arpad, and speaks against me or against my son or against my grandson or against my descendant in the way
2. that a man seeking asylum usually does, or if he speaks evil words without (justification), you shall (not) accept the words from him; you must surrender them into my hands; and your son
3. shall surrender (them) to my son, and your descendant shall surrender (them) to my descendant, and the descendants of [any of the] kings of Arpad shall surrender (them) to me. Whatever seems fitting to me, I shall do to them.
4. If you do not do so, you have been false to all the gods of the treaty which is in [this] inscription. If any of my officers flees from me as a fugitive or any of my kinsmen or any of
5. my eunuchs or any of the people who are under my control, and they go to Aleppo, you shall not provide them with food, nor shall you say to them, Enjoy yourselves in your place, nor shall you alienate
6. them from me; you must conciliate them, and send them back to me. If they will not [remain] in your land, be conciliatory (and keep them) there, until I come in person and make reconciliation with them. But if you alienate them
7. from me and provide them with food and say to them, Remain where you are and do not return to his allegiance, you have been false to this treaty. In the case of any of the kings with whom
8. I have trading relations or any who is an ally of mine, when I send my envoy to him to ask after his welfare or on any matter of business that I have, or he sends his envoy to me,

9 ה֯ לי ארחא לתמשל בי בזא ולתרשה לי על֯י[ה ו]הן להן
ש[ק]ר֯ת [בע]די֯א אלן והן מן חד אחי או מן חד בי
10 ת אבי או מן חד בני או מן חד נגד֯י או מן ח[ד פ]קדי או
מן חד֯ ע֯מ֯[מי]א זי בידי או מן חד שנאי ו
11 יבעה ראשי להמתתי ולהמתת ברי ועקר[י] הן א[ית]י יקתלן
א֯ת תאתה ותקם דמי מן יד שנאי וברך יאתה
12 יקם דם ברי מן שנאוה ובר ברך יאתה יקם ד[ם ב]ר֯ ברי֯
ועקרך יאתה יקם דם עקרי והן קריה הא נכה
13 תפוה בחרב והן חד אחי הא או חד עבדי או [חד] פק֯ד֯י
או חד עמא זי בידי נכה תכה איה ועקרה ושר֯
14 בוה ומודדוה בחרב והן להן שקרת לכל אלהי [ע]דיא זי
בספרא זנה והן יסק על לבבך ותש֯א֯ על ש
15 פתיך להמתתי ויסק על לבב בר ברך ויש[א] על ש֯פתוה
להמתת בר ברי או הן יסק על לבב עקרך
16 וישא על שפתוה להמתת עקרי והן יסק על [ל]בב מל֯כ֯י
ארפד בכל מה זי ימות בר אנש שקרתם לכ
17 ל אלהי עדיא זי בספרא זנה והן ירב בר[י] זי ישב על
כהסאי חד אחוה או יעברנה֯ לתשלח לש
18 נך בניהם ותאמר לה קתל אחך או אסרה וא֯[ל] ת֯שריה
ו֯הן רקה ת֯[ר]קה בניה֯ם ליקתל וליאסר
19 והן לתרקה בניהם שקרת בעדיא אלן ו[מ]לכן [זי סחר]תי
ויקרק קרקי אל חדהם ויקרק קר
20 קהם ויאתה אלי הן השב זי לי אהשב֯ [זי לה וא]ל תעשקני
את והן להן שקרת בעדי֯א א
21 לן ולתשלח לשן בביתי ובני בני ובני א[חי ובני ע]קרי ובני
עמ֯י֯ ותאמר להם קתלו מרא

9. the road shall be open to me. You shall not overrule me in this respect, nor shall you assert authority over me therein. If you do not do so, you have been false to this treaty. If any of my brothers or any member of
10. my father's house or any of my sons or any of my peers or any of my officers or any of the people who are under my control or any of my enemies
11. seeks my head to put me to death or to put to death my son or my descendant, if they kill me, you shall come in person and avenge my blood at the hand of my enemies, and your son shall come
12. (and) avenge my son's blood upon his enemies, and your grandson shall come (and) avenge my grandson's blood, and your descendant shall come (and) avenge my descendant's blood. If it is a city, you must
13. strike it with the sword. If it is one of my kindred or one of my servants or [one] of my officers or one of the people who are under my control, you must strike him, his family,
14. the members of his clan and his relatives with the sword. If you do not do so, you have been false to all the gods of the treaty which is in this inscription. If the idea comes to your mind and you take it upon
15. your lips to put me to death, or if the idea comes to the mind of your grandson and he takes it upon his lips to put my grandson to death, or if the idea comes to the mind of a descendant of yours
16. and he takes it upon his lips to put my descendant to death, or if the idea comes to the mind of (any of) the kings of Arpad—when someone dies, you have been false to all
17. the gods of the treaty which is in this inscription. If my son, who sits upon my throne, is in dispute with one of his brothers, or he banishes him, you shall not let loose your
18. tongue among them, and say to him, Kill your brother or imprison him, but do not let him go free. If you truly make reconciliation between them, he will not be killed or imprisoned.
19. But if you do not make reconciliation between them, you have been false to this treaty. In the case of kings with whom I have trading relations, when a fugitive of mine flees to any of them, or a fugitive of theirs flees
20. and comes to me, if he has returned mine, I shall return [his, and] you yourself shall not misrepresent me. If you do not do so, you have been false to this treaty.
21. You shall not let loose your tongue in my house nor among my sons nor among my [brothers nor among] my descendants nor among my people, and say to them, Kill your lord

22 כם והוי חלפה כי לטב הא מך ויקם חד [דמי והן ת[עבד
מרמת עלי̊ או על בני או על̊ עקרן[י]

23 [שק]רתם לכל אלהי עדיא זי בספרא זנ[ה ותלאי[ם וכפריֹה
ובעליה וגבלה לאבי ול

24 [ביתה עד] עלם וכזי הבזו אלהן בית [אבי הא ה]ו̊ת לאחרן
וכעת השבו אלהן שיבת בי

25 [ת אבי- - - -בית] אֹבי ושבת תלאים ל[- - - -]עֹ ולברה
ולבר ברה ולעקרה עד עלם ו

26 [הן ירב ברי וירב בר ב]רֹי וירב עקרי [עם עקרך ע]ל̊
תלאים וכֹפריה ובעליה מן ישא

27 . . . . c. 14 . . . . [מל]כֹי ארפד . . . . c. 16 . . . .
לנֹה שקרת בעדיא אלן והן

28 . . . . c. 42-3 . . . .
וֹישחדן כל מה מלך זי י

29 . . . . c. 38-9 . . . . [כל מה
ז]י̊ שפֹר וכל מֹה זי ט[ב - -]

NOTES

The following is a summary of the clauses:

1–4   provides for the surrender of rebels and plotters, who seek safety or assistance in Arpad.

4–7   seems to concern deserters or fugitives who are only potential rebels; the king of Arpad is to attempt reconciliation in their case.

7–9   guarantees freedom of passage for envoys.

9–14   provides for the king of Arpad's intervention to avenge his ally's assassination.

14–17   warns against the king of Arpad himself organizing such an assassination.

17–19   arranges for the king of Arpad's good offices should his ally's successor quarrel with family rivals.

19–20   warns the king of Arpad not to interfere in arrangements between his ally and other monarchs.

22. and be his successor; for he is not better than you. Someone will avenge [my blood. But if you] commit acts of treachery against me or against my sons or against my descendants,

23. you have been false to all the gods of the treaty which is in this inscription. [Tal'ayim], its villages, its citizens and its territory belong to my father and to

24. [his house for] ever. When the gods struck down [my father's] house, [it] went to another; but now the gods have restored the fortunes of

25. [my father's] house . . . . my father's [house], and Tal'ayim has returned to . . . . and to his son and to his grandson and to his descendants for ever.

26. [If my son quarrels or my grandson quarrels] or a descendant of mine quarrels [with a descendant of yours] over Tal'ayim, its villages and its citizens, whoever raises

27. . . . . the kings of Arpad . . . . , you have been false to this treaty.

28. If . . . . and they bribe any sort of king who

29. . . . . [every] fair and every good thing . . . .

21–3 warns the king of Arpad not to encourage dynastic squabbles in his ally's court.
23–7 acknowledges that a territory in dispute between the two parties should remain in the control of Arpad's ally.
27– is only partially preserved; see the note.

There are parallels to most of the clauses in the extant Hittite, Egyptian, and Akkadian treaties; see *ANET*, 199 f., 531 f. The sections referring to internal dynastic quarrels are of particular help in elucidating the difficult second half of the Hadad inscr.; q.v. no. **13** introduction; a number of biblical passages showing similar anxiety over a peaceful succession and the continuance of the royal house are cited there.

1. If we are dealing with a stele on the pattern of i and ii, the surviving face is the reverse, and the text is continued from a missing side to its right; in that case the inscr. prob. finished on a missing side to its left. There is, however, no evidence of a pyramid shape, and the first part of the inscr. may have been written on a slab of stone above the present one. ברך = [brāk]. כים is prob. a prepos., i.e. 'like, in the manner of any man who . . . . . .' (Akkad. *kīma*), although elsewhere in Syrian Sem. the form is always כ; thus with the enclitic,

Hebr. [kmō]; Aram. [kmā]. Fitzmyer connects the word with Hebr. כי, 'indeed, surely', a meaning which is disputed (see Brown, Driver, and Briggs, ad loc.), and which is in any case not found with a resumptive force in the middle of a sentence.

2. יבעה = [yibʿē]; 11. רוח; note the internal *mater lectionis*. אפוה = ['appawh]; dual. The phrase, clearly idiomatic, means lit. 'who seeks the breath of his nostrils'; cp. Lament. iv 20; a rebel or plotter seeking political asylum would not unnaturally have harsh things to say about his former ruler. Alternative renderings are 'who blows hot' (Rosenthal, 1960) and 'who rants' (Fitzmyer); these are based on a meaning 'make to boil' carried by the verb in Isa. lxiv 1, but not attested for Aram., lit. 'who causes the breath of his nostrils to boil'; cp. also Exod. xv 8. Rosenthal compares Prov. i 23, where the verb NBʿ (Hiph.) is used along with רוח; he thinks a form of BʿY may have been original. Garbini (1959, 43) derives the verb (with [b] for [p]) from PʿY; later Aram. 'bleat'; Arab. partic. 'foaming with rage'; ['afʿā], 'viper'; Hebr. ['apʿē], idem, and Isa. xlii 14 (*NEB* 'whimper'; 'hiss'?). He suggests, 'who emits venom through his nostrils like a viper'. וימלל could, but less satisfactorily, be construed with זי. לחית; i C 20. לעלי; the י is very uncertain; we may have here a compound prepos. equivalent to על and going with ימלל; but the ל suggests rather the common Aram. and Syriac adverb [lʿēl(ā)] or prepos. [lʿēl(ā) min], 'above, over and beyond'. I assume that a noun is missing in the lacuna, and that we have another idiomatic phrase meaning 'beyond what is merited', 'unjustified', or the like; cp. Syriac [lʿēl men melltā], 'ineffable', lit. 'beyond word(s)'. A negative has also to be supplied before תקח. Rosenthal takes ל as the negative and restores לעלי ועל ברי תקח, 'you must not, to my detriment and the detriment of my son, accept . . . .'; but there is not room for six letters in the lacuna, and the syntax is very infelicitous. מן יד; Mal. ii 13. הסכר = [haskēr]; infin. absolute; the normal infin. Haph. would end in [ā] as in later Aram.; the constr. of this occurs in המתת (11). The base SKR, found also in Hebr. (Isa. xix 4; Piel) is an alternant of Phoen. and Hebr. SGR; *KAI* no. 14 Eshmunazar 9, 21 (Yiph.); 1 Sam. xvii 46 (Piel); xxiii 11 (Hiph.). תהסכרהם = [thaskirhōm] or the like. In view of later Aram. practice and of vol. I no. **16** Mesha 18, where a dot precedes the suffix הם after a verb, it is tempting to write the suffix separately here, i.e. = [hēm], a short form of the biblical [himmō(n)]; but this would be impossible in the case of תרקהם (6).

3. יסכר; an Aphel form, which exists alongside the Haph. in biblical and Egyp. Aram., or simply a scribal mistake for יהסכר; cp. אהאבד and אהבד (ii C 4, 5). יהסכרן; note the collect. subj. עקר. חד; also possible is כל. After 'me' understand 'and my son, etc.'. מה; cp. no. **13** Hadad 12. אעבד = ['aʿbēd]; for the comparable idiom in Hebr. see 2 Sam. x 12; xix 38, etc. להם = [lhōm].

4. הן להן; cp. Syriac ['ellā 'ēn], 'if not', 'except'. שקרתם = [šqartūm]; Peal; so (with ל) in 14, 16, 23; see at i A 14. Here and in 16 the form is plur., no doubt to emphasize that every generation of kings listed in the protasis is under an obligation; cp. הם in 2 referring to a series of sing. subjects in 1 f.; similarly יהכן (5). In 7 and 23 the plur. is used against the syntax, there being no explicit mention of sons, grandsons, etc., in the protasis. In all other cases (9, 14, 19, 20, 27) the sing. שקרת is used. יקרק = [yiġru/ōq]; no. **20** Ashur ostracon 9; later Aram. ʿRQ; not now (as Brockelmann, *Lexicon Syriacum*) to be connected with Arab. and Hebr. ʿRQ. קרק; partic.; cp. 19, where a suffix is added. פקדי = [pqīday]; Gen. xli 34; Judg. ix 28. אחי = ['aḥay];

prob. in this context 'kindred' in general; no. 13 Hadad 24; 2 Sam. xix 13; in 9 on the contrary, 'brothers' are distinguished from other royal relatives.

5. סרסי = [sārīsay]; 2 Kgs. xxiv 12, etc. יהכן = [yhākūn]; note the absence of a following prepos.; Driver vi 2 (after אזל); Ps. c 4 (after בוא). Aleppo, as a shrine of Hadad (i A 10), may have been an international or at least inter-Aramaean place of refuge; in that case the fugitives need not have been seeking asylum with the king of Arpad personally, and this rather than my suggestion in the summary above about them being only potential rebels could explain the peculiar nature of the duty imposed on him here. תסך; i A 26, though here with a more general meaning; cp. Dan. ii 46 (Pael). שלו = [šlaw]; imper. plur.; cp. Ps. cxxii 6; Dan. iv 1. על אשרכם = [ʿal ʾaṯrkōm]. תהרם = [thārēm] or [tahrēm]; on the form see at אהלד (i C 18). נבשהם = [nab-šhōm]; the phrase means lit. 'you will not make his soul high away from me', or perhaps 'higher than me'; cp. Dan. v 20; Deut. xvii 20. Alternatively, 'you will not remove his soul from me'; cp. Isa. lvii 14.

6. רקה = [raġġē]; Pael infin. absol. against the normal infin. חויה (i A 13). תרקהם = [traġġēhōm] or the like; if the suffix were separate, the verb would have been written with a final ה. The base is related to later Aram. RʿY; Hebr. RṢY; Arab. RḌY; the Peal occurs in no. 13 Hadad 18, 22. The sense is as Syriac Pael, 'to appease, reconcile, placate, etc.'; cp. Peshitta 1 Sam. xxix 4 (Ethpa.); cp. also Job xx 10. Dupont-Sommer thinks this meaning is incompatible with the previous clause, and proposes a connection with Hebr. RṢṢ, lit. 'crush, oppress, shatter', i.e. [tēruġhōm] or the like, which he would render 'arrest, detain'; but it is impossible to derive an infin. form רקה from this base. תהשבהם = [thāṯībhōm] or [tahṯībhōm]; see at אהלד (i C 18). ישבן = [yiṯṯbūn]; the restoration is Dupont-Sommer's; presumably the fugitives, not being guilty yet of any crime, could refuse to return, and were free to go elsewhere; in that eventuality, the king of Arpad was to try to dissuade them. Rosenthal, 'If not, they shall remain in your land, etc.' רקו = [raġġaw]; imper. plur., most easily explained as a careless mistake for the sing. (רקי = [raġġī]), induced by שלו in the previous line, although it may like שקרתם in 7 be employed to generalize the reference and implicate future kings; cp. הוי (22) following a plur. שם = [ṯām]; no. 13 Hadad 8; later only [tammā] or [tammān]; Hebr. [šām]. Degen, *Grammatik*, 20 gets rid of the non-Aram. form of the adverb by assuming ש to be an error for ה and reading רקוהם. עד; note the omission of זי; Ezra iv 21. אנה; for emphasis.

7. שבו = [ṯēbū]. לתחתכם = [lathōtkōm]; see at i A 6 and for the equivalent Hebr. idiom Exod. xvi 29, etc. תפנו = [tipnaw]; jussive, lit. 'do not turn after him'. באשרה; i A 5; cp. Ezek. xxix 16. שקרתם = [šaqqērtūm]; with ב and a non-personal object prob. Pael; so also in 9, 19, 20, 27; see again at i A 14. כל מלכיא; *casus pendens*, beginning the next section. זי = 'of', a usage not otherwise found in Old Aram.; 19. סחרתי is usually interpreted as a noun with the sense 'vicinity, neighbourhood'; cp. Palest. Aram. [saḥrānīn], plur.; but in Syrian Sem. the base means 'to trade' (Hebr. and later Aram.), 'be a beggar' (Syriac) rather than simply 'to go around', and the first of these nuances should perhaps be read into the phrase here.

8. רחם; active partic. (Syriac). ואשלח; the ו continues the *casus pendens* and adds a conditional or circumstantial force; Job xxix 12. מלאכי = [mal'kī]. אלוה = ['lawh]. לשלם; 2 Kgs. x 13 (after ירד); there is argument about the final letter, which Dupont-Sommer insists is ח, i.e. '(to ask him) to send

(a message to me)'; see Fitzmyer, ad loc. חפצי = [ḥipṭī]; the meaning is as in Hebr. [ḥēpṣ] (Isa. lviii 3; Eccles. iii 1); Syriac ḤPṬ, passive partic., 'diligent'; Pael 'urge, entreat'; Arab. ḤFẒ. פתחה = [ptīḥā]; passive partic. fem. agreeing with ['urḥa'] (emph.), which is fem. in later Aram. (and in Prov. xv 19).

9. תמשל; Exod. xxi 8; this verb does not occur in later Aram. תרשה; see the discussion on this verb at no. **13** Hadad 27, where it is one of the cruces of the inscr. Rosenthal, 'you must not contest its use with me', but the nearest usage to this (Egyp. Aram.) occurs always in a context of lawsuits, which is inappropriate here. עליה = [ʿlayh]; fem. suffix agreeing with [d̲a'], 'this matter'. מן חד = [man ḥad].

10. נגדי = [ngīday]; Job xxix 10; 2 Chron. xxxv 8. Also possible, since the downward stroke of ד is rather long, is the reading נגרי = [nāgray], a loanword from Akkad. *nāgiru*, 'prefect, overseer'. עממיא = [ʿam(ᵉ)mayya'] as in later Aram.; plur. as against sing. collect. in 5; Dupont-Sommer reads עמיא, but there seems to me to be room for three faded letters between ע and א. שנאי = [śān'ay]; vol. I no. **16** Mesha 4. The final ו begins the apodosis; it may be a scribal error, induced by the ו in the previous section (8) following a *casus pendens*, though it did not introduce the main clause; cp., however, the one following [man] in ii C 10; no. **20** Ashur ostracon 16(?).

11. ראשי = [ri'šī]; cp. the frequent biblical phrase בקש נפש, 'to seek the life of'. להמתתי = [lahmātūtī]; constr. infin.; Dan. vi 4. איתי = ['iyyātī]; no. **5** Zakir B 5. יקתלן; with [t] as in Arab. and the Zenjirli dialect (no. **14** Panammu 8). תאתה = [ti'tē]. תקם = [tiqqōm]; base NQM; Deut. xxxii 43; 2 Kgs. ix 7 (Piel, but with מיד). יאתה יקם; asyndeton, much commoner in Aram. than in Hebr., where in prose the Waw consecutive construction dominates; for examples in poetry see Exod. xv 9; Hos. v 15.

12. קריה = [qiryā]; fem. abs. הא = [hi']. נכה = [nkā]; infin. absol. Peal; cp. Hebr. גלה = [galō]; the normal infin. prob. ended in [ē]; see at לבנא (no. **13** Hadad 13). Peal and Aphel forms of NKY occur in Syriac; Hebr. only Hiph.

13. תפוה. The פ is certain, but later in the line כ is to be read (תכה), so we most prob. have a scribal error. Hebr. has a base TPP, Qal, Poel, 'to beat the timbrel', which Dupont-Sommer thinks may be represented here (imper. plur.), but there is no evidence for this verb being used in other than its primary sense. Vocalize [tikkawh]; 2 plur., with suffix (fem.); the form seems to be jussive; cp. תשריה (18; with אל). In the case of the 3 plur. suffixes in 2, 6, one does not expect [inn], later Aram. lacking such a suffix, but here its absence is awkward; see further in the introduction. Later in the line תכה = [tikkē]. Note the mistake איה for איתה. עקר; collect.; prob. the offender's immediate offspring are meant rather than a distant descendant, as elsewhere in the inscr. שרבוה; a plur. noun with suffix, connected with Syriac [šarbtā], 'generation, family, clan' (Rosenthal). The reading ר is preferable to Dupont-Sommer's ג, i.e. שגבוה = [śgībawh], 'his exalted ones, nobles'; the base ŚGB occurs in *KAI* no. 222 i B 32.

14. מודדוה = [mawd(ᵉ)dawh]; no. **13** Hadad 24; base YDD; a form like Hebr. מסגר, 'smith', since the Haph. or its equivalent does not occur in any Sem. language. יסק = [yissaq]; base SLQ; with the phrase cp. Ezek. xxxviii 10. תשא = [tiśśa']. שפתיך = [śiptayk] or the like; dual; cp. Ps. xvi 4.

16. מה זי is here prob. temporal, though Fitzmyer prefers to render, 'in whatever way a man dies'. ימות = [ymūt] with internal *mater lectionis*. בר אנש; this is the earliest occurrence of the term; Dan. vii 13.

17. ירב = [yrīb] with direct object as in Job x 2; Isa. xxvii 8. כהסאי = [kuhs'ī], a loan-word from Akkad., which has the two forms *kursū* and *kussū*; the [h] may therefore be in place of [r], which is usually retained in Aram., or we may have a case of dissimilation, [hs] substituting for the geminate consonant. I can adduce no parallel to either change. יעברנה = [yaʿbrinnēh]; imperf. (H)aph. with suffix; cp. 1 Kgs. xv 12. In the present context we have presumably to think of a dispute over the succession; the successful claimant may appropriately banish his rivals, but is not to be encouraged to go further. אחוה = ['aḥawh]. תשלח; for comparable metaphors see Ps. l 19 (Qal); Prov. vi 19 (Piel); cp. also no. **13** Hadad 9.
18. בניהם = [bēnayhōm] with reduced diphthong in the first syllable. תאמר; the negative has to be understood, as in 21. אחך = ['ḥūk]. אסרה = ['isrēh] or the like; imper. with suffix. תשריה = [tišrayh]; jussive with suffix. רקה; 6, where the verb is followed by a direct object. The verbs at the end are best regarded as passives, since they lack suffixes, though cp. יהסכר, etc. (3); יאסר therefore = either [yu'sar] or [yi'su/ōr].
19. מלכן; *casus pendens* as in 7 f. קרקי = [ġārqī]; see at 4. חדהם; numerals with suffixes are rare in Sem.
20. יאתה = [yi'tē]. השב = [hšīb]; Haph.; note the perf. in the protasis. אהשב; see at i C 18. תעשקני = [taʿšuqnī] or the like; jussive with suffix; in Hebr. 'to oppress, extort, do wrong'; cp. no. **19** Nerab ii 8; thus here perhaps 'hinder'; but with the fuller context of 4–7 for comparison, a sense like Syriac 'slander, accuse' is more suitable.
21. The new section begins abruptly with what biblical critics would call an apodeictic formula as opposed to the casuistic formulas (with 'if', etc.) used previously; see Alt, *Essays on Old Testament History, etc.* (Oxford, 1967), 77 f. The change of style underlines the solemn nature of the injunction, as does the ominous חד, 'someone', in the next line. בני בני; the first word is prob. the prepos. 'between' (cp. 18), but may (Fitzmyer) mean 'sons of', i.e. 'my grandsons, etc.' with ב understood. מראכם = [māri'kōm] or the like.
22. הוי = [hwī]; imper. sing.; note the change of person. חלפה = [ḥālpēh] or [ḥlīpēh]; vol. I no. **16** Mesha 6; Ahiqar 18; less likely is the prepos. [ḥlāp], 'instead of, in the place of', which in later Aram. adds suffixes to a plur. stem; cp., however, תחת (i A 6; iii 7). See further on this phrase Fitzmyer (1969). מך must be a mistake for מנך, this prepos. always retaining [n] before suffixes in Aram. לטב, etc.; 1 Sam. xv 28; 1 Kgs. xix 4. יקם; 11. מרמת = [mirmāt]; fem. plur. abs.; Dan. xi 23; Ps. x 7.
23. תלאים = [tal'aym]; the vocalization depends on Noth's (1961) identification with *Ta-al-ḫa-yi-im(ki)*, a city mentioned frequently in the Mari archives and situated somewhere in northern Mesopotamia east of the Euphrates; see Bottéro and Finet, *Archives royales* XV (1954), index. Phonologically, this is quite acceptable, since in the Akkad. of Mari symbols with [ḫ] are sometimes used in representing Syrian Sem. [']; cp. *si-im-ḫa-al* for שמאל, 'north', in the name of the tribe Banū Sim'al. For the bearing of the identification on the historical and geographical background of this and the other two stelae see the introduction. It does not seem from the wording here, notably אחרן in 24, that Arpad had ever possessed Tal'ayim, but apparently Matiʿel has had designs upon it, or has been interfering in its affairs, and the ally of stele iii now extracts from him an agreement to desist in the future. כפריה = [kpīrayh]; no. **13** Hadad 10 (with internal *mater lectionis*); no. **14** Panammu 10 (in conjunction with בעל as here); Neh. vi 2; the later Aram. form is [kpar];

cp. Mari Akkad. *kaprum*, 'encampment' (Bottéro and Finet, op. cit., lexicon). בעלי; or 'its rulers, commanders'; see at i A 4. גבלה = [gbūlah]; no. **14** Panammu 15; this word does not occur in later Aram.

24. The restorations in this and the following line are Dupont-Sommer's. עד עלם; no. **5** Zakir C. כזי = [kd̲ī]; later כדי. חבז; Arab. [ḫabaza], 'strike' (Fitzmyer) and [ḥafaza], 'push' (Rosenthal) both give suitable meanings; if the second is accepted, we have another case of [b] for [p]; cp. Hebr. ḤPZ, 'flee in haste, be alarmed'. The form is Pael, since an infin. with the ending [ā] occurs in *KAI* no. 223 ii B 7. With the thought cp. vol. I no. **16** Mesha 5; no. **14** Panammu 2. אלהן; see at i A 30. הא = [hī']. הות = [hwāt]. אחרן = ['uḥrān]; Dan. ii 44; Deut. xxiv 2. כעת = [k'at]; Ezra iv 17. השבו שיבת = [ht̲ību t̲ībat]; Ps. cxxvi 1, 4; note the internal *mater lectionis*. If חבזו is translated 'drove out', the phrase should be taken lit., i.e. 'brought about the return of'; cp. possibly vol. I no. **16** Mesha 8–9.

25. A verb prob. stood in the middle of the lacuna, either with אלהן or בית אבי as the subject. שבת = [t̲ābat]. After ל comes a proper name; ברגאיה is read by Dupont-Sommer, but the final letter, which he takes as a dubious ה, looks to me more like ע; see further in the introduction.

26. There is no room for the expected phrases to be written out in full; the scribe may have been preserving space at the bottom of the stele. Note that in the second lacuna a prepos. has to be supplied with ירב, which in 17 was followed directly by its object. ישא may begin a similar phrase to the one in 14 f.

27. הן לתקת[ל]נה], 'if you do not kill him'; so Dupont-Sommer.

28–9. ישחדן = [yišḥdūn]; the subject may be the kings of Arpad, who in this new section, which would clearly have to be continued on a further portion of the stele, are being warned against bribery. The phrase in 29 will in that case refer to the bribes they offer. Alternatively, the subject could be אלהן, the verb having the sense of 'reward', though this is not attested elsewhere. The phrase in 29 then describes the blessings which faithfulness to the treaty will bring, and could be among the final words of the inscr. כל מה; i A 26. שפר = [šappīr]; so Syriac.

10. Upper Mesopotamia: Tell Halaf   Fig. 5

The tiny inscr., the oldest in Aram. but unfortunately too fragmentary to be satisfactorily deciphered, is written on three sides of what seems to have been a socle or plinth from an altar. It was found in 1931 at Tell Halaf, the ancient Gozan (2 Kgs. xvii 6) on the Habur river, capital of one of the small Aramaean states which sprang up in upper Mesopotamia in the 11 cent. B.C. and after a short independent existence fell to the Assyrians at the beginning of the 9 cent. Formerly in a museum at Berlin, it is now lost. Words are divided by large strokes. The script belongs to the late 10 or very early 9 cent., and witnesses to an early spread of Aram. writing across the Euphrates from Syria. Thus with the triangular ד, which lacks a downward stroke and the elongated ז cp. Gezer (vol. I no. **1**) and the 10-cent. Phoen. inscrs. The ח with only two cross-bars (?) is paralleled on the Mesha stele. The כ is like a 10-cent. Phoen. כ,

only upright. Previously the Aramaeans of the Gozan area had used Akkadian, as other inscrs. unearthed in the same excavation show. The only certain word is זי, the relative, but this is enough to establish the dialect as Aram.

The transcription is made from the plate in the original publication by J. Friedrich and others, *Die Inschriften vom Tell Halaf* (Berlin, 1940), 69 f., with reference to the sketch in the article by R. A. Bowman in *AJSL* 58 (1941), 359 f.; see also Dussaud's review in *Syria* 23 (1943), 106 f.; *EHO*, 23; Koopmans, *Chrest.* no. 3; *KAI* no. 231; Degen, *Grammatik*, 23. Other sketches in Driver, *Writing*, fig. 73; *KAI* pl. XII.

זדית̊ ׀ כע̊י ׀ זי ׀ כחי.....

NOTES

The first phrase consists of a fem. noun in the constr. followed by what is prob. the name of a person or a deity. Bowman reads זבית, with the demonstrative written defectively, i.e. [ḏē bayt], 'This is the house, abode of'; but the form of this pronoun elsewhere in Aram. is זנה or דנה; Phoen. ז; Hebr. זה. זי = [ḏī]. כחי; Bowman, 'who is my strength', i.e. [kōḥī], a word only attested for Hebr.; cp. Gen. xlix 3. Alternatively, restore כחיי = [kḥayyay], 'who is, was as my life'; Deut. xxx 20; Prov. iv 13; with the use of the prep. cp. Ps. cxxii 3; Song viii 10.

11, 12. Luristan i, ii Fig. 8 (i)

Inscr. i (no. **11**) is written round the neck of a bronze juglet measuring 15 cm. in height, inscr. ii (no. **12**) round the outside rim of a bronze cup measuring 3·9 cm. high and 14·7 cm. in diameter. The objects were found in tombs in western Iran in the area of Luristan in the Zagros mountains north of Elam, and are now in the Foroughi collection in Teheran. The script of i belongs to *c.* 750 B.C. or even earlier. The writing on ii points to the end of the 8 cent. about the same period as the Nineveh weights (see Table of scripts) and the Nerab inscrs. (nos. **18**, **19**). See further Naveh, 'Script', 12 f. The names on the texts are difficult to analyse, but some at least seem to be Syrian Semitic in origin. Since inscr. i, if not ii, predates the expansion of the Assyrian empire under Tiglathpileser III and his successors and the mass deportations which this brought about, it is reasonable to conclude that the people who made and inscribed the juglet and cup belonged to a group of ethnic Aramaeans from Babylonia, who migrated to Luristan in the early 8 cent. and maintained themselves in that mountainous region for several generations thereafter. A scarab decoration on the inside base of the cup shows an Egyptian influence, which was prob. mediated through contacts between the Aramaeans of Syria and Babylonia before the migration took place. The inscrs. are unfortunately too small to allow identification of the dialect, but it was doubtless related to the dialects of the Kaldu (Chaldaeans) and other Aramaean tribes, who were active in southern and eastern Babylonia from the 9 cent. onwards and were not finally pacified till the rise of the neo-Babylonian empire; see on their history Dupont-Sommer, *Araméens*, 73 f.

The inscrs. were published with plates and sketches by Dupont-Sommer in *Iranica Antiqua* 4 (1964), 108 f.; see further Naveh, 'Inscrs.', 20–1 and Garbini, *AION* 17 (1967), 92 f. A second inscr. on a bronze jug (= Luristan iii) is published by Dupont-Sommer in the same article; it is dated by him around 600, but seems to me to be considerably later. I would place it in the early 5 cent.; cp. ס; ע and especially צ and ש. An inscr. on a 3-cent. silver plaquette from Iran is published by Dupont-Sommer in a separate article in the same periodical.

No. **11**

1 i -- א' זי' עבדת' פראתן' אלסתר

2 לׄעתרמצרן' נגש

1. The (juglet) which PR'TN, (daughter of) 'LSTR, had made
2. for ʿTRMṢRN, (son of) NGŠ.

NOTES

1. For the first word Dupont-Sommer suggests plausibly כדא = [kadda'], though in the Bible and Targums this indicates a large pottery jar for carrying water and not a small jug; Gen. xxiv 14; Judg. vii 16. עבדת = [ʿabdat]; fem.; the meaning approaches 'dedicated', as on the 3-cent. plaquette, where ל with a deity's name follows. פראתן may be short for '(The god . . . .) has given (me?) a posterity'; cp. בלאתן on an Aram. endorsement (Driver, *Iraq* 4 (1937), 16–18); *Nabū-zēr-iddina* (Tallqvist, *Names*, 164); *Zēr-iddin* (ibid. 248); פרור (no. **20** Ashur ostracon 1). אלסתר = ['il sattēr] or the like, 'God has concealed, sheltered'; the Pael is regular in Aram., where Hebr. has the Hiph.; cp. Hebr. סתרי (Exod. vi 22). The daughter's name, if correctly interpreted, is Babylonian, witnessing to a partial integration of Babylonians and Aramaeans in the period before the family moved to Luristan.
2. The third name may be that of a husband, who had died. For the divine element see on עתרסמך (no. **7** Sefire i A 1). The second element is translated 'our fortress' by Dupont-Sommer; cp. no. **5** Zakir A 9; Hebr. מצור in 2 Chron. viii 5; Hab. ii 1. The base is found in Palest. Aram., though not in Syriac; the meaning 'confine, besiege, etc.' is not very suitable for personal names. If the derivation is accepted, we may vocalize [mṣūran] or the like; the shorter suffix is as in Syriac, but it is also common in the Egyp. papyri, so cannot be taken as the mark of an eastern dialect. Garbini thinks rather of a place-name, thus making the recipient a deity, 'Athtar of Muṣur'. A land of this name east of the

Tigris in the Zagros region is known from Assyrian sources; e.g. *ARAB* II, 120; it is to be distinguished from the מצר of Sefire i A 5 (q.v. note). Garbini does not explain the final [n], nor how a West Semitic deity came to be associated with so distant a region, only recently penetrated by a few Aramaeans. נגש; cp. Hebr. [nōgēš], 'taskmaster, ruler'; on Garbini's interpretation, this will be an epithet of Athtar rather than a personal name.

No. **12**

ii לכמרא̊ל̊ה . בר . אלסמך . עבד . ע̊זר

Belonging to KMR'LH, son of 'LSMK, servant of 'ZR.

NOTES

If composed of the elements כמר (no. **18** Nerab i 1) and אלה (= ['lāh]), the first name means lit. 'A priest is a god' or 'Priest of a god', structures which have no parallel. Dupont-Sommer suggests 'Kimir is (a) god', comparing Greek *Κιμμέριοι* for Akkad. *Gi-mir-ra-a-a*; Hebr. גמר (Ezek. xxxviii 6). The Cimmerians were a people from the area SE. of the Black Sea, who caused the Assyrians trouble in the reigns of Esarhaddon and Ashurbanipal; see *ARAB*, index. There is no evidence, however, of a deity Kimir, nor is the structure of the name improved; Dupont-Sommer compares Hebr. יואל, but this means 'Yahweh is El'. With אלסמך cp. again עתרסמך (Sefire). With the last name cp. Hebr. עזר (Neh. iii 19; Jerem. xxviii 1); the editor reads ג, which gives an unknown name, but he mentions ע as a possibility.

II

INSCRIPTIONS IN THE DIALECT OF ZENJIRLI

13. Hadad

Pl. III

THE colossal statue of Hadad, erected by Panammu I, which in its original state was about 4 m. high, contains the inscr. carved in relief across its lower portion; the area of writing measures 1·40 m. in height and from 0·90 to 1·30 m. in width. The monument was found in a village a little to the NE. of Zenjirli in 1890, and is now in the Staatliche Museen, Berlin. On the two ancient names of Panammu's kingdom, שמאל and יאדי, see respectively at no. **5** Zakir A 7 and below, 1.

Contents

The script is clear and neat, but the lacunas and smudges, several of which occur at crucial points, make interpretation very difficult. The contents, as I understand them, are as follows:

1–13 (a). After a statement that he has erected the statue, Panammu acknowledges that his authority derives from the gods, and describes the prosperity of the land during his reign. The first part of the Karatepe inscrs. (*KAI* no. 26) is couched in not dissimilar terms; contrast the opening of no. **14** the Panammu (II) inscr.; cp. in the Bible Ps. lxxii 3 f., 16 f., etc.

13 (b)–15 (a). Panammu has erected the statue at the command of Hadad and alongside it has made a tomb for himself.

15 (b)–18. He instructs his successors to sacrifice to 'this Hadad', and in particular to keep praying for the soul of Panammu.

19. A building (?) is constructed to house the statue.

20–24 (a). His successor is warned of the dire consequences that will follow if he does not pray for the soul of Panammu; cp. the list of curses in no. **7** Sefire i A 14 f.

24 (b)–26. His successor is adjured not to engage in the kind of wholesale slaughter of members and adherents of the royal house, which so often accompanied an accession in the ancient Near East; cp. in the context of a treaty no. **9** Sefire iii 9 f., 17 f., 21 f., and in the Bible Solomon's execution of Adonijah, Joab, and Shimei (1 Kgs ii); cp. further 1 Kgs. xvi 11; 2 Kgs. x 6 f.; xi 1, etc.

27–31 (a). In the event of internecine strife in the royal house, a rigorous process of trial by peers, to be supervised by the king, is laid down, whereby an aggrieved party may obtain justice; the punishment of the guilty is to be by stoning; cp. in Israelite law passages like Deut. xiii 6 f.; xxi 18 f.; xxii 13 f.

31 (b)–34. The vengeance of the gods is invoked on his successor (now addressed directly), if he takes part himself in such persecution of rivals; provocation is no excuse.

There is nothing in the last two sections about tampering with the statue, a view widely held, but based on an erroneous reading of יגנב, 'he steals' for יגמר, 'let him assemble' in 28, and a mistranslation of זכרי, '(his kindred) male' in the same line as 'my memorial'.

Historical circumstances

The dynasty to which Panammu belonged began with his father קרל, who may have been a usurper like Zakir of Hamath, but was not a Semite. Panammu, however, gave a Semitic name to his son Barṣur (Panammu 1, 3), which bears witness to the growing importance of the Aramaean element in his kingdom, as does the language he employs in this inscr.; the previous dynasty of Kilamuwa used Phoen. The inscr. gives no historical information, except indirectly. Thus the buoyant tone of its opening section, and the absence of references to external troubles point to a date in the first half of the 8 cent., when Syria enjoyed freedom from Assyrian intervention. This was the period which further south saw the long and prosperous reigns of Jeroboam in Israel and Uzziah in Judah. The opening lines here imply that, having come to the throne at an early age, Panammu's reign had so far been equally long and happy. The final part (24 f.) introduces a more querulous note, and shows his concern about a bloodless succession. It seems likely that the dynastic squabbling described in the first two or three lines of the Panammu (II) inscr. had already commenced, which would make the erection of the statue belong to the final years of his reign. If my interpretation of these lines (see at Panammu 4) is correct, Panammu I met his death in the ensuing coup.

Writing and date

A comparative study of the writing confirms these deductions. All the inscrs. from Zenjirli share a similar script, which in so far as the two can be distinguished is nearer to the Aram. than the Phoen. style, even where the latter language is used. Of the letters where a development can be traced the א; ה; ז; ט; ס; and ק of this inscr. retain the shapes of the older (late 9 cent.) Kilamuwa inscrs. (*KAI* nos. 24, 25), whereas ד; ו; ח; י; and כ resemble more the shapes of the later Panammu and Barrakkab inscrs. (nos. **14–17**) which date to between 733 and 727 B.C. The closest single relative is the Sefire inscrs. (nos. **7–9**); a similar date, around 760–50 B.C., is indicated; on this basis we may put the years of Panammu I's reign at roughly 780–743. Words are separated by dots.

The letters ו and י operate as internal *matres lectionis* in קירת and כפירי (10); יהבית (11); מומת (24) and יומו (for יומת; 26); איח(י)ה (27, 28, 30) and איחתה (28, 31).

A noteworthy feature of the orthography, and one that does not make interpretation any easier, is the large proportion of writing errors that can be detected. I have found the following: אנהו for אלהו (2); דדד for הדד (2); חלבת(י) for חלבבתי (10, 12); לבבתה for חלבבתה (19); שם. נ for לשמש (18); יומו for יומת (26); and possibly אן for הן or אם (15); and אנו for הנו (30). There may be one or two more. This suggests a rather careless mason, but perhaps also (though cp. Sefire) one unpractised in writing the dialect, which may therefore have only recently replaced Phoen. as an official medium.

Language

This dialect, which is also found in the next inscr., is basically Aram. in character, as the majority of isoglosses in both phonology and grammar and the bulk of the vocabulary show; but there is a substantial minority of features that link it more closely with the Canaanite dialects, and a few where it is independent of either group, or at least preserves an earlier stage of development. We may regard it as standing in an analogous relation to the Aram. dialects as Moabite does to Hebr. (see in vol. I 72 f.). It should not be called Ya'udic; see again on יאדי (1).

In *phonology*, the interdentals and emphatics behave as outlined in the Note at the beginning of this volume; thus ק = [ġ] in ארק (*passim*); ארקו (13) and ירקי (18, 22); not, however, in צרי (30). Another feature of the phonology, shared by the Phoen. inscrs. of Kilamuwa, but also by Sefire (see nos. **7–9** introd.), is the occasional substitution of [b] for [p]; thus נבש (*passim*); תאלב (34) and perhaps the word חלבבה (see at 3) and לבתכה (23). In רש (Panammu 12) there is possibly a case of the elision of ['] in pre-consonantal position, but the text is very uncertain. The use of א instead of ה as a *mater lectionis* in שתא (9) and *passim* in fem. nouns shows, however, that ['] has regularly lapsed at the end of words; cp. פא (17, 33); וא (Panammu 12). There is assimilation of ['] to [t] in יתמר (10). Prosthetic א is quite common; אשם (16); ארקרשף (11) and ארקו (13); אגם (Panammu 5). As usually in Aram. the [n] of מן, 'from', does not assimilate with the following consonant. Diphthongal reduction is widespread but, against the normal orthographic practice elsewhere, is not always reflected in the orthography, giving a number of historical spellings; thus הושבת (19) against משב (8); יומי (Panammu 9) against ימי (9); איחיה (27) against איחה (30; Panammu 17).

In *grammar*, the pronouns אנך (1) and אנכי (Panammu 19); זן (*passim*) and זנה (Panammu 22), fem. זא (18), connect the dialect respectively with Canaanite and Aram., although זן occurs in the Phoen. of Byblos (*KAI* no. 1 Ahiram 2). The longer forms אנכי and זנה are prob. historical spellings, preserving an ending no longer pronounced. The plur. 'these' is ['ēl] as in no. **5** Zakir. 'Who?' is מן as in Aram. (Hebr. מי). Nouns have neither an emph. state nor definite article; cp. vol. I no. **1** Gezer; *KAI* no. 1 Ahiram. With masc. plur. nouns the abs. endings are [ū] for the nominative, [ī] for the oblique, without mimation or nunation; the constr. of both is [ay] or [ē], possibly dropped in the nominative; thus אלהי (Panammu 22) but אלה (Panammu 2); cp. and contrast Gezer in Hebr., where [ū] is the nom. constr. (abs. presumably [ūm]). Fem. plur. nouns end in ת as in Canaanite, not ן as in Aram. (abs.); contrast nos. **7–9** Sefire, which have ת in nouns and adjectives, but ן in verbal partics. There are a number of fem. abstract nouns ending in [ū] or [ī]; constr. [ūt], [īt], a typical Aram. structure. The 3 masc. sing. suffix with masc. plur. nouns is [ēh] from [ayh]; א(י)ח(י)ה (27, 30); contrast both Hebr. יו and Aram. וה. Suffixes are added to אב and אח in the Aram. manner; אבוה (Panammu 2). In verbs, the endings of the perf. 1 sing. (ת); perf. 3 fem. sing. (ת), and the imperf. 3 fem. plur. (ן) are the regular Aram. The imperf. 3 masc. plur. has [ū] as in Canaanite, but this ending is found (as a jussive) at Nerab (nos. **18**, **19**) and not infrequently at Sefire and in biblical and Egyp. Aram.; such forms should be vocalized with penultimate stress; cp. יאבדו = [yēbádū] (Jerem. x 11). The Peal infin. lacks the [m] prefix of Aram., but there are parallels to this at Sefire (בשט; i A 24; לשגב; *KAI* no. 222 i B 32) and in biblical Aram. (לבנא; Ezra v 3). A Hithpeel form occurs in יתמר (10) where Hebr. has a Niphal. The dialect has a Huphal, formed as in Hebr.; מומת (24); יומת (26). In the imperf. of the Haphel, the ה is dropped, i.e. Aphel; יקם (28). Against Canaanite (and general Old Aram.) practice, verbs final ['] and final [w, y] are not always distinguished; thus שתא (9); תשתי (22); לבנא and יקרני (13). Aram. is the י in הרפי (Haph. perf.; Panammu 8) and before the suffix in בכיה (Pael perf.; Panammu 17, 19). As normally in the Hamath dialect (no. **5**) suffixes with verbal imperfs. are not preceded by [inn]; תהרגה (33); see further in the introduction to Sefire (nos. **7–9**).

In *vocabulary*, the following lists of common words show the respective relationships with the Canaanite and Aram. groups; references are given where my readings differ from previous ones. Typically Aram. are באשר, 'after'; בר; דלח; הוה, 'to be'; הן; חד; יהב (11, 12); יומי (plur.); כבר (verb); מז (from מה זי); מצע (Panammu 10); מרא; פם; קדם, 'before'. Typically Canaanite are אם, 'if'; גם; הרג; זר, 'stranger'; חלל, 'to slay' (Panammu 3); ישר (33); כרת; מקם, 'place'. Arabic gives the nearest parallels to גמר; הוה, Pael, 'to let fall'; the precative particle ל; the conjunction פ or פא; the [t] in קתל (the last two, however, occur at Sefire; for פ see *KAI* no. 223 ii B 4, 6). Akkad. loan-words are נש, 'oath', and several technical terms, especially in Panammu. The transposition of consonants in לגר, 'foot', is as in Mandaic. Not attested elsewhere are הנו, 'if, behold'; חלבבה; the adverb מת; the plur. form קירת and several other words or (if the base is known) particular forms.

Bibliography (including no. **14** Panammu)

Original publication in F. von Luschan and E. Sachau, *Ausgrabungen in Sendschirli* I (Berlin, 1893), 49 f.

The early treatment I have most used is D. H. Müller, *WZKM* 7 (1893), 33–70, 113–40.

See further:

NSE p. 440 f.

NSI nos. 61, 62.

J. A. Montgomery, 'Babylonian *niš* 'oath' in West Semitic', *JAOS* 37 (1917), 329 f.

A. Poebel, *Das appositionell bestimmte Pronomen der 1 Pers. Sing. in den westsemitischen Inschriften*, etc. (Chicago, 1932), 43 f.

No. **13**

1 ——— אנך [.] פנמו . בר . קרל . מלך . יאדי . זי . הקמת . נצב .
זן . להדד . בעלמי [.]

2 קמו . עמי . א̊נהו . דדד . ואל . ורשף . ורכבאל . ושמש . ונתן .
בידי . הדד . ואל .

3 ורכבאל . ושמש . ורשף . חטר . חלבבה . וקם . עמי . רשף . פמז .
אחז .

4 ביד[י] - - - מ̊א . פלח̊ - - י̊ . ומז . אשא̊[ל . מן .] אלהי . יתנו . לי .
ושנם . על . ויו .

5 .... *c.* 29 letters missing .... ל̊ - . ארק .
שער̊י . האע -

6 .... *c.* 31 .... [א]רק . חטי
[. ו]ארק [.] שמ̊י [.]

7 וארק ..... *c.* 10 ..... אז . ב̊ - - - - שפי .... *c.* 7 ... יעבדו .
ארק . וכרם .

8 שם . יש[בו] .... *c.* 8 .... [ע]ם̊ . פנמו . גם [.] ישבת . על . משב .
אבי . ונת̊ן . [ה]ד̊ד̊ [.] בי[ד]י̊ .

Ginsberg, 'Problems', *passim*; see also *JAOS* 62 (1942), 183 f.
B. Landsberger, *Sam'al: Studien zur Entdeckung der Ruinenstätte Karatepe* (Ankara, 1948).
J. Friedrich, *Phönizisch-punische Grammatik* (Rome, 1951), Anhang: 'Skizze der Sprache von Ja'udi im nördlichen Syrien'.
EHO, 61 f. (a disappointing treatment).
Garbini, 'Antico', 256 f.
Koopmans, *Chrest.* nos. 9, 11.
KAI nos. 214, 215.
J. Friedrich, 'Zur Stellung des Jaudischen innerhalb der nordwestsemitischen Sprachgeschichte', *Studies in Honor of Benno Landsberger* (Chicago, 1965), 425 f.
J. C. Greenfield in *Leshonenu* 32 (1968), 359 f. (Hebrew article with English summary).

Plates and figures (Hadad)

Von Luschan, loc. cit., Tafn. VI–VII; *NSE* Taf. XXII (a drawing, which is unreliable in certain respects); Birnbaum, *Scripts*, no. 016.

---

1. I am Panammu, son of QRL, king of Y'DY, who have raised this statue for Hadad. In my youth

2. there stood with me the gods Hadad and El and Resheph and Rakkabel and Shemesh, and into my hands did Hadad and El

3. and Rakkabel and Shemesh and Resheph give the sceptre of authority; and Resheph stood with me. So whatever I grasped

4. with my hand . . . . . . cultivated; and whatever I asked from the gods they used to give to me; . . . . . .

5. . . . . a land of barley it was over

6. . . . . a land of wheat, and a land of garlic,

7. and a land . . . . they used to till land and vineyard;

8. there did dwell . . . . with Panammu. Moreover, I sat on my father's throne, and Hadad gave into my hands

9 חטר . חל[בבה . גם . הכר]ת . חרב֯ . ולשן . מן . בית . אבי . ובימי .
גם . אכל . ושתא [. יא]ד֯י [.]

10 ובימי . יתמ֯ר . ל֯ - - - - - י . לנצב . ק֯יר֯ת . ולנצב . זררי . ולבני .
כפיר֯י . חלבת֯[י . ג]מ֯ . יקח[ו .]

11 אשר֯ו . יה֯[ב]י֯ת֯ . ה[ד]ד - - - אל . ורכבאל . ושמש . וארקרשף .
וכברו . נתנה . לי . ואמן . כ֯רת .

12 בי . ובימי . חלבת֯[י .] - ד֯ת֯ - . א֯הב . ל֯אלהי . ומת . יקחו . מן .
יד֯י . ומה . אשאל . מן . אלהי . מת . ית֯[נ]ו֯ [.]

13 ל֯י . וארק֯ו . ד֯ש - [בר] . קרל . אלהי . מ֯ת . פ֯לו . נתן . הדד .
מת . ל[י . מ]ת [.] יקרני . לבנא . ובח֯לבבתי .

14 נתן . מ֯ת . ו֯[מ]ת֯ [. קר]א֯נ֯[י .] ל֯בנא . פבנית . מ֯ת . ו[ה]קמת .
נצב . ה֯דד . זן . ומ֯קם . פנמו . בר . קר֯ל . מלך .

15 יאדי֯ [.] ו֯מן . אנ֯ . חד֯ [.] לפנמו . בני . יאחז [. חט]ר . וישב . על .
משבי . ויסעד֯ . אברו . ויזבח .

16 הדד . זן [. פא] . יא[מ]ר֯ [.] את֯ [.] נשי . ויזבח . [הדד . ז]ן . פ֯כ֯א [.]
יזבח . הדד . ויזכר . אשמ֯ . הדד . או .

17 כ֯א . פא . יאמר֯ [. תאכל . נב]ש . פנמו . עמך . ותש[תי . נ]בש [.]
פ֯נמו [.] עמ֯ך . עד֯ . יזכר . נבש . פנמו . עמ֯ [.]

18 [ה]ד֯[ד] . ב֯י֯מ֯ . . . . *c.* 8 . . . . - ב֯אה֯ [.] זא . י֯תן . ל֯[הדד . וי]רקי .
בה [.] ש֯י [.] להדד . ולאל . ולרכבאל . ושם . נ֯

19 - - - - - מ֯נ֯ - - - - ב֯כ֯ - - - - - י֯ . קי֯זא . פ֯ב֯נ֯[ית]ה . והושבת . בה֯ .
אלהי . ו֯בלבבתה֯ . חנאת .

20 [ואלהו .] נתנו . לי . זרע . חבא . . . *c.* 6 . . . י - - ו֯מ[ן . חד .] בני .
יאחז . חטר . וישב . על . משבי֯ . מ֯ל֯ך֯ [.]

21 על֯ . [יאדי] . ויסעד . אברו . וי֯ז֯[בח . הדד . זן . ולא . יזכ]ר .
אשם . פנמו . י֯אמר [.] ת[א]כ֯ל . נבש . פנ֯מ֯ו֯ [.]

9. the sceptre of authority; [he also cut off] sword and slander from my father's house; and in my days also Y'DY ate and drank.
10. In my days command was given . . . . to establish cities and establish towns; and to the inhabitants of the villages my authority extended; the
11. districts received the bounty of Hadad and El and Rakkabel and Shemesh and 'RQRŠP; and greatness was granted to me, and a sure covenant struck
12. with me. In the days of my authority . . . . would I offer to the gods, and they used to accept (them) from my hand; and what I asked from the gods, they used always to give
13. to me. Favour did my god . . . . the son of QRL continually. Then if ever Hadad gave to me, he used always to call on me to build; and during my rule
14. he did always give, and did always call on me to build. So I have built, and I have raised a statue for this Hadad, and a place for Panammu, son of QRL, king
15. of Y'DY. Now, if one of Panammu's sons should grasp the sceptre and sit on my throne and maintain power and do sacrifice
16. to this Hadad, and should say, By thee I swear, and do sacrifice to [this Hadad], whether in this way he does sacrifice to Hadad and invokes the name of Hadad or
17. in another, let him then say, May the soul of Panammu [eat] with thee, and may the soul of Panammu drink with thee. Let him keep remembering the soul of Panammu with
18. Hadad; in the days . . . . this . . . . . let him give to [Hadad], and may he look favourably upon it as a tribute to Hadad and El and Rakkabel and Shemesh;
19. . . . . this . . . . . .; so I built it, and I have made my god to dwell in it, and in his authority I have found rest.
20. [Now the gods] have granted me a seed to cherish . . . . If (however), [any] of my sons should grasp the sceptre and sit on my throne as king
21. over [Y'DY] and maintain power and do sacrifice [to this Hadad, and should not] remember the name of Panammu, saying, May the soul of Panammu eat

22 עם . הדד . ותשתי . נבש . פנמו . עם . ה֯[דד] . הא . . . . *c.* 12
. . . . . . חהן . זבחה . ואל . ירקי [.] בה [.] ומז .

23 ישאל . אל . יתן . לה . הדד . והדד . חרא . לבתכ֯ה . . . .
c. 17 . . . . [א]ל . יתן . לה . לאכל . בר֯גז .

24 ושנה . למנע . מנה . בלילא . וד֯לח֯ . נתן . ל[ה] . . . . *c.* 16
. . . . [א]יח[י . ומ]ו֯דדי [.] מ֯ו֯מת֯ [.] מ֯ - ת֯י .

25 יאחז . חטר . ביאד֯[י] . וישב . על . משבי . וימ֯ל[ך . מלך . אל .
יש]ל֯ח . ידה . בחרב . ב[בית . אב]י . או .

26 [בחמא . או . ב]חמ֯ס [.] אל . יהרג [.] או . ברגז . או . על . א֯ - - א֯ .
א֯ל֯ [.] י֯ומו . מת . או . על . קשתה . או . על . אמרתה .

27 . . . . *c.* 14 . . . . [א]חה . ירשי . שחת . ב֯אשר֯ . חד . א֯יחיה .
או . בא֯שר . חד֯ . מודדיה . או . באשר .

28 חדה . איח[תה . או . מן . חד . בית]י֯ . ירשי . שחת . יגמר֯ . א֯י֯[ח]יה .
זכ֯רי . ויקם . ותה . במאה . מ֯ת[.]נ֯שה .

29 יאמר . אחכם . השחת . הנ . . . *c.* 6 . . . [י]ש֯א . יד֯יה . לאלה .
אבה . נ֯שה . יאמר . הן֯ . אם . שמת . אמרת . אל . בפם .

30 זר֯ . אמר . קם . עיני . או . ד֯לח . או֯ [. שמת . אמרת]י . בפמ֯ .
אנשי֯ . צרי . פ֯א֯נו . זכר . הא . לתגמר֯ו֯ . איחה .

31 זכ֯רו . פלכתשה . באבני . והנו . ר֯ת֯ . . . *c.* 6 . . . [לתגמ]רן .
א֯יחת[ה .] פלכתשנה . באבני . והנו . לו . שחת .

32 באשרה . ות֯לעי . עינך . בא[ש]רה֯ [. א]ו֯ . . . *c.* 6 . . . [או .] ע֯ל [.]
קשת֯ה [.] או . על . גברתה . או . על . אמרתה .

33 או . על . נדבה . את . פא . ישר . הא֯ . א֯ - - ר [.] וה[ן] . . . . . . *c.* 11
. . . . . א֯ו . תהרגה . בח[מס . או .] ב֯חמ֯א . או .

34 תחק . עליה . או . תאלב . אש . זר [.] ל֯הרגה . י . . . . . *c.* 9 . . . .
[יהר]גו . - . . . .

22. with Hadad, and may the soul of Panammu drink with Hadad, as for him . . . . his sacrifice, and may he not look favourably upon it, and what
23. he asks, may Hadad not give to him, but with wrath may Hadad confound him, ... may he not allow him to eat because of rage,
24. and sleep may he withhold from him in the night, and may terror be given to him . . . . my kinsmen or relatives . . . . . . put to death . . . .
25. (and) he should grasp the sceptre in Y'DY and sit on my throne and reign [as king, let him not] put forth his hand with a sword against my [father's house], either
26. [in anger or in] violence; let him not do murder, either in rage or by . . . .; let no one be put to death, either by his bow or by his command.
27. . . . . his kinsman should plot the ruin of one of his kinsmen or one of his relatives or
28. one of his kinswomen, [or if any member of my house] should plot ruin, let him (sc. the king) assemble his male relatives, and stand him before a hundred (of them). On his oath
29. let him (sc. the aggrieved party) say, Your brother has caused (my) ruin. If (he denies it, and) he (sc. the aggrieved party) lifts up his hands to the god of his father, and says on his oath, If I have put these words in the mouth
30. of a stranger, say that my eye is fixed or fearful or [that I have put my words] in the mouth of enemies, then if it is a male (sc. who has plotted), let his male relatives
31. be assembled, and let them pound him with stones, and if it is . . . ., let her kinswomen be assembled, and let them pound her with stones. But if you (sc. the king) have persecuted any such,
32. your eye being wearied by him, either on account of . . . . or of his bow or of his power or of his command
33. or of his instigation—yes you—, then he is in the right, you are . . . ., and if . . . . or you slay him in violence or in anger, or
34. you issue a decree about him, or you incite a stranger to slay him, may (the gods) . . . . slay . . . .

NOTES

1. אנך = [ʾnāk]; cp. Moabite אנך = [ʾanōk]; Hebr. אנכי; in Panammu 19 אנכי is a historical spelling, unless we suppose both forms were used interchangeably. פנמו; Akkad. (*m*)*Pa-na-am-mu-u*; ו therefore = [ū]; the original Hittite ending is [muwa]. קרל is doubtless another Anatolian name; it is not recorded in the Assyrian sources. יאדי; the pronunciation is unknown. An equation with the (*kur*)*Ia-ú-da-a-a* of an undated and ill-preserved portion of Tiglathpileser III's annals (*ANET*, 282b; see also *DOTT*, 54), describing a campaign in the north of Syria, is to be resisted. Elsewhere in Assyrian records this name refers indubitably to Judah (see, e.g., *ANET*, 282a). The Azriau mentioned as its king can therefore only be Azariah (Uzziah), who *c.* 743 B.C. at the end of his long reign must have organized a coalition of Syro-Palestinian states against Tiglathpileser's invasion in much the same way as Hadadezer of Damascus a cent. previously at the time of the battle of Qarqar; see further in the introduction to Sefire (nos. **7–9**). On Judah's strength and international reputation in Uzziah's day see 2 Chron. xxvi 6–15. Panammu's kingdom is called Samʾal by Tiglathpileser (*ANET*, 282–3) and by his own successors (no. **15** Barrakkab i 2); see further at no. **5** Zakir A 7. הקמת = [hqēmit]; Dan. iii 14. הדד; see at no. **1** Barhadad 2. נצב = [nṣīb]. זן = [d̲ēn]; זנה, the form in other inscrs., is in Panammu 22 probably a historical spelling. עלמי = [ʿlūmay]; Job xxxiii 25 and (another word) Eccles. xii 1; hardly [ʿālmī], lit. 'in my eternity', i.e. 'as my eternal abode' or the like (cp. *KAI* no. 1 Ahiram 1); a suffix is never found with this word (in Eccles. xii 5 and similar phrases it belongs with the first member of the constr. relation).

2. קמו עמי; no. **5** Zakir A 3. Note the mistakes in writing אלהו (= [ʾlāhū]) and הדד. אל; see at Zakir A 3. רשף = [ršēp]; cp. Deut. xxxii 24; Hab. iii 5; the Syrian god of pestilence, worshipped also at Carthage, where he had a temple, and earlier at Mari (cp. the name *A-bi-ra-sa-ap*, Huffmon, *Amorite Personal Names* (Baltimore, 1965), 20); he was equated by the Greeks with Apollo. רכבאל = [rākēb] or [rakkab ʾēl], 'rider, charioteer of El', according to *KAI* no. 24 Kilamuwa i 16 and Panammu 22 the patron deity of the royal house. The (*d*)*be-ʾ-li-ra-kab-bi ša* (*uru*)*Sa-ma-al-la* of an Assyrian letter (Harper, *Assyrian and Babylonian Letters*, 1892 f., 633, 7), i.e. 'the lord of the chariotry' is doubtless the same; in Greek mythology we may think of Iolaus, nephew and charioteer of Heracles; cp. also the epithet used of Baal in the Ugar. myths, *rkb ʿrpt*, 'rider on the clouds'; in the Bible of Yahweh Ps. lxviii 5. שמש = [šmēš]. נתן; sing. verb with a list of subjects as often in Daniel (iii 29; v 14, etc.). ידי = [yday]; dual with suffix.

3. חטר = [ḥṭōr]. חלבבה; a fem. noun with reduplicated third radical from (1) the base ḤLB; [ḥlab], 'milk', i.e. prosperity or the like; cp. the metaphorical uses in Exod. iii 8; Isa. lv 1; Joel iv 18, etc., or (2) the base ḤLP, 'to succeed (as king)' with [b] for [p], i.e. 'successorship, caliphate, legitimate rule' or the like; cp. no. **9** Sefire iii 22; vol. I no. **16** Mesha 6. It is written twice (10, 12) without the second ב (an alternative form?) and once (19) without the ה. מז = [mad̲] from [mā] and [d̲ī]; biblical מה די; Palm. מדי. אחז = [ʾēḥu/ōd̲]; the absence of a second א does not mean that the א in יאחז (15) was not pronounced; even in Arab. two hamzas are not tolerated in close proximity. The imperfs. in this and the following lines are frequentatives.

4. בידי; sing. as in 25 or dual. פלח; perhaps part of a noun or a verb from the base PLḤ, which means 'to serve (god)' as well as 'to labour, cultivate';

either suits the context. יתנו = [yittēnū]. The words at the end are presumably agricultural terms; they have not been identified.

5. שערי = [śʿārī]; plur. obl.; in Panammu 6, 9 שערה is fem. sing.; Hebr. also has two forms. At the end perhaps read הא[.]על.

6. חטי = [ḥiṭṭī]; plur. שמי = [ṯūmī]; Hebr. שומים (Num. xi 5); Palest. Aram. תומין; Arab. [ṯūmun].

7. אז; possibly as in Panammu 9 = [ʾaḏ], 'then'; Hebr. אז; biblical Aram. אדין. יעבדו = [yaʿbĕdū].

8. שם = [ṯām]; see at no. **9** Sefire iii 6. ישבו = [yiṯṯēbū], continuing the series of imperfs. There is room for a subject (people, gods?) and an adverbial phrase or phrases as in Isa. xxxii 17, 18; Ezek. xxviii 26; cp. also vol. I no. **16** Mesha 9. גם is only found in this dialect and in Moabite outside of Hebr. ישבת = [yiṯbēt]. משב = [mōṯab].

9. The restoration הכרת is Müller's; Haph.; the base is not found in later Aram., but the Peal occurs in 11; cp. Ps. xii 4 and with a similar verb Hos. ii 20. לשן = [liššān]; for an additional example in this sense see Ps. cxl 12. ימי = [yōmay] from [yawmay]; cp. יומי (Panammu 10; constr.); the plur. in the Canaanite dialects is [yamīm]. With the final phrase cp. 1 Kgs. iv 20. שתא; the א may be regarded as a replacement for ה due to the partial merging of bases final [ʾ] and [w, y].

10. יתמר = [yittmar]; (H)ithpeel imperf. with [ʾ] assimilated to [t]; cp. יתסר (Ahiqar 80); the meaning 'command' is suggested by the next readable phrase; it is rare for this verb in Hebr. Afterwards supply לבני ארקי (?); instead of ל, however, perhaps read ו. קירת = [qīrāt] with internal *mater lectionis*; the sing. may have been [qīr] as in Moabite, although the plur. there is קרן (vol. I no. **16** Mesha 29); see further at 19, where קר is a possible reading; the usual Aram. is קריה. זררי; an unknown plur. form, translated to accord with the context. כפירי = [kpīrī] with internal *mater lectionis*; see at no. **9** Sefire iii 23. יקח[ו] = [yiqqáḥū]; no dot is visible after ח; if the interpretation of the next difficult phrase is accepted, a ו must have been crushed in at the end of the line, unless it was carelessly omitted.

11. Lidzbarski reads (*NSE*) יקח . אש . רעיה . ויתר הדד, i.e. 'each received his neighbour; and Hadad and El, etc., were abundantly gracious ......'. רעיה = [rēʿēh]; prob. sing.; cp. רעיך (2 Sam. xii 11) and for the reduced diphthong איחה (30); this word is absent from Aram. except for Ahiqar 222 (רעה). יתר; presumably Pael, lit. 'make to increase, abound'; cp. Deut. xxviii 11 (Hiph.). But decisive against this reading is the dot after ו (not ע; note the down-stroke) and after ת (there is no room for ר). אשרו = [ʾaṯrū]; nom. plur.; the meaning 'region, district' is common in Syriac, though I have found no example without a qualifying adjective or following noun. יהבית = [yahbīt]; constr.; Targum Eccles. v 10; note the internal *mater lectionis*. ה[ד]ד; better perhaps הד[ד . ו]אל with wide spacing. ארקרשף = [ʾarġē ršēp], 'favourite of Resheph'; passive partic. with prosthetic [ʾ]; cp. רצוי (Deut. xxxiii 24); a noun and verb from this base (later Aram. RʿY; Arab. RḌY) occur in 13, 18, 22. For prosthetic [ʾ] in a divine name see ארשף on a Punic inscr. from Ibiza (*KAI* no. 72, A 1). כברו = [kabbīrū]; fem. sing. נתנה = [ntīnā]; passive partic. אמן = [ʾmōn]; Hebr. [ʾōmn]; כרת = [krīt]; with the whole phrase cp. Neh. x 1. In a more general sense cp. this section with 2 Sam. xxiii 5 and other passages on the Davidic covenant.

12. אהב = [ʾēhab] from [ʾihhab]; cp. תהב (*KAI* no. 222 Sefire i B 38); in later Aram. the imperf. of this verb is replaced by יתן from NTN. A word meaning

'gifts' or the like may have preceded. מת; a troublesome adverb, which can occupy any position in the clause. It is usually rendered 'surely, indeed', a colourless translation which naturally fits every context, but also suitable, especially in conjunction with the frequentative imperfs., in a meaning 'always, ever', and this has the merit of allowing an etymological link with Arab. [matay]; Akkad. *ina matē*; Hebr. [matay]; Syriac ['emat] (with [y] written but not pronounced); all 'when?', but Akkad., Syriac, also 'whenever'; vocalize therefore [mat]. מה; cp. no. 9 Sefire iii 3.

13. ארקו = ['arġū]; fem. sing. with prosthetic [']; cp. Syriac *'r't*, Luke ii 14 (Sinaiticus); Hebr. רצון in Ps. v 13; cxlv 16. The following letter, which could also be ר (or ו) will then begin a verbal perf. meaning 'bestow' or the like; the ש could be מ. אלהי; sing. with suffix, giving more room for a preceding verb and perhaps prepos. בר; בת, 'house', would be better (cp. 9), but in the Zenjirli inscrs. this word is always written בית, for which there is no space. Alternatively וארקו = [warġaw/ō] with the א belonging to the copula; cp. Panammu 12; אלהי is then plur. with suffix, or a mistake for אלהו. A possible restoration in the gap is בשי בר, i.e. 'and favourably upon the tribute of the son of QRL did my (the?) gods look always'; cp. 18. לו; with the perf. as in 31 and as normally in Hebr. יקרני = [yiqrēnī] with the diphthong reduced as in verbs final [w, y]; cp. יענני (no. 5 Zakir A 11). לבנא = [libnē] with א as in למבנא (Ezra v 2); לבנא (ibid. 3; note the false vocalization, as if to suggest מבנא) and other infins. in biblical and Egyp. Aram. from bases final weak, whether the last radical was originally ['] or [w, y]. A vocalization [ā] is impossible in a form from the base BNW, although an infin. like מקרא (Cowley xxviii 4) may at an earlier stage have stood for [miqra'] or [miqrā]; base Proto-Sem. QR'.

14. קראני = [qar'ánī] with the ['] retained in non-final position; cp. חנאת (19). בנית = [bnayt] as in biblical suffixed forms (Dan. iv 27) or [bnēt] as in free forms (Dan. iv 2). מקם = [mqām]; here 'tomb'; cp. *KAI* no. 14 Eshmunazar 4; this word is rare in later Aram., and does not have the meaning 'place'.

15. For ו perhaps read פ; the letter is very faded. The phrase beginning with מן (= [man]) is difficult to analyse, but cp. the formula הן מן חד followed by a plur. noun (or its equivalent) in no. 9 Sefire iii 9–10, 'If any of my brothers, etc.'. There is no justification for Lidzbarski's reading עם . נצב . חד - - מן . מן, i.e. 'a place for Panammu, king of Y'DY, together with a statue. Now, whoever from among my sons, etc.'. For אן perhaps read אם (29) or regard as a mistake for or by-form of הן; cp. אנו (30); it would look better before מן. יאחז = [yi'ḥu/ōd]; see at אחז (3). ישב = [yittēb]. יסעד = [yis'ad]; for the sense cp. in Hebr. Isa. ix 6; Prov. xx 28. אברו = ['abbīrū]; fem. sing. יזבח = [yidbaḥ]; later DBḤ; Arab. ḎBḤ. The verb is followed by a direct object as in Sabaean; Hebr. requires [l].

16. The restoration פא is suggested by the occurrence in 17. יאמר = [yi'mar]. The following phrase means lit. 'Thou art my oath'; the writing is very faded, and the ת seems to be written over another letter; but cp. the idiom אמר נשה, lit. 'he said his oath' in 28, 29. It is difficult to avoid linking this idiom with the Akkad. *nīš zakāru*, lit. 'to speak the oath of', i.e. 'swear by' such and such a deity. Akkad. *nīšu* comes from the base NŠW/' (Hebr. NŚ') and also means an act of 'lifting'. The word here and Syriac [nīšā], 'banner, sign, portent' are prob. Akkad. loan-words; but Syriac also possesses a plur. form [nessē], 'signs', which is connected with Hebr. [nēs], 'standard'; Ps. lx 6, 'warning'; Palest. Aram. [nissā], 'sign, miracle'; the base NSS does not exist in a verbal

form (the verb in Ps. lx 6 is from NWS, 'to flee'), but may have meant 'to be high, conspicuous'. The semantic overlapping shown in these words and phrases allows us with Montgomery (1917) to bring the strange phrase יהוה נסי, 'Yahweh is my banner' ('oath'?) in Exod. xvii 15 into the reckoning; notice verse 16, which involves the solemn cursing of Amalek. כא = [kā], 'thus, here'; the reading is suggested by the first word in 17, where the left top corner of כ is visible; cp. the double כה (= [kō]) in passages like Exod. ii 12; Num. xi 31; xxiii 15; 1 Kgs. ii 30. יזכר = [yid̲ku/ōr], 'remember', or more likely (H)aphel [yad̲kēr], 'make mention of, call upon, invoke'; cp. Isa. xxvi 13, etc.; for the dropping of [h] in the imperf. see יקם (28). אשם = ['ušm]; so no. **7** Sefire i C 25 but not no. **5** Zakir C. The passage 15 f. is not easy to piece together accurately, although the general drift is clear; we have stereotyped phrases repeated a number of times, but the linking words are unfortunately missing or faded. It is also impossible to say with certainty where the main clause begins; *NSI* not till עד . יזכר (end of 17); the translation at פא . יאמר (start of 17); but it could be at the earlier פא . יאמר in this line.

17. For the restoration see 21–2. תאכל = [ti'ku/ōl]. נבש = [nbaš]. תשתי = [tištay/ē]; jussive, though the imperf. also has י (ירשי; 27) in contrast with the ה of Sefire (q.v. nos. **7–9** introduction). עד is taken here = [ʿōd] from [ʿawd], 'still, yet, again, etc.', though the word is found elsewhere in Aram. only a few times in the Egyp. papyri; this is the only possibility if the next sentence begins with בימ (18). But these three letters are uncertain; if (with י for ב) they begin a verbal form, [ʿad], 'until, as long as' may be read here, i.e. 'As long as . . . . . , may . . . . .'. For examples of עד without the relative see no. **9** Sefire iii 6; Driver vi 5. יזכר; here Peal, since the object is not divine.

18. An acceptable restoration is perhaps בימי חלבבתה, 'Throughout the days of his rule let him, etc.'. This leaves room for a letter before באה; the faint traces visible could be of ז, in which case we may have yet another mistake, for זבחה as in 22; but though a fem. form [dibḥā] exists in Syriac, the word for 'sacrifice' is always masc. in the Canaanite and west Aram. dialects; nor do I know of an example construed with נתן, 'to give'. ל[הדד]; the faint shape two after ל may be another ל; ל[א]ל[הה], 'to his god'(?). ירקי = [yirġay/ē]; jussive; cp. no. **9** Sefire iii 6 (Pael). בה = [bah]; fem. שי = [šay/ē]; Ps. lxviii 30; lxxvi 12; Isa. xviii 7; Ugar. *šy*. שם . נ; the dot is faded, but the נ is clear; nevertheless we must have a mistake for שמש; cp. 2–3; no other line in the inscr. finishes in the middle of a word; the prepos. ל is also missing.

19. קיזא; unknown; the י is very doubtful; perhaps read קר[.]זא, i.e. 'this city'; see at 10 (קירת) and cp. *KAI* no. 26 Karatepe ii 9, 18; *KAI* no. 14 Eshmunazar 15 f. If the capital is meant, בניתה (= [bnaytah]; see at 14) has the meaning 'rebuild', 'reconstruct'; cp. vol. I no. **16** Mesha 21 f.; no. **5** Zakir B 4, 10. Also possible is נצבתה = (nṣabtah); cp. 10. אלהי; sing. with suffix in this context. הושבת = [hōt̲bēt]. Note the omission of ח in the second last word. חנאת = [ḥan'ēt]; from a base final ['], not in this case merged with a form from a base final [w, y], and therefore dubiously connected with ḤNW, Hebr. 'encamp'; Syriac 'aim at'; Arab. 'bend'. In any case the meaning 'rest' usually assigned it (and adopted here for want of a better) does not follow obviously from any of these; the Pael occurs in Panammu 12. According to Caquot (in Ingholt and others, *Recueil de tessères de Palmyre*, Paris, 1955, 144) a form from the base may occur on a tessera from Palmyra, but no other instance has been found.

20. נתנו = [ntánū]. חבא; there is a fem. noun [ḥibbā] in Mishnaic Hebr. meaning 'love', and this gives a reasonable sense; in the classical period only [ḥōb]; Aram. [ḥubbā], masc. emph., 'bosom'. Panammu was an old man in 750 B.C., so the gift of progeny is clearly unconnected with the action of 19. ומן; the ו is unclear; perhaps הן should precede.

21. על; the ל appears to have been written over another letter, perhaps ט. לא = [lā] is required in the lacuna; it does not occur elsewhere in this inscr., or in Panammu. יאמר; the י is uncertain; read ל (?).

22. הא = prob. the personal pronoun, but possibly [hā], 'behold'; no. **15** Barrakkab i 17. זבחה; if the restoration in 18 is rejected = [d̲ibḥēh]; masc. with suffix.

23. חרא; a fem. noun from the base ḤRW; Hebr. חרון. לבתכה; no base BTK is known; the translation assumes a connection with Syriac PTK, Peal, 'to mix, mingle'; Pael, 'to vary, confuse'; i.e. [lbattkēh]. Lidzbarski (*NSE*) reads ליתכה = [lyattkēh]; Haph. from NTK with suffix (fem.), i.e. 'As for wrath, let Hadad pour it forth'; but the ב is clear; and in למנע (24) the [y] of the imperf. is replaced by [l]; the suffix also comes in very awkwardly. ל; a precative particle; Akkad. *lū*; Arab. [li]; Ugar. *l*. יתן; cp. 2 Chron. xx 10. לאכל = [li'ku/ōl]. רגז = [rgōz].

24. שנה = [šēnā]; cp. עטה (Dan. ii 14); or [šinnā] as in Palest. Aram. and Syriac. בלילא; no. **7** Sefire i A 12; vol. I no. **16** Mesha 15; the ending, which is identical in form if not in function with the locative, was *h* = [ah] in Ugar., now in this dialect [ā] as in Hebr.; the א is therefore a *mater lectionis*. דלח = [dlūḥ] as in Palest. Aram., where the base is common; Hebr. only Ezek. xxxii 2, 13, 'to make turbid'. נתן; one is tempted, in view of the mistake נ for ל in 2, to read לתן = [littēn] and bring the syntax into accord with the previous clauses; but it is prob. a passive partic. in lieu of a finite verb as in 11. After לה perhaps read ימם = [yōmām] or [yēmām]; cp. Hebr. יומם; Targum יימם; Exod. xiii 22; the first מ is visible, but the writing is much too faded for certainty. A fresh section begins in the lacuna. It is likely that the first clause, which is missing or damaged beyond recovery, speaks of an intention to kill rather than an actual execution of relatives, otherwise the following lines are contradictory; cp. the phrases used in no. **9** Sefire iii 10, 14. איחי = ['īḥay]; cp. Ugar. *'iḫh*, 'his brothers' (NK 35); perhaps the plural of אח (27?, 29) in this dialect, or a special form meaning 'kindred' in general, 'colleagues' or the like; cp. Panammu 17. מודדי = [mōd(ᵉ)day]; no. **9** Sefire iii 14. מומת = [mūmat]; apparently Huphal partic., masc. sing. with internal *mater lectionis*; in Hebr. cp. 1 Sam. xix 11; 2 Kgs. xi 2; or could it be an infin. like the strange forms מפרש and משרא in Dan. v 12? The bottom curl of מ can be seen in the last word; is it מ(י)תי, 'dead', masc. plur., to be construed with איחי, etc. (cp. מת; 26) or מ(ו)תי, 'my (Panammu's) death'?

25. A ו is expected before יאחז or another הן. The context demands אל in the lacuna. ידה = [ydēh]; sing.

26. For the restoration see 33. חמא = [ḥmā]; fem. חמס = [ḥmas]. יומי; in the light of מומת (24) this must be a mistake for יומת; Huphal imperf.; the next word is prob. [mīt], lit. 'be killed dead'; in Hebr. the infin. absolute is used. אמרתה = ['imrtēh]; Targum ['imrā] is masc.

27. אחה = ['ḥuh], 'his brother'; cp. אבוה (Panammu 2); or perhaps מן . חד .] אי[חה, '(If) any of his brothers'; cp. איחה (30). There is room before this for another phrase, either carrying on from the previous line or beginning the new section. ירשי; this difficult word is one of the cruces of the inscr.

There seem to be three bases or at least three different ranges of meaning. (1) Akkad. *muraššū*, 'accuser, calumniator' (D partic.); Egyp. Aram. רשי, 'to take a person to law'; 'to bring a suit against a person' with two direct objects; Syriac Peal, 'to blame, censure a person'; Aphel 'to lay something to the charge of' with [b] or [bātar] of the person. (2) Akkad. *rašū*, 'to obtain, take, possess'; Š, causative; Syriac Pael, Aphel, 'to give, confer'; Palest. Aram. Aphel, 'to lend'. (3) No. **9** Sefire iii 9, Peal, 'to assert authority over' with [l] of person; Nabat. and Palest. Aram. adjective רשי = [raššay], 'authorized, allowed'; Palest. Aram. Peal, 'to have power, authority'; Aphel, 'to allow, permit'; Hebr. רשיון (only Ezra iii 7); late Hebr. Hiph., 'to allow, empower'. The choice here is between meanings (1) and (3), (H)aph., i.e. [yaršay/ē], either '(If) his brother should bring a charge of destruction against (באשר)' or '(If) his brother should permit, allow, authorize, encourage destruction'. The second is preferred because in 31–2 באשר seems to go with שחת, though it is possible to argue that an abbreviated phrase is being used there, i.e. 'If (sc. the charge of) destruction (is brought) against him'. שחת; in 31 a perf., here an infin.; since there is no example in Aram. of an infin. Pael without the fem. ending, it is perhaps best to regard it as an infin. Peal; Palest. Aram. Peal, 'to mutilate'; Hebr. Piel, 'to destroy, spoil, pervert'. From a parallel base comes Sefire ישתחט (no. **7** i A 32); Palest. Aram. ŠḤṬ, Peal, 'to slay'; Mishnaic Hebr., Qal, idem; Syriac, Peal, 'to harm, impair'. באשר = [ba'ṯar]. The phrase means lit. 'to destroy after', i.e. 'persecute and destroy' or perhaps 'try to destroy'; cp. Hebr. בער אחרי, 'to burn, consume after' (1 Kgs. xiv 10; xxi 21).

28. חדה; in Hebr. the constr. would be used, or מן. איחתה = ['īḥātēh]; cp. 31. With the restoration cp. no. **9** Sefire iii 9–10. יגמר = [ygammēr]; Pael; the meaning is as in Arab. (conjug. II); Hebr. and later Aram., 'to come to an end; to complete, fulfil'. The usual reading is יגנב, but the מ seems to me clear, and if the final letter is more like ב, exactly the same may be said of the ר in לתגמרו at the end of 30. זכרי = [ḏikrī], masc. plur. of [ḏkar], 'male'; Palest. Aram. [dikrā]; Hebr. [zakār]; Arab. [ḏakarun]; cp. Nabat. אחוהי דכרין (*CIS* ii 209, 5). יקם = [yqīm]; (H)aph.; the subject is prob. the king, who is instructed to see that the due process of law is carried out. ותה = [wātēh], i.e. the subject of the last clause; cp. Syriac [lwāt], 'towards'; contrast Zakir (no. **5**) and Sefire (nos. **7–9**) אית; later Aram. ית. מאה; presumably the minimum number for a trial of nobility. Lidzbarski's reading (*NSE*) במצעה, 'in the midst' (fem.) is suggested by Panammu 10, not by the photograph. נשה; see at 16.

29. אחכם = ['ḥūkōm]. השחת; Haph. instead of Peal; cp. Hebr. Hiph. In the lacuna understand, 'If he (the accused) denies it' or the like. The next clause is best taken as a solemn declaration on the part of the accuser that his evidence is true; if it is a plea of innocence by the accused, then the person to be stoned must be the accuser, and death by stoning seems a rather harsh verdict. ישא = [yiśśā]; no. **5** Zakir A 11; also possible in this dialect is [yiśśē]; cp. שא = [śē] (Ezra v 15); לבנא (13). ידיה; dual. The god will be Rakkabel (2). הן and הנו (= [hinnū]?) are interchangeable like הן and הנה in Hebr., and have the same double meaning of 'if' and 'behold'; in later Aram. הן becomes ['in] (Palest.) or ['en] (Syriac), and is restricted to 'if'; 'behold' is הא (here in 22?); אם is only found here outside the Canaanite dialects. שמת = [śāmit]; Ezra vi 12. אמרת; see at 26; here plur. פם = [pum].

30. זר = [zār]; this meaning elsewhere only in Hebr. and Phoen. (*KAI* no. 26

Karatepe iii 16). קם = [qīm]; passive partic.; cp. 1 Kgs. xiv 4. דלח is also prob. passive partic., agreeing with עין. אנשי = [ʼanšī]. צרי = [ṣāray] with suffix or abs. [ṣārī]; ק is expected (cp. Arab. [ḍarra]), but perhaps [ġ] was no longer retained in initial position. On the other hand, the base is very rare in Aram., only Syriac [ʻar(r)tā], 'rival wife', so we may have a loan-word from Phoen.; cp. צרא (Targum 1 Sam. i 6). For another example of צ = Proto-Sem. [d̲] see no. 7 Sefire i A 28 (חצר). אנו; mistake for or by-form of הנו. לתגמׂרו = [litgammárū].

31. לכתשה = [liktšūh]. אבני = [ʼabnī]; plur. obl. In the lacuna supply a word (or phrase) meaning 'female', followed by הא = [hī]; cp. the phrases with בת in Gen. vi 2; Dan. xi 17. לתגמרן = [litgammrān]. לכתשנה = [liktšānah]. שחת; I take as 2 masc. sing., i.e. [šḥat(t)](Peal) or [šaḥēt(t)](Pael). In his desire to emphasize that the continued well-being of the royal house depends on the king's impartiality and lack of malice and his refusal to be provoked, Panammu addresses his successor directly. Alternatively (see on ירשי; 27), 'If the charge of persecution is brought against him (i.e. the king), and your eye, etc.', in which case the 'you' of the following lines is the people in general, and the crime being condemned is regicide.

32. תלעי; Palest. Aram. Lʻ'Y; perhaps connected with the base L'Y. גברתה = [gbūrtēh].

33. נדבה prob. = [nudbēh]; infin. with suffix; there is no masc. noun from this base in Aram. or Hebr. ישר = [yšar]; cp. Arab. [yasara]; unknown in Aram., and in Hebr. with the meaning 'upright, straight' rather than 'in the right', but the photograph is clear. Thereafter perhaps restore את . ישר, i.e. 'he is as much in the right as you are', though there is scarcely room. On the base HRG see further at no. 7 Sefire i A 24.

34. תחק = [tiḥu/ōq]; cp. מחן (Dan. iv 24); the base is ḤQQ. עליה = [ʻlēh]. תאלב; Pael, lit. 'teach' (with [b] for [p]). הרגה = [hurgēh]. The subject of the final clause is prob. the gods. One expects the suffix ך after [יהר]גו, but there appears to be a dot.

14. Panammu   Pl. IV

The inscr., discovered near Zenjirli in 1888, was written across the lower half of a monument erected by Barrakkab to his father, Panammu II; the edge of the overskirt of the statue runs through it; the top half, with the rest of the statue of the king, and much of the left-hand portion of the inscr. itself are missing. The area of writing measures about 1 m. high and, where whole lines survive, 1·50 m. broad. Like the previous inscr. it is housed in the Staatliche Museen, Berlin.

Again like Hadad it is technically a votive inscr., but Barrakkab uses much of his space rehearsing the career of his father. He gives sufficient information to enable us to date the inscr. and the events it records within quite accurate limits. Panammu, after eluding capture in a conspiracy or coup, which resulted in the death of his father Barṣur, and perhaps also of his grandfather Panammu I, appealed to Tiglathpileser III of Assyria, and with his assistance gained the throne, and crushed the dissident faction. It is prob. that these events took place during Tiglathpileser's campaign against Arpad in the years 743–740, and that the faction which ousted the ruling family for a time was nationalistic and anti-Assyrian (*ANET*, 282 f.; *DOTT*, 53 f.). For all we know, they may have been allies of Azariah of Judah in the coalition he forged at this time to resist the Assyrian advance (see further at Hadad 1). Having acceded, Panammu nursed his stricken country back to prosperity, and from time to time accompanied Tiglathpileser on his campaigns, meeting his death on one such expedition at Damascus. This can only have been in 733–732 B.C., when Tiglathpileser defeated Damascus and incorporated it within his empire, and subdued Israel, replacing Pekah with Hoshea (*ANET*, 284; *DOTT*, 55). At the end of the inscr. Barrakkab mentions his own accession and its confirmation by Tiglathpileser, which suggests that it was made early in his reign, in 732 or 731. The inscr. offers illuminating parallels to contemporary events and politics in Israel; cp. 2 Kgs. xv 17–31; xvi 5–10; xvii 1–6, 24.

On the relation of the script to earlier inscrs., and on the Zenjirli dialect see the introduction to Hadad. As there, dots are used as word-dividers. Internal *matres lectionis* are even more frequent than on Hadad; thus פלטוה (2); אבוה (2); איחי (3); קירת (4, 15); הוית (5); אשור (7 and *passim*, but note אשר; 18); קתילת (8); (possibly) קנואל (8); מוכרו (10); כפירי (10); איחה (17); בכיתה (17); possibly also משות and יושא (21). In מוכרו and יושא the vowels so represented are apparently short.

The transcription is made from the photograph in von Luschan and Sachau (1893), Taf. VIII with reference to the copy in NSE Taf. XXIII; see also Birnbaum, *Scripts*, no. 017. For bibliography see Hadad, and add for this inscr. Dupont-Sommer in Rosenthal, *Handbook*, sect. I, 3.

1 נצב . זן . שם . בררכב . לאבה . לפנמו . בר . ברצר . מל֯ך֯ [.
יאדי] - - י֯ . - - ב֯ - . שנת֯ [.] מ֯פלט[ה . א]בי . פ֯נ[מ]ו֯ [.] ב[צ]ד֯ק

2 אבה . פלטוה . אלה . יאדי . מן . שחתה . אלה . הות . בבית .
אבוה . וקם . אלה . הד֯[ד . ע]מ֯ה֯ [. ו]ק - - - משבה . ע֯ל [.]
ו֯ - - ו - - לא֯ד֯וש - - - - . שחת - - -

3 בבית . אבה . והרג . אבה . ברצר . והרג . שבעי *10 20 20 20* איחי .
אבה֯ . - - - - - . - ל . רכב . - ה . - - - - - - בך . עלמ֯ - - - - - ך .
בעל . - - - - חלל֯ [. ב]נ֯[י .] פ֯נ֯מ֯ו֯ [.] ב֯ר֯ . ק֯[רל]

4 ויתר֯ה . מת . מלא . מסגרת . והכבר . קירת . חרבת [.] מן . קירת֯ .
ישב֯ת .... *c.* 35 letters missing ....
תשמ[ו]

5 חרב . בביתי . ותהרגו . חד . בני . ואגם . הוית . חרב . בארק .
י֯אדי֯ . וה֯ל[לו .] א֯ל . פ֯נמו [.] ב[ר .]קרל . א[ב . אב] . אבי֯ -
מ֯ - ד֯ם . בנ֯ר֯ . אבד ..... *c.* 10 .....

6 שאה . ושורת֯ . וחטה . ושערה . וקם . פרס . בשקל . ושט֯רבת .
- - - . בשק֯ל . וא֯סנב֯ . משת֯ . בשקל . ויבל [.] אבי . בר֯ .....
..... *c.* 10

7 עד . מלך . אשור . ומלכה . ע֯ל . בית . אבה . והרג . אב֯ן֯ . שחת .
מן . בית . אבה [.] - - - - מן . אצרת֯ [. ב]כ֯[ל] . ארק֯ [.] יאדי .
מן . במ֯ .... *c.* 16 ....

8 ופשש . מסגרת . והרפ֯י֯ . שבי . יאדי . וק[ם .] אבי . והרפ[י] . נשי֯ .
בס ...... *c.* 11 ..... בא - . בית . קתילת . וקנ֯ו֯אל ....
...... *c.* 13

9 בית . אבה . והיטבה . מן . קדמתה . וכבר֯ת . חטה . ושערה .
ושאה֯ . ושורת֯ . ביומיה֯ . ואז [.] אכלת [.] ושת֯[י]ת֯ ....
.... *c.* 16

10 זלת . מוכרו . וביומי . אבי . פנמו . שם . מת . בעלי . כפירי֯ .
ובעלי . רכ֯ב . ו - ח - ב [.] אבי . פנמו . במצעה֯ ....
.... *c.* 25

1. This statue has Barrakkab set up for his father Panammu, son of Barṣur, king of [Y'DY] . . . . . . the year of his deliverance. As for my father Panammu, because of his father's righteousness
2. the gods of Y'DY delivered him from destruction. There was a curse on his father's house, but the god Hadad stood with him, and . . . . . . his throne against . . . . he destroyed . . . . . .
3. in his father's house, and he slew his father Barṣur, and he slew seventy kinsmen of his father . . . . (the commander) of the cavalry . . . . the commander of . . . . he executed the sons of Panammu, son of QRL;
4. and with the rest of them he kept on filling the prisons; and desolate towns he made more numerous than inhabited towns . . . . shall you set
5. the sword against my house, and slay one of my sons? So have I caused the sword to fall upon the land of Y'DY. Then these men executed Panammu, son of QRL, my [great-grand]father . . . . perished . . . .
6. corn and millet and wheat and barley; and a peres stood at a shekel, and a ŠTRBH of . . . . . . at a shekel, and a 'SNB of . . . . . . at a shekel. Then my father carried . . . .
7. to the king of Assyria, and he made him king over his father's house; and he slew the stone of destruction, ridding his father's house of it . . . . from treasuries throughout the land of Y'DY, from . . . .
8. and he made away with the prison-houses, and released the captives of Y'DY; and my father arose and released the women in . . . . the house of the women who had been killed; and QNW'L . . . .
9. his father's house, and he made it better than it was before; and wheat and barley and corn and millet were plentiful in his days; and then did (the land) eat and drink . . . .
10. cheapness of price. In the days of my father Panammu he always appointed commanders in the villages and commanders of the cavalry; and he gave my father Panammu authority in its midst . . . .

11 בי . לו . בעל . כסף . הא . ולו . בעל . זהב . בחכמתה . ובצדקה . פי̊ . אחז . בכנף̊ . מ[ר]אה . מלך . אשור . ר[ב] .... c. 20 ....

12 אשור . פחי . ואחי . יאדי . וחנאה̊ . מראה . מלך . אשור . על . מלכי̊ . כבר[י .] בר̊ש .... c. 28 ....

13 בגלגל . מראה . תגלתפלסר . מלך . אשור . מחנת . ת̊ - . מן . מוקא . שמש . וע̊ד . מערב .... c. 24 ....

14 רבעת [.] ארק . ובנת . מוקא . שמש . יבל . מערב . ובנת . מערב . יבל . מו[קא . ש]מש . ואב[י] .... c. 18 .... [והוסף . ל]

15 גבלה . מראה . תגלתפלסר . מלך . אשור . קירת . מן . גבל . גרגם . ---ו̊י̊ . [וא]בי . פנמו . בר̊ . ב̊[רצר] .... c. 18 ....

16 שמגר . וגם . מת . אבי . פנמו . בלגרי . מראה . תגלתפלסר . מלך . אשור . במחנת . גם [. בכיה . מראה . תגלתפלסר . מלך . אשור]

17 ובכיה . איחה . מלכו . ובכיתה . מחנת . מראה . מלך . אשור . כלה . ולקח . מראה [.] מלך̊ . [א]שור̊ ...... c. 12 ...... [תאכל . ותשת]

18 י . נבשה . והקם . לה . משכ̊י . בארח . והעבר . אבי . מן . דמשק . לאשר̊ . ביומי . ש̊ר .... c. 21 .... [ובכ]

19 יה . ביתה . כלה . ואנכי . ברכב . בר . פנמ[ו . בצ]ד̊ק̊ . אבי . ובצדקי̊ [.] הושבנ̊י̊ . מרא[י . תגלתפלסר . מלך . אשור . על . משב]

20 אבי . פנמו . בר . ברצר . ושמת [.] נצב . זן . [לאב]י . לפנמו . בר . ברצר . ומל̊כ̊ת̊ . בט̊ .... c. 24 ....

21 ואמר . במשות . ועל . יבל . אמן . יסמ̊[ך] . מלכ----- . ויבל . יוש̊א . קד̊ם̊ . קבר̊ . אבי . פנ[מו] .... c. 21 ....

22 וז̊כר . זנה . הא . פא . הדד . ואל . ור̊כבאל . בעל . בית . ושמש . וכל . אלה̊י . י̊אדי .... c. 21 .... [בית]

23 י . קדם . אלהי . וקדם . אנש .

11. my father, though he possessed silver and though he possessed gold, because of his wisdom and his righteousness. Then did he grasp the skirt of his lord, the [great] king of Assyria . . . .
12. of Assyria; then did he live, and Y'DY lived; and his lord, the king of Assyria, positioned him over powerful kings as the head . . . .
13. (ran) at the wheel of his lord Tiglathpileser, king of Assyria, in campaigns from the east to the west, and . . . .
14. (over) the four quarters of the earth. The daughters of the east he brought to the west, and the daughters of the west he brought to the east; and my father . . . . [and added to]
15. his territory did his lord Tiglathpileser, king of Assyria, towns from the territory of Gurgum . . . .; and my father Panammu, son of Barṣur . . . .
16. . . . . Then my father Panammu died while following his lord Tiglathpileser, king of Assyria, in the campaigns; even [his lord, Tiglathpileser, king of Assyria, wept for him],
17. and his brother kings wept for him, and the whole camp of his lord, the king of Assyria, wept for him. His lord, the king of Assyria, took . . . . [may]
18. his soul [eat and drink]; and he set up an image for him by the way, and brought my father across from Damascus to Assyria. In my days . . . .
19. all his house [wept] for him. Then me Barrakkab, son of Panammu, because of my father's righteousness and my own righteousness, did my lord [Tiglathpileser, king of Assyria,] make to sit [upon the throne]
20. of my father Panammu, son of Barṣur; and I have set up this statue for my father Panammu, son of Barṣur; and I have become king in . . . .
21. . . . . (untranslatable) . . . .
22. which this memorial is, then may Hadad and El and Rakkabel, lord of the dynasty, and Shemesh and all the gods of Y'DY . . . . [my house]
23. before the gods and before men.

NOTES

1. ברכב is short for בר רכבאל; see at Hadad 2. ברצר = [bar ṭūr], lit. 'son of the rock'; see for this divine element פדהצור (Num. i 10); צוריאל (Num. iii 35); later Aram. טורא. אבה = ['būh]; cp. אבוה (2). שמאל may be restored instead of יאדי; no. 15 Barrakkab i 2; thereafter perhaps זי with a verb. One expects ב before שנת, and the dot may be part of it; the reference is not, of course, to the time of the erection of the statue, which followed Barrakkab's accession (20). מפלטה = [mipltēh]; cp. Ps. lv 9; there is just room for the suffix. Otherwise the noun goes with אבי, and a new sentence begins in the previous lacuna. בצדק; cp. 11, 19; no. 15 Barrakkab i 4; in these passages with the nuance of loyalty towards an overlord (not paralleled in the Bible), here of devotion to the gods; Gen. vii 1; Mal. iii 18.
2. פלטוה = [palltūh]; Pael. אלה = ['lāh] from an earlier ['lāhay/ē] (22); nom. constr. שחתה = [šaḥtēh] or the like; the suffix is awkward, but the noun is masc. in 7. אלה = ['lā]; a word only known from Hebr., lit. 'oath, curse'; with the sense here cp. Deut. xxx 7; Jerem. xxiii 10; Prov. iii 33 (another word, but with ב). It is usually taken as 'conspiracy', but this meaning is unattested. הות = [hwāt]. קם; there is scarcely room for עמה (cp. Hadad 2), so we may have a reference to Hadad rising in anger; cp. vol. I no. 16 Mesha 5; no. 9 Sefire iii 24. The name of the rebel may follow על; for an Anatolian name beginning with [w] see no. 35 Saraïdin. A new sentence begins at the end of the line with the usurper as subject.
3. שבעי = [šib'ī]. The number consists of three sets of two large dots (:) followed by a single dot. The number 30 occurs on a fragment found at Zenjirli, and is formed of two short horizontal lines (the Phoen. 10) followed by one. Regularly in Phoen. numbers like 30 and 70 are made up of the sign for 20 plus 10 or 3 by 20 plus 10; but in a Hebr. inscr. from an area where Phoen. influence was strong (vol. I no. 4 Tell Qasile) a number 30 occurs, composed of three horizontal lines one on top of another, a method similar to that used on the Zenjirli fragment and in this inscr., where the dots evidently stand for lines. See Table of numerical signs and for Hebr. see the Table in vol. I. The middle of the line is beyond recovery. The word before רכב (= [rkēb], collect.; Hebr. [rēkb]) could be בעל as in 10, as could the על in the sequence עלמ, the reference being to the slaughter of high officials, whose replacement is alluded to in 10. חלל; the second ל is just visible; presumably Pael, lit. 'to pierce'; the base does not occur in later Aram. with this sense, but in Hebr. cp. Ezek. xxviii 9 (Piel); Isa. liii 5 (Pual), and the common adjective [ḥalāl], 'slain'. The restorations at the end are by no means certain, but בר and ק are reasonably clear; the brothers of Barṣur will be meant.
4. יתרה = [yitrēh] with suffix referring to בית; presumably the less important members of the royal house, whose release is mentioned in 8. מת; a meaning 'always, ever' (see at Hadad 12) is distinctly awkward in this context. מלא; Pael. מסגרת = [misgrāt]; Ps. xviii 46. הכבר; a common base in Aram.; a verbal form in Hebr. only in Job xxxv 16; xxxvi 31 (Hiph.) חרבת = [ḥārbāt]; Targum Ezek. xxvi 19. ישבת = [yāṯbāt]; Targum Isa. liv 1. Alternatively, the forms may be vocalized as passive partics. תשמו = [tśīmū]. Müller rather imaginatively supposes the speaker to be Hadad, announcing a divine oracle. I prefer him to be Panammu I, with the corollary that he must still have been king at the time of the rebellion. When, towards the end of his long reign, the Assyrians moved westwards, he probably decided to come to

terms with the new power, thus initiating the policy so faithfully followed by Panammu II and Barrakkab. The usurpers, no doubt nationalists, concerned to maintain their country's independence and perhaps of royal blood themselves, seem to have spared the aged king but, after his intervention, they decided to put him to death also (5). Perhaps Barṣur was the effective ruler, a regent like Jotham in contemporary Judah (2 Kgs. xv 5); there Azariah's (Uzziah) ill health led him to hand over the day-to-day administration to his son, but it did not prevent him organizing international resistance to Tiglathpileser, as the Assyrian annals show (see at Hadad 1). As it turned out, neither Panammu's currying of Assyrian favour nor Azariah's arrogant resistance made much difference to their countries' ultimate fate. The assumption that Barṣur was regent, incidentally, would account for the references to his 'house' in 2, 3; he was to all intents the head of the family. The final clause may have begun with 'if' or 'because' but, in view of the ו in 5, unusual in an apodosis, I treat it as a question; a statement with 'behold' is also possible.

5. **אגם**; prob. prosthetic ['] with a word of similar structure to **שם** (Hadad 16, 21). **הוית**; for HWY(') in the sense of 'to fall' see Job xxxvii 6, where it is usually taken as an Arabism, but not necessarily so in the light of this passage; the form is Pael, i.e. [hawwīt] with internal *mater lectionis*. **חללי**; Dupont-Sommer suggests **חל[י·ש]אל**, 'Panammu asked those who had been killed', apparently thinking of some conversation in the after-world; one would require more evidence that this unusual meeting was taking place before accepting the proposal. **אבד** prob. refers to the collapse of the economy during the civil war, alluded to in the next line; cp. Joel i 11; the words before it will then be unknown agricultural terms (see Hadad 4).

6. **שאה**; loan-word from Akkad. *šēu*. **שורת** = [śōrāt] from [śawrāt]; a species of grain, usually thought to be millet or sorghum; the sing. of this word may occur in Isa. xxviii 25. Not possible (see 9) are vocalizations [ṯ'ā], 'ewe' and [ṯōrā], 'cow' (cp. Arab. masc. [ṯawrun]; later Aram. **תורא**); cp. no. 7 Sefire i A 21, 23 (q.v. for the etymology of the first). **חטה** and **שערה** are fem. sing. against the plur. forms in Hadad 5, 6. For QWM in Hebr. referring to prices see Lev. xxvii 14, 17, and for **ב** in a similar passage to this see 2 Kgs. vii 1. **פרס** = [prēs]; Dan. v 25, 28; Akkad. *parsu* is a half-mina. **שקל** = [ṯqēl]; the mina (Akkad. *manū*) contained 60 shekels. **שטרבה**; an unknown weight. **אסנב**; the word occurs without prosthetic ['] on a lion-weight from Nineveh (*CIS* ii 7), where it is explained in the Akkad. version as two-thirds of a mina; cp. Akkad. *šēnēpū*, 'two-thirds'. **משת**; an unknown commodity; Lidzbarski (*NSE*) reads **משח**, 'oil'. **יבל**; Pael; the Hebr. form is Hiph.

7. **אשור** = ['aṯṯūr]; note the *mater lectionis* against **אשר** (18; *KAI* no. 24 Kilamuwa i 8); Ahiqar **אתור**. **מלכה**; Pael; 2 Kgs. xxiv 17 (Hiph.); no. 5 Zakir A 3 (Haph.). **אבן שחת**; presumably the leader of the rebellion, a strange phrase, perhaps a commercial term used metaphorically; cp. Isa. viii 14. **אצרת** = ['ōṣrāt]; cp. Syr. ['awṣar]; the plur. here is fem. as in Hebr.; the **ת** and a shape like **כ** can just be traced in the lacuna. The passage may be illustrated from 2 Kgs. xvi 8.

8. **פשש**; the base may be connected with PWŠ, Syriac 'remain, desist from'; i.e. here Pael, 'to abolish' or the like; Palest. Aram. **פשפש**, Pilpel, 'to search' does not give a very suitable meaning. **הרפי** = [harpī]. **שבי**; collect. as in Hebr. and later Aram., i.e. [šbī]; cp. Isa. xx 4. Before **בית** a possible restoration (Dupont-Sommer) is **[רכ]בא[ל]**, which suggests that **קנואל** may also be a divine name; some kind of proper burial ceremony may be being alluded to.

קתילת; note the internal *mater lectionis* and [t] as Sefire no. **9** (iii 11) against the [ṯ] of later Aram. and of Hebr.

9. היטבה = [hay/ēṭbēh] with ʼ as in no. **15** Barrakkab i 12 and Hebr. against later Aram. [ʼōṭēb] (Aphel) with ו. קדמתה = [qadmtēh]; cp. Ezek. xxxvi 11. כברת = [kibrat]. אז; Hadad 7. שתית = [šatyat] or as later [štiyyat] (though this may be a secondary vocalization); the form is Peil, as in Palest. Aram., usually with prosthetic [ʼ]; note, however, שתא (Hadad 9). The subject is prob. ארק rather than יאדי, which is masc. in Hadad 9.

10. זלת = [zōlat] or [ḏōlat] with [ō] from [aw]; Palest. Aram. זולה; base ZWL (rare); cp. Hebr. ZLL; Arab. ḎLL; Aram. DLL (rare) or ZLL. מוכרו = [mukrū]; fem. sing. abs. with *mater lectionis* for a short vowel; cp. Hebr. מכר (Num. xx 19); in later Aram. the base has the restricted meaning 'to betroth, marry'. The roaring inflation of 6 has apparently been countered. On בעלי see at no. **7** Sefire i A 4. כפירי; Hadad 10. רכב; see at 3. Possibly restore ב[ה]ח[ל]ב; Haph., lit. 'he caused to succeed', although it is conjug. II which has this meaning in Arab.; see on חלבבה (Hadad 3). מצעה = [mṣīʿah], the suffix referring to the land; Palest. Aram. מציעא. Lidzbarski (*NSE*) makes the word fem. and reads (cp. 12) במצעת̊]. מ[ל̊כ̊י .[כ̊ב̊ר̊]י], but the writing is very faded.

11. A verb implying obedience or the like may be supplied at the end of 10; the sense appears to be that, though he was self-sufficient, Panammu was wise enough to seek Assyrian patronage; the clauses with לו slightly mitigate the sycophantic tone. פי is generally regarded as an alternative form of פא; perhaps the dot is a mistake, and we should read פ followed by an imperf. implying that this was his habit; cp. the imperfs. in Hadad 4 f. אחז with ב; contrast Hadad 15 f. With the phrase (כנף = [knēp]) cp. Zech. viii 23. מראה = [mārʼēh]. רב; from the Akkad. title *šarru rabū*; cp. in Hebr. Nimrud 2 (vol. I no. **6**); 2 Kgs. xviii 19.

12. ואחי = [wāḥay]; cp. Gen. iii 22 where, as often in Hebr. before the stress and presumably here, [w] becomes [wā]. In Hadad 13 there may be a case of וא = [wa]. This rendering (Ginsberg) is preferable to Cooke's (*NSI*), 'the governors, and the princes of Y'DY', where פחי is a masc. plur. form; the plur. elsewhere is פחות or פחוות (Hebr.); פחון (Aram.); the word is derived from the Akkad. title *bēl pāḫāti*, governor of a province. חנא; Pael; see at Hadad 19. With the phrase cp. 2 Kgs. xxv 28. ברש = (?) [brēš]; cp. 2 Chron. xx 27; vol. I no. **16** Mesha 20.

13. גלגל = [galgal] as in biblical Aram., Hebr., or [gilgal] as in Palest. Aram. At the end of the previous line restore רץ = [rāṣ]; Hebr. RWṢ; no. **15** Barrakkab i 8; later Aram. רהט; cp. 1 Sam. viii 11; 1 Kgs. xx 33; 2 Kgs. x 15, 16. תגלתפלסר as in 2 Kgs. xvi 7 against תגלתפליסר (no. **15** Barrakkab i 3); תכלתפלסר (no. **20** Ashur ostracon 15); תגלתפלאסר (2 Kgs. xv 29); תגלתפלנסר (1 Chron. v 26); Akkad. *Tukulti-apil-é-šar-ra*, 'My confidence is the son of Ešarra'; note the various means of preserving the full syllable [pil] and the Assyrian pronunciation of [š] as [s]. מחנת = [maḥnāt]; plur., formed as in Hebr.; contrast מחנות (no. **5** Zakir A 9). For a similar omission of prepos. in Hebr. see Ps. cxxvii 2 ('in sleep'). After this comes a word of two or three letters; מ[ת] is a possibility, especially since it occupies a variety of positions, though the first letter looks more like ת. מוקא = [mōğā]; Hebr. מוצא; Egyp. Aram. מועא. In the lacuna Dupont-Sommer restores ומן . צפון . ועד . דרום . על ., i.e. 'and from the north to the south over .....'; but

this is not enough, even with the repetition of מחנת. There should be no *mater lectionis* in דרם (= [dārōm]). צפון = [ṣippūn]. I suggest reversing the word-order in the previous phrase, as happens in the next line; i.e., 'and in campaigns from the west to the east over (על)'.

14. רבעת = [ribʿāt]; cp. Hebr. רבע; no. **15** Barrakkab i 4, where with מרא the phrase translates the Akkad. 'lord of the four quarters', a frequent title in neo-Assyrian texts. בנת; cp. Ps. xlv 13; Jerem. iv 11; Ezek. xvi 27, etc. For the well-known Assyrian policy of transplanting peoples see also 2 Kgs. xvii 6, 24. הוסף = [hōsēp]; no. **5** Zakir B 4.

15. גבלה = [gbūlēh]; in no. **9** Sefire iii 23, but not in later Aram. גרגם; see at no. **5** Zakir A 6. Thereafter Dupont-Sommer restores ו[דנני]°, 'the Danunians'; *KAI* no. 24 Kilamuwa i 7; *KAI* no. 26 Karatepe i 2 f.; this is plausible, but the second last letter, though faint, looks more like ו.

16. שמרג; unknown; perhaps a place-name. מת = [mīt]; perf. 3 masc. sing. בלגרי = [bligray/ē], lit. 'at the feet of'; dual constr.; cp. Mandaic ליגרא and for the idiom 1 Sam. xxv 27. The restoration at the end (with the addition of the king's name) is Dupont-Sommer's. בכיה and in 17 (plur.) = respectively [bakkyēh] and [bakkyūh]; the retention of י before the suffix suggests a Pael, as commonly in Syriac; cp. Ezek. viii 14 (Piel).

17. איחה = ['īḥēh]; Hadad 30. בכיתה = [bakkītēh]; the form without suffix would be [bakkyat]. מחנת = [maḥnāt]; sing. constr. from a base final weak, identical in form with the plur. (13). כלה = [kullah]. The restoration at the end is made on the basis of Hadad 17, 21–2, though there is not much room for a sensible filling out, e.g. 'he took his body and said, With his god may . . . .'

18. משכי = [maśkī]; fem. abs. sing.; Hebr. משכית; Num. xxxiii 52; Lev. xxvi 1; Ezek. viii 12. ארח = ['rōḥ]. דמשק = [dammśak] or the like; on the importance of this reference for dating the inscr. see the discussion in the introduction. אשר; note the omission of the *mater lectionis*. In the lacuna understand, 'In my days he sent my father back to his own land, and I wept for him and . . . .' or similar. Illustrate the passage from Gen. l 4 f. Dupont-Sommer suggests שר[גן], i.e. 'In the days of Sargon (I brought back), etc.'; but Sargon did not begin his reign until 722, and the following line implies that Barrakkab erected the statue soon after his accession. If the restoration is accepted, the date of the inscr. has to be brought down to about 720, which would be awkward, since in his other inscrs. Barrakkab uses the Aram. lingua franca.

19. אנכי; see at Hadad 1. ברכב; note the careless omission of ר. For the restoration at the end see no. **15** Barrakkab i 4–7, where instead of משב we have כרסא; but cp. 2.

20. לאב[י] does not fill the space, but a piece of the design comes in at this point. מלכת = [milkēt]; cp. vol. I no. **16** Mesha 2; the reading is very uncertain.

21. This line has defeated interpretation; it prob. concerns the maintenance of rites at Panammu's tomb; cp. Hadad 15 f. אמר may be a part of the verb 'to say' or = ['immar], 'lamb'. משות (with internal *mater lectionis*?) may be the same as משת (6). יבל is a verb in 6, but is here a noun; cp. Hebr. [ybūl], 'produce, fruit of the earth'; here of a victim? אמן; cp. Hadad 11; here perhaps an adjective ['ammīn], 'constant, perpetual', as in Syriac. In Hebr. and Syriac [s(a)mak yad ʿal] is frequently used in a context of sacrificing; here, 'let the king lay his hand upon it' (?) יושא; Huphal from NŚ' (?); if so,

the *mater lectionis* indicates a short vowel. Dupont-Sommer proposes יו[ק]א; Haph. from YĠ' = Hebr. YṢ'; cp. מוקא (13). קדם = [qdām], the Aram. equivalent of Hebr. לפני. The suffix in אבי is awkward if instructions are being given to Barrakkab; could he be addressing his successor?

22. זכר = [d̲kēr] or [d̲kōr]; cp. Hebr. [zēkr]; Syriac [dukrānā]; a translation 'this is a memorial' is not possible. The drift seems to be that if the rites are properly maintained, the blessing of the gods will follow. On the deities see at Hadad 2. אלהי; nom. constr.; the ending is perhaps silent; cp. אלה (2).

23. אנש = ['nāš]; collect.; cp. *KAI* no. 10 Yehaumilk 15–16.

III

EARLY INSCRIPTIONS IN IMPERIAL OR OFFICIAL ARAMAIC

15–17. Zenjirli: Barrakkab i–iii   Fig. 11 (ii)

INSCR. i, found in 1891, is carved on a block of stone alongside a relief of Barrakkab in Assyrian dress, beginning under his outstretched arm. The stone, measuring 1·31 m. high by 0·62 m. broad, formed part of a new palace, whose building is celebrated in the final lines of the inscr. The bulk of the inscr., however, is taken up with Barrakkab's protestations of loyalty to Tiglathpileser and praise of his magnanimity in allowing him to succeed his father.

Inscr. ii was unearthed in the same excavations, but remained unpublished until 1955. It consists of a large fragment (44·5 cm. by 45·5) from a similar stone, showing on the right a part of the face and raised arm of a man bearded in the Assyrian manner; his hand holds a drinking-vessel. The nine incomplete lines of writing begin left of the forearm. Comparison with several uninscribed reliefs from Zenjirli suggests that the original written surface occupied a rough square between the upper parts of two carved figures, that on the right being the king, who is seated, the missing figure on the left being a servant, who is standing with a fan in his hands; centre bottom there would be a table, marking the lower limit of the writing. The complete inscr., therefore, can hardly have exceeded twelve lines. The extant lines are in a similar vein to the long preamble of i; the absent final two or three prob. stated briefly the purpose behind the inscr.

Inscr. iii, also discovered in 1891, is carved along the top of a large stone 1·06 m. in height. Below it there is a relief of the king seated on the left and a servant standing on the right; unlike the kind of picture on ii there is no table between the figures.

Inscr. i is now in the Museum of Antiquities at Istanbul, the other inscrs. in the Staatliche Museen, Berlin.

The inscrs. are to be dated a few years later than Panammu; q.v. introduction for the historical background. On the relation of their scripts to those of the earlier Zenjirli and other Old Aram. inscrs. see the introductions to no. **13** Hadad and nos. **7–9** Sefire. On i words are separated by dots, on ii and iii by little strokes. Internal *matres lectionis* are less common than on Hadad and Panammu (no. **14**); they occur only in the place-name אשור (i 9; ii 9) and in Tiglathpileser's name (*passim*; see at i 3).

Language

The Barrakkab inscrs. are the earliest to employ the language commonly called official or imperial Aram., which is best known from rather later sources like the Egyp. papyri and the biblical books of Ezra and Daniel. The prevailing view (Ginsberg, 'Problems'; Garbini, 'Antico'; Rosenthal, *Grammar*, 6) derives this lingua franca from the Aram. dialect spoken in Assyria, but the evidence is very tenuous. The only Old Aram. texts from this or a neighbouring region, no. **10** Tell Halaf and no. **11** Luristan i, give no dialectal information. There are admittedly certain features shared with Akkad., which are not found either in Old Aram. or in the western dialects of the Christian era, but are prominent in Syriac and Mandaic, and on which Ginsberg in particular places great weight. These features are not, however, universal, and they may just as easily be put down to an influence exercised independently by Akkad. on the lingua franca and on the ancestors of the later eastern dialects. It seems to me much more probable that the dialect of the leading Aramaean power (Damascus) would be the one to commend itself to Assyrian administrators and traders, when in their constant dealings with other countries their own cumbersome cuneiform began to prove a liability. For similar opinions see Dupont-Sommer, *Araméens*, 85 and *EHO*, 29, 64, though these, I think, overstress the unitary nature of the Old Aram. dialects, as if an official language was already in use in Syria before the Assyrian advance in the late 8 cent.; see further my remarks in the introduction to nos. **7–9** Sefire.

The chief differences from the native dialect of Zenjirli are in grammar, notably the pronoun אנה and the system of endings in nouns. We can assume that other exceptional grammatical features of the Hadad and Panammu inscrs., e.g. the suffix [ēh] (from [ayh]) with masc. plur. nouns, were also dispensed with. In verbs, the influence of Akkad has been traced in a Hittanaphal form supposed to occur in i 14; but there is a simpler explanation (see the note). In vocabulary, the forms מצעת (i 9) and אחי (i 14) contrast with the indigenous מצע (no. **14** Panammu 10) and איחי (no. **13** Hadad 24). In the case of the verb היטבתה, however, it is likely that the native form is retained; see the notes to i 12. In phonology, too, there is distinct evidence that the spoken dialect affected the new medium, notably in the matter of diphthongal reduction, which is more widespread than in either the Nerab inscrs. (nos. **18**, **19**) or the Ashur ostracon (no. **20**). Reduction of [ay] is shown by the form of Tiglathpeleser's name, of [aw] by the suffix in לישה (i 16). The [b] in נבשת (ii 7) is also prob. due to local influence. I assume this influence extended to the final ['], which I mark silent as in the Hadad and Panammu inscrs. The only clear instance of Akkad. influence on the phonology is the dissimilation of [q] in כיצא (i 19).

Bibliography

Inscrs. i and iii were officially published in von Luschan, *Ausgrabungen in Sendschirli* IV (Berlin, 1911), 345 f.
For inscr. ii see H. Donner in *Mitteilungen des Instituts für Orientforschung* 3 (1955), 73–98.
See further:
D. H. Müller, *WZKM* 10 (1896), 194 f.
NSE p. 443 f.
NSI no. 63.
Poebel (1932): see bibliography to no. **13** Hadad.
EHO, 29 f.
Garbini, 'Antico', 273 f.
Koopmans, *Chrest.* no. 12.
KAI nos. 216–18.
Rosenthal, *Handbook*, sect. I, 4.
Degen, *Grammatik*, 8–9 and index.

Translation

ANET, 655 (i).

Plates and figures

Von Luschan, op. cit., Tafn. LXVII (i), LX (iii); Donner, loc. cit. (ii); *NSE* Taf. XXIV (i, iii); Diringer, *Alphabet*, fig. 126 (i); Driver, *Writing*, pl. 31 (i, iii); *ANEP*, nos. 281 (i), 460 (iii); Birnbaum, *Scripts*, no. 018 (i); *KAI* Tafn. XXXII (i), XII (ii).

No. **15**

i 1 אנה . בר[ר]כב .
2 בר . פנמו . מ֯לך . שמ
3 אל . עבד . תגלתפ֯ליסר . מרא .
4 רבעי . ארקא . בצדק . אבי . ובצד
5 קי . הושבני . מראי . רכבאל .
6 ומראי . תגלתפליסר . על .
7 כרסא . אבי . ובית . אבי . ע֯
8 מל . מן . כל . ורצת . בגלגל .
9 מראי . מלך . אשור . במצע
10 ת . מלכן . רברבן . בעלי . כ
11 סף . ובעלי . זהב . ואחזת .
12 בית . אבי . והיטבתה .

מן . בית . חד . מלכן . רברב 13

ן . והתנאבו . אחי . מ̊לכי 14

א . לכל . מה . טבת . ביתי . ו 15

בי . טב . לישה . לאבהי . מ 16

לכי . שמאל . הא . בית . כלמ 17

ו . להם . פהא . בית . שתוא . ל 18

הם . והא . בית . כיצא . ו 19

אנה . בנית . ביתא . זנה . 20

1. I am Barrakkab,
2. the son of Panammu, king of
3. Sam'al, servant of Tiglathpileser, lord
4. of the four quarters of the earth. Because of my father's righteousness and
5. my own righteousness, my lord Rakkabel
6. and my lord Tiglathpileser seated me upon
7. my father's throne. My father's house
8. laboured more than all others; and I have run at the wheel
9. of my lord, the king of Assyria, in the midst
10. of powerful kings, possessors of
11. silver and possessors of gold. I have taken over
12. my father's house, and have made it better
13. than the house of any powerful king.
14. My brother kings were envious
15. because of all the good fortune of my house. Now,
16. my fathers, the kings of Sam'al, had no suitable palace.
17. They had indeed the palace of Kilamuwa,
18. and it was their winter palace
19. and also their summer palace.
20. But I have built this palace.

NOTES

1. אנה; for the native forms see at no. 13 Hadad 1. ברכב; no. 14 Panammu 1.
2. שמאל; no. 5 Zakir A 7.
3. תגלפליסר; see at no. 14 Panammu 13; the י here is a *mater lectionis* for [ē], showing that the reduction [ay] to [ē] must have taken place. מרא רבעי ארקא = [mārē rib'ay/ē 'arġā]; contrast רבעת (no. 14 Panammu 14). With the masc. plur. form cp. in Hebr. Ezek. i 8; xliii 16; since the phrase does not occur elsewhere in Aram., we cannot say whether the change is due to the new dialect. The Akkad. title is *šar kibrāt erbetti*.

4. צדק; no. **14** Panammu 1.
5. הושבני = [hōṯbánī]; no. **14** Panammu 19. רכבאל; see at no. **13** Hadad 2.
6. The conjunction of god and Assyrian king is interesting; cp. ii 1–3.
7. כרסא = [kursē] from [kursi']; cp. כהסאי (no. **9** Sefire iii 17); כרסאה (Cowley vi 2). Later, like מרא, the forms were accommodated to a final weak base; thus with a suffix כרסיה (Dan. vii 9). עמל; Barrakkab is perhaps simply claiming that his family was the most zealous in the suzerain's service, but there may be a nuance of profit or gain, as is sometimes carried by the base in Hebr.; cp. Ps. cv 44; Isa. liii 11; Eccles. *passim*, especially ii 10; iv 4; v 17.
8. מן כל; Dan. xi 2. רצת = [rāṭit]; see at no. **14** Panammu 13; the base in Egyp. and later Aram. dialects is RHṬ.
9. מצעת = [miṣ'at]; fem. constr.; so Syriac; contrast the masc. form in no. **14** Panammu 10.
10. רברבן = [rabrbīn]; the usual plur. of [rab] in biblical and Palest. Aram.; cp. Ezra v 11. בעלי, etc.; no. **14** Panammu 11.
11. זהב = [ḏhab]. אחזת = [aḥḏēt]; no. **13** Hadad 15 f.; the reference is to assuming the headship of the dynasty.
12. היטבתה = [hay/ēṭabtēh]; no. **14** Panammu 9; note that the form in the papyri (Cowley vi 11) and later Aram. dialects has ו in the first syllable.
13. lit., 'one of powerful kings'.
14. התנאבו is a difficult form. It is usually explained as Hittanaphal from Y'B and due to the influence upon the lingua franca of Akkad., where forms with infixed [tan] are known; Moscati, *Comparative*, 129. The base Y'B is common in Syriac in the Ethpa. with [l] in the sense 'long for, desire eagerly'. Vocalize therefore [hitnō'ábū] with reduction of the diphthong [aw]. Poebel's explanation (1932, 51) as Hithpe. or Hithpa. from a base N'B, not otherwise attested, is preferable. The meaning required is different from that of Syriac Y'B, though perhaps near enough to justify the two bases being regarded as alternants; cp. Ugar. and Phoen. YTN with Hebr. and Aram. NTN; Ugar. NP', 'shoot up' (I D 65) with Arab. YF', 'be grown up, climb'. אחי = ['aḥay]; contrast איחי (no. **13** Hadad 24). מלכיא = [malkayyā].
15. ל either goes with the verb in 14 (cp. Syriac) or means 'because of' (cp. Isa. lv 5). כל מה; no. **7** Sefire i A 26, 30. טבת = [ṭābat] (adjective as noun) or [ṭūbat]; cp. Ps. lxv 5.
16. בי . טב prob. = [bay/ēṭṭāb] with the [t] assimilated to a following [ṭ]. Cp., however, Egyp. Aram. בי (absol.); Palest. Aram. בי (constr.); Syriac [bay] (absol.). לישה = [lay/ēṭōh] with reduction of the second diphthong; cp. לא איתוהי (Dan. ii 11). אבהי = ['bāhay]; Cowley xxx 13; biblical and Palest. Aram. have a fem. form, emph. אבהתא; Syriac has both forms.
17. הא = [hā], 'behold'; contrast הן, הנו (no. **13** Hadad 29 f.). In 18 and 19 הא is the pronoun [hū]. The point seems to be that until Barrakkab built this new palace, the one built by Kilamuwa (now pronounced with final [ū]) had to suffice for both summer and winter use; cp. Amos iii 15; Jerem. xxxvi 22.
18. להם = [lhōm]. שתוא = [śitwā]; Palest. Aram. [sitwā]; Hebr. סתו (Song ii 11; prps. loan-word); Arab. [šitā'un].
19. כיצא = [kay/ēṯā] with dissimilation of [q] to [k] before [ṯ]. Similar instances of dissimilation of [q] before emphatic consonants are found in no. **18** Nerab i 11 (יכטליך); no. **24** Carpentras 2 (כרצי); Ahiqar 101 (כצפה); 127 (כציר); 158 (כשיטא). This phonetic feature is attested elsewhere only for Akkad.

(von Soden, *Grammatik*, 1952, 53) and, in an area where Akkad. was previously spoken, for Mandaic (Nöldeke, *Grammatik*, 1875, 39). Note that of the western examples Carpentras 2 alone takes us beyond the era of the Assyrian and neo-Babylonian empires. The Ahiqar romance, of course, originated in Assyria, prob. in the 7 cent.; see Rowley in *DOTT*, 270 f.

20. **בנית** = [bnay/ēt]; no. **5** Zakir B 4, 10; no. **13** Hadad 14.

No. **16**

אנה ברכב בר פנמו מלך שמא[ל עבד תגלתפ] 1 ii
ליסר מרא רבעי אר[קא עבד ---] 2
ואלהי בית אבי צ[דק אנה עמ מ] 3
ראי ועם עבדי בית[מראי מלך אשור] 4
וצדק אנה עמ[ה מן כל וצדקן בני] 5
מן בני כ[ל].................. 6
נבשת הם ....[ונתן ר] 7
כבאל חני קד[ם מראי מלך] 8
אשור וקדם[ ]ב........... 9

ii 1. I am Barrakkab, the son of Panammu, king of Sam'al, [servant of Tiglath]
2. pileser, lord of the four quarters of the earth, [servant of . . . .]
3. and of the gods of my father's house. [Loyal have I been towards]
4. my lord and towards the servants of the house [of my lord, the king of Assyria.]
5. Loyal have I been towards [him more than any other, and loyal have my sons been]
6. more than the sons of any other . . . .
7. their souls . . . .
8. Rakkabel [has shown] favour to me in the presence [of my lord, the king of]
9. Assyria and in the presence of . . . .

NOTES

1–3. Cp. the opening lines of i. At the end of 2 was perhaps the name of Hadad or other deity of Zenjirli; Rakkabel, the dynastic god, is prob. to be included in the next phrase. Note again the juxtaposition of earthly ruler and gods. **צדק** = [ṣaddīq]. With the use of **עם** cp. Deut. xviii 13; 1 Kgs. viii 61.

4. עבדי בית are prob. the Assyrian officials with whom Barrakkab had to deal; cp. no. **9** Sefire iii 13; 2 Sam. ix 2; Jerem. xlvi 26. The restoration at the end is Donner's.

5. At the end of the line Donner proposes a phrase beginning with מן = [man], i.e. '[If any] of (lit. from) my sons . . . .'; cp. no. **13** Hadad 15, 20. This would require the letter following בני in 6 to be י, beginning an imperf. verb; but the surviving traces seem to me rather to suggest כ. The restoration in the text is based on i 7–8 and takes מן as the comparative 'than'. It makes a line slightly longer than 4, which is in its turn slightly longer than 1–3; we have to assume that the fan and arm of the missing servant lent a little forward.

6–7. נבשת'הם = [nabšāthōm]; the suffix is written separately as in no. **5** Zakir A 9, an interesting isogloss between a text in official Aram. and one of the more independent Old Aram. dialects. The sense may be filled out as follows or similar, 'As for my brother kings, their souls hated me, were vexed with me, and they . . . . . .; but Rakkabel showed favour . . . . .'; cp. i 14–15; 2 Sam. v 8; Judg. x 16.

8. חני = [ḥinnī], lit. 'gave my favour'; cp. Gen. xxxix 21, where we have the only occurrence of this noun in the Bible with a suffix.

9. Instead of ב perhaps read ע and restore 'the servants of the house' as in 4. In the final 2 or 3 lines there was prob. a brief statement about the occasion of the inscr.

No. **17**

iii מראי'בעלחרן'אנה'בררכב'בר'פנמ[ו]

My lord is Baal Harran. I am Barrakkab, the son of Panammu.

NOTE

The moon-god was doubtless worshipped at Zenjirli under his West Semitic name Sahar, but he was not prominent enough to be mentioned in the lists of deities in no. **13** Hadad 2–3, 11; no. **14** Panammu 22. This suggests that the introduction of the cult of the Babylonian Sin, whose chief shrines were at Ur and Harran, was motivated by political considerations on Barrakkab's part; cp. the worship of the Tyrian Baal at Damascus (no. **1** Barhadad 3) and in Israel (1 Kgs. xvi 31–2).

18, 19. Nerab i, ii

The two inscribed reliefs, respectively 0·93 and 0·95 m. high and 0·35 and 0·45 m. broad, were found in 1891 at Nerab, a small village 7 km. SE. of Aleppo, and are now in the Louvre in Paris. The upper part of inscr. i (no. **18**) surrounds the head and upraised hands of a human figure at prayer, no doubt that of the priest mentioned in 1; the lower part is written across his robe. Inscr. ii (no. **19**) is written entirely above the relief; the priest here is represented sitting, in the act of offering a libation before an altar; facing him and behind the altar stands an attendant, holding a fan. The style of execution is in both cases thoroughly Assyrian as on the Barrakkab stones (nos. **15–17**). This and the fact that the priests' names are both Akkad. and contain the element Sin make it likely that they served in a sanctuary of the Babylonian moon-god, though on the inscrs. the deity is called by his West Semitic name Sahar; the other deities mentioned (i 9; ii 9) are, however, Babylonian. Perhaps the sanctuary was a daughter-sanctuary of the great temple of Sin at Harran, the importance of which was already acknowledged in northern Syria in the late 8 cent.; see no. **17** Barrakkab iii. Clermont-Ganneau suggests that after the destruction of Harran in the final decade of the 7 cent. (*ANET*, 311; *DOTT*, 77) the shrine of Sin was transferred to Nerab, and that his worship was centred there until Nabonidus restored the Harran temple in the mid 6 cent. But the date thus given for the inscrs., 600–550, is too low. The script shows cursive influence, and finds its nearest relative in the Nineveh weights (see Table of scripts). The כ of Nerab seems a little later; but the ק is more archaic, resisting in this respect the cursive influence already visible in the ק of the Panammu and Barrakkab inscrs. (nos. **14–17**). In the case of two letters, inscrs. i and ii have different forms. The ח of i has a single bar, that of ii a double; compare these with the ח of no. **14** Panammu, which has three bars, that of no. **15** Barrakkab i, which has two, and that of the Nineveh weights, which has one. With the ס of i cp. no. **14** Panammu and no. **15** Barrakkab i, with that of ii cp. the Nimrud ostracon (see Table of scripts). A date early in the 7 cent. is indicated.

With very few exceptions inscr. i lacks dividing spaces between words; on ii about half the words are separated by small spaces, and about half are run together. There are only two cases of internal *matres lectionis*; יכטלוך (i 11) and שמוני (ii 7).

The dialect is the official or imperial, as is shown by the Akkad. influence on its phonology, certain in the case of dissimilation in i 11 (יכטלוך), but rather less so in the several instances of nasalization in place of gemination (see the notes to i 5, 12). A dialect akin to that of Arpad was doubtless, however, still spoken in the region; the absence of [inn] before a 1 pers. suffix with the imperf. (ii 9) may be due to its influence. The word ארצתה (i 4) is a loan-word from Akkad. The conjunction למען (ii 7) is only found here outside Hebr.

Bibliography

The inscrs. were first published by Ch. Clermont-Ganneau in *Études d'archéologie orientale* 2 (1897), 182 f. See further:
NSE p. 445.
NSI nos. 64, 65.
Gevirtz, 'Curses', 147 f.

Koopmans, *Chrest.* nos. 17, 18.
KAI nos. 225, 226.
Rosenthal, *Handbook*, sect. I, 5.
S. Kaufman, 'Si'gabbar, priest of Sahr in Nerab', *JAOS* 90 (1970), 270 f.

Translation

ANET, 661 (ii).

Plates and figures

NSE Taf. XXV; *NSI* pls. V, VI; Driver, *Writing*, pl. 54; *ANEP*, nos. 280, 635; *KAI* Tafn. XXIV, XXV.

No. **18**

i

1 שנזרבן כמר
2 שהר בנרב מת
3 וזנה צלמה
4 וארצתה
5 מן את
6 תהנס צלמא
7 זנה וארצתא
8 מן אשרה
9 שהר ושמש ונכל ונשך יסחו
10 שמך ואשרך מן חין ומות לחה
11 יכטלוך ויהאבדו זרעך והן
12 תנצר צלמא וארצתא זא
13 אחרה ינצר
14 זי לך

1. Sin-zer-ibni, priest
2. of Sahar at Nerab, deceased.
3. This is his picture
4. and his grave.
5. Whoever you are
6. who drag this picture
7. and grave
8. away from its place,
9. may Sahar and Shamash and Nikkal and Nusk pluck
10. your name and your place out of life, and an evil death

11. make you die; and may they cause your seed to perish!
But if
12. you guard this picture and grave,
13, 14. in the future may yours be guarded!

NOTES

1. There are traces of what may be another letter before the ש, but since the writing is exceptionally clear throughout, they should preferably be regarded as scores on the relief and not, as in most editions of the text, a second faded ש. This reading depends on a misinterpretation of the name in ii 1, which led to the first letter there being taken as the relative pronoun ש (Phoen. ש; אש; Mishnaic Hebr. ש; Akkad. *ša*), used in the sense 'belonging to', 'appertaining to'. Since ש occurs nowhere else in Aram., its use at Nerab was put down to Akkad. influence. The priest's name means 'Sin has created a seed'; cp. *Marduk-zēr-ibni* (Tallqvist, *Names*, 134) and the names cited at no. **11** Luristan i 1. כמר = [kmōr]; Syriac emph. [kumrā]; Hebr. [kōmr] (in the Bible always *in sensu malo* of a heathen priest).
2. שהר; no. **5** Zakir B 24. נרב; the modern Arab. name is [nayrab], with a diphthong, apparently reduced here; there is no other evidence from either inscr. of diphthongal reduction. מת = [mīt]; passive partic.
4. ארצתה = ['irṣtēh]; a loan-word from Akkad. *irṣitu*, the equivalent of Hebr. ארץ; Aram. ארקא; ארעא; this explains צ instead of ק. It is used here in its special Akkad. meaning of 'underworld', thus 'grave'.
5. את; no. **9** Sefire iii 11; no. **20** Ashur ostracon 2, 19. Egyp. and biblical Aram. (Kethibh) have אנת, prob. a secondary form due to nasalization; see further at 12.
6. תהנס; no. **5** Zakir B 20.
7. זנה; here with צלמא (= [ṣalmā]); cp. in 12 זא with ארצתה; prob. the pronoun should in each case be construed with both nouns.
8. אשרה = ['aṯrēh]; no. **5** Zakir B 21.
9. For the gods see the notes to no. **5** Zakir B 24; no. **7** Sefire i A 8 f. I give Shamash here in the Akkad. spelling. יסחו = [yissáḥū]; jussive; base NSḤ; cp. Ezra vi 11; Prov. ii 22.
10. שמך = [šmāk]. חין = [ḥayyīn]; Dan. vii 12. מות = [mawt]. לחה = [lḥē]; abs.; the fem. occurs in no. **7** Sefire i A 26; C 6.
11. יכטלוך = [yikṭlūk]; jussive with suffix; for the feature of dissimilation see at no. **15** Barrakkab i 19. יהאבדו = [yha'bēdū] with ['] retained as in no. **8** Sefire ii C 4; contrast biblical הובד.
12. ינצר = [yinṭu/ōr] with nasalization substituted for gemination, a common feature of Egyp. Aram. (e.g. הנעלת; Cowley xv 6; base ʿLL) and of the biblical dialect (e.g. תנדע; Ezra iv 15; base YDʿ), though also found in later dialects. An analogous process is met with in Akkad. (von Soden, *Grammatik*, 1952, 33, 125), but unlike the much rarer instances in Aram. of dissimilation of [q], the feature is too widespread in Aram. dialects for it to be put down to external influence. It may even have occurred in Old Aram. dialects, for it is strictly speaking a sub-phonemic phenomenon, which need not always be reflected in the orthography; cp. יסחו in this inscr. (9) with the forms containing נ in no. **30** Tema i 14; Ahiqar 156; הסק with להנסקה in the same verse in Dan. (vi 24; base SLQ); and the various examples of את and אנת noted above (5), particularly the Kethibh and Qere of the biblical text.

13. אחרה = ['áḥrā] or ['ḥórā]; cp. לאחרה (ii 8); Palest. Aram. לאחרא, though the latter has only the meaning 'backwards'. The ending is, however, the so-called locative, which can sometimes have a temporal sense; e.g. ימימה (Exod. xiii 10); Ugar. *'lmh*, 'forever' (I D 154). For an example of a word with this ending in Hebr. preceded by a prepos. see Ps. ix 18 (לשאולה); on the origin of the ending see at vol. I no. **16** Mesha 15. ינצר = [yunṭar]; Peil (passive) jussive with nasalization.

No. **19**

1 ii שאגבר כמר שהר בנרב

2 זנה צלמה בצדקתי קדמוה

3 שמני שם טב והארך יומי

4 ביום מתת פמי לאתאחז מן מלן

5 ובעיני מחזה אנה בני רבע בכונ

6 י והום אתהמו ולשמו עמי מאן

7 כסף ונחש עם לבשי שמוני למען

8 לאחרה לתהנס ארצתי מן את תעשק

9 ותהנסני שהר ונכל ונשך יהבאשו

10 ממתתה ואחרתה תאבד

1. Si'-gabbari, priest of Sahar at Nerab.
2. This is his picture. Because of my righteousness before him,
3. he afforded me a good name, and prolonged my days.
4. On the day I died, my mouth was not closed to words,
5. and with my eyes I was beholding children of the fourth generation; they wept
6. for me, and were greatly distraught. They did not lay with me any vessel
7. of silver or bronze; with my garments (only) they laid me, so that
8. in the future my grave should not be dragged away. Whoever you are who do wrong
9. and drag me away, may Sahar and Nikkal and Nusk make
10. his dying odious, and may his posterity perish!

NOTES

1. שאגבר; Akkad. *Si'-gab-ba-ri*, 'Sin is a warrior'; see Kaufman (1970) and Tallqvist, *Names*, 194, where other names with the element *Si'* = *Sin* are listed. The base GBR is not found in Akkad. outside proper names, and the elements accompanying *Si'* in Tallqvist's lists seem frequently to be Syrian

Sem.; it is likely therefore that *Si'* is a Syrian Sem. form of *Sin* and that the bearers of the names with this element were Aramaeans by race, who had become devotees of the Babylonian moon-god. If ש = 'pertaining to', the name of the priest is אגבר, which cannot be paralleled.

2. צדקתי = [ṣidqtī]; cp. no. **14** Panammu 1, where the form is masc. קדמוה = [qdāmawh].
3. שמני = [śāmánī]; cp. 2 Sam. xiv 7 and for the omission of [l] with a verb of giving Isa. xxvii 4. שם = [šum]. הארך; with א retained against later Aram. הורך or אורך. יומי = [yawmay]. With the sentiment cp. Job xxix 18, etc.
4. יום; constr. before the subordinate clause; cp. Exod. vi 28; Job iii 3. מתת = [mētit]. לאתאחז = [lā 'it'ḥad]; Ithpe; there are several examples in the Old Aram. inscrs. of ה being dropped in the imperf. Haph., Hithpe., etc., but this is the earliest instance of its omission in a perf. The meaning 'shut, close' is common for this base in later Aram; cp. Syriac [pūmā 'eḥad]. With the sentiment cp. Deut. xxxiv 7; Job xxix 22, etc.
5. מחזה = [mḥazzē]; Pael partic.; cp. no. **7** Sefire i A 13, where an infin. Pael occurs. This gives a more felicitous syntax than the usual interpretation [mā ḥāzē], 'What am I seeing?'; also, elsewhere in Aram. [mā] is only joined in the orthography to the relative זי (מז; no. **13** Hadad 3; Palmyr. מדי) or the particle [dēn] (Palest. Aram. and Syriac). רבע = [ribbē'] or the like; in Hebr. this adjective is used in the plur. with the sense of fourth generation, lit. 'fourth ones in a series'; Exod. xx 5. With the sentiment cp. Ps. cxxviii 6; Job xlii 16, etc. בכוני = [bkawnī]; Gen. xxiii 2; Jerem. viii 23; cp. no. **14** Panammu 16, 17 (Pael).
6. הום = [hawm], a noun from the base HWM, 'discomfit, distract', not otherwise attested for Aram.; cp. Hebr. מהומה in Prov. xv 16. The form is prob. not an infin. absol., which derives from an original [kitābu]; thus in Hebr. [qōm], but in Aram. the long [ā] would be retained. אתהמו = ['itthámū]; Ithpe.; cp. Ruth i 19 (Niph.). מאן = [ma'n]; cp. Dan. v 2. For similar statements on grave inscrs. see vol. I no. **8** Silwan 1–2; *KAI* no. 13 Tabnit 4 f.
7. נחש = [nḥāš]. לבשי = [lbūšay]. שמוני = [śāmúnī] with internal *mater lectionis*. למען; cp. Hebr.
8. לאחרה; see at i 13. לתהנס = [lā tuhnas]; Peil; i 6. מן את; i 5. תעשק; no. **9** Sefire iii 20.
9. תהנסני = [tihnsēnī]; in contrast with no. **5** Zakir B 20 (a 3 pers. suffix) and general practice in official Aram., [inn] is not inserted before the suffix; cp., however, the omission in no. **5** Zakir A 11 (יענני) and generally with 1 pers. suffixes in the Sefire texts (nos. **7–9**). יהבאשו = [yhab'éšū]; jussive, with ה retained.
10. ממתתה = [mmāt(ᵉ)tēh]; cp. Palest. Aram. ממתא (masc. emph.); Hebr. מרוצה, 'manner of running' (2 Sam. xviii 27). אחרתה = ['aḥrītēh]; cp. Ps. xxxvii 38; cix 13; Dan. ii 28 (with a different meaning); the form in later Aram. is ['aḥrāytā], which in Syriac sometimes means 'posterity'. תאבד = [ti'bad]; Peal.

20. The Ashur ostracon

Pl. V

The text was pieced together from six fragments of potsherd discovered during a German expedition to Ashur at the beginning of this century.

The maximum height is around 42 cm., the maximum breadth around 60. The right-hand margin is largely preserved, but on the left we have the ends of only two lines (14, 15); probably the lines in their immediate vicinity are nearly complete, but it is otherwise impossible to estimate where the left edge came. The ostracon is now in the Staatliche Museen, Berlin.

Writing

Together with the Nimrud ostracon (see Bibliographical notes) and the Adon papyrus (no. **21**), the Ashur text gives us our earliest sure data on Aram. cursive writing, though the influence of this style is already noticeable in the Hamath graffiti (no. **6**), the Nineveh weights, and even on the Nerab stones (nos. **18**, **19**). The most striking departure from the lapidary style is the opening of the heads on ב, ד, and ר; cp. also ע; this feature is found on all three texts. Equally all three texts share shapes which clearly predate the 5-cent.-Egyp. papyri, notably ו, צ, and ש. The Nimrud script is earlier than the other two, being closer to the lapidary parent; cp. א, ז, י, מ. At first glance Adon seems earlier than Ashur, agreeing with Nimrud in several shapes where Ashur agrees with the Egyp. papyri; e.g. נ, ס, ת. In the case of צ, however, Ashur seems nearer to the lapidary not only than Adon but also than Nimrud. Particularly interesting letters are א, ה, and ק, all of which on Ashur and the first two of which on Adon present several variants, sometimes archaic, sometimes advanced, sometimes distinctive, as if cursive practice was in a state of considerable flux during the 7 cent. The Nimrud script is very similar in its basic contours to the lapidary of Nerab, and prob. belongs to about the same time (700 B.C.). On historical grounds the Ashur ostracon has to be dated around 650 (see below) and the Adon papyrus around 600, though on the evidence of the writing alone I should be inclined to have a larger gap between Nimrud and Ashur, and a smaller between Ashur and Adon. The explanation of this discrepancy doubtless lies in a quicker development of cursive forms in Assyria, the centre of empire, than in the fringe area on the Levantine coast, from which the Adon letter originated. See further Naveh, 'Script', 15 f.

As is usual in Semitic cursive writing, ligatures are present, though never frequent. The most notable are מ, ligatured 11 times with a following letter, 6 with ו and 4 with ר; א, ligatured 9 times, 2 with ל; and ה, ligatured 6 times, 3 with מ. The proportion of ligatures seems not dissimilar to that on the Lachish ostraca (vol. I no. **12**).

Words are generally separated by spaces, but in a large number of cases they are run together. Lidzbarski and Dupont-Sommer indicate several of these in their transcriptions, but in my estimation, as the transcription below shows, by no means all of them. I have counted a total of twenty-three missing spaces, of which no less than seventeen seem to possess some significance, either for phonology or for syntax or for both. These are (in order of frequency) before המו in 9, 12, 13 (*bis*), and 16; after בית in place-names in 15 and 21; after מן in 9 and 15 (*bis*); within the phrase 'my lord the king' in 7 (*bis*); after the small words כי in 8, זי in 13, and בר in 14; before the small words כא in 8 and לן in 14. Note, however, the missing space before the conjunction 'and' in 16. There are also a considerable number of broad or even double spaces; but of these only three can claim to be significant as possibly indicating the end of a sentence or phrase; those after the first המו in 9 and the last המו in 12, and that after אלה in 13. Rather awkward in the light of the tendencies revealed in the seventeen cases of absence of space mentioned above are the broad spaces between אמר and לי and between מראי and מלכא in 8, and after מן in 16. Finally, a few instances of a space within a word, obviously due to carelessness, are to be noticed; e.g. in פרור (1) and לאמר (8). On the importance of investigations into this kind of feature see Gibson in *Archivum Linguisticum* 17 (1969), 131 f.

Matres lectionis occur internally in אחוך (1) and in a few place- or personal names; חפירו (5); נבוזרכן (10); and other names with the same divine element in 14, 19; אשור (11 *et passim*).

Historical circumstances

The first 18 lines of the ostracon comprise a letter sent by Bel-etir to Pir'i-Amurri. Due to lacunas caused by missing pieces or faded writing, the contents are very difficult to reconstruct, but it is now generally accepted that two of the people mentioned, Bel-etir himself and his companion Arbai, are to be identified with high Assyrian officials of the same names who appear together several times in Akkad. correspondence between Ashurbanipal and Nabu-ushabshi, governor of Uruk; for the texts see Waterman, *Royal Correspondence of the Assyrian Empire* IV (Chicago, 1936), nos. 273, 543, 1108, 1244. In each of the letters the governor dispatches Bel-etir and Arbai to the king with a troop of cavalry. The letters belong to the period of the revolt of Shamash-shum-ukin, Ashurbanipal's brother and king of Babylon, which was crushed by Ashurbanipal after three years in 648 B.C.; *ARAB* II, 301 f. In the present letter Bel-etir and Arbai are stationed at Uruk with Pir'i-Amurri and some other officials. The latter group left for Ashur, while Bel-etir and his companions proceeded to Bit-Amukkani in southern Babylonia, where, at a place called Hafiru in the desert, they captured four individuals (named in line 10), who had in their possession a letter from Shamash-shum-ukin. The contents of the letter are not divulged, but it was important enough for it and the four men to be sent on immediately to Ashurbanipal. If, as seems likely, it concerned Shamash-shum-ukin's plans for the rebellion, the ostracon will date just before its outbreak. Later (6), another individual called Abai was captured; a second letter, addressed to him, had, it appears, been carried by the prisoners (10). Bel-etir then himself visited Assyria and found his captives being treated as royal or state prisoners. Ashurbanipal gave all five to him as his personal slaves (7–8), but when Bel-etir returned to Babylonia, he left them behind in Ashur in the care of someone called Upaqa-ana-Arbaili (10). He now writes to Pir'i-Amurri to ask for them to be sent on to him (11). A subordinate of Pir'i-Amurri (13) may have been the messenger, or the one whom Bel-etir intended should take the prisoners back to him. A person called Pileser (12) had meanwhile expressed doubts, either about the captives' guilt or about the authenticity of Bel-etir's claim upon them, and Bel-etir reiterates the story for his benefit. Some other individuals, again probably slaves, were also to be dispatched to him (14). The next section of the letter (15 f.) rehearses certain campaigns of former kings of Assyria, in which captives had been deported. It is not immediately apparent why these allusions are brought in. Dupont-Sommer believes the references to the pursuing or fettering of these prisoners and to their destruction by fire were to underline the harsh treatment accorded to rebels in general. I argue that the references are more particularly relevant to the rest of the letter, and concern fugitives who escaped after being taken to Assyria. This would enable us to understand the verb קרק (9, 13, 16, 17, 18) in its obvious sense 'to flee', as on the Sefire inscrs., and to see in the five prisoners, with whose fate the letter is so occupied, descendants of peoples previously deported to Assyria from Babylonia, who defected to Shamash-shum-ukin and were subsequently captured while engaged on a mission for him. But the whole section is extremely problematic.

Lines 19 f. form a postscript, addressed to another person, by name Nabu-zer-ushabshi, who is possibly the same as the Nabu-ushabshi, governor of Uruk, mentioned earlier. The section is in a very poor state of preservation, however, and little can be squeezed from it beyond the fact that Nabu-zer-ushabshi is displeased at something. If the governor is meant, he must at the moment be in Ashur; perhaps he exercised some control over the activities of Bel-etir and Arbai and, learning of the incident of the prisoners, had complained about their sending them to Assyria without first reporting to him.

Several other names from the ostracon are paralleled in Ashurbanipal's correspondence, but in most cases a connection is very unlikely; see further in Dupont-Sommer's commentary, *in locis*, and for the Akkad references Waterman, op. cit., index. Bel-etir's companion in line 3 (גרצפן) is possibly to be equated with Gir-ṣapunu, eponym for the year 660 (*ARAB* II, 439), but his status does not seem to be high enough.

Language

The language is imperial Aram., showing no trace of the eastern Aram. dialects later spoken in this region; see further in the introduction to nos. **15–17** Barrakkab. In phonology, we have the change [ṯ] to [t] in יהתב (11), but not in אשור (*passim*; later אתור) or מן שנה (16). Lapse of ['] internally is shown by מרי (6; cp., however, מראי; 7, 8, 17), at the end of a word by אחזא (14; cp. תחזה; 20). The substitution of [w] for [m] in certain place- and personal names is prob. inner Akkad.; see at no. **5** Zakir A 1. The only direct evidence of diphthongal reduction is ימן (16) = [yōmīn] from [yawmīn]; see, however, on המו (4) and איתהם (6). The בית in place-names should perhaps be pronounced [bīt] in the Akkad. manner. In grammar, the pronoun המו has also a shortened form הם (17); the fem. is הני (12). The jussive is distinguished from the imperf.; תחזו (17). The old infin. without prefixed מ is found in לאמר (8, 10). In 9 קרק is prob. an infin. absol. Verbs final ['] and [w, y] have sometimes merged; אחזא (14); but כסא (16, 18) retains [']. There is an example of a dual noun construed with two 3 sing. fem. verbs in 9, a feature not attested in later Aram. In vocabulary, the [h] in the plur. of יד (5, 9) and the Akkad. loan-word לבת (19, 20) are noteworthy. There has been much discussion about the meaning of קרק (9 *et passim*)

No. **20**

1 [אל א]חי פרור אחוך בלטר שלם לש̊ ....

2 [-----] עמי את במתכדי ואנה וערבי ומ ....

3 [----אזל]ת מן ארך עם גרצפן ועם וגמ̊ר א ....

4 אנה.....*c.* 10.....ב̊ית אוכן *1 3* המו אגרת מלך בבל..........

5 בידה[יה]ם י̊[אמר לאמר אל זי] בית אוכן בחפיר̊ו במדברא אחזן המ[ו] ....

6 איתהם ....*c.* 13.......[ה]ו̊שרת למר̊י מלכ̊א אזי [אבי] אחזן - מן - נ̊ה̊..............

7 ואתית----ק̊ד̊ם̊ [מרא]ימל[כא] ---ן עם כלביא שמן יהב̊ המו לי מרא̊ימלכ̊א..............

8 כיזא זא אמר לי מראי מלכא לא̊מר [זלך] המז ולטחנו לה̊ י̊טעמכ̊א ח̊זית ב..............[עם זי]

and כסא (16, 18). The syntax is very abrupt, as commonly on Aram. letters.

Bibliography

The first publication was by Lidzbarski in *ZA* 31 (1917–18), 193 f.
See further:
D. H. Baneth, 'Zu dem aramäischen Brief aus der Zeit Assurbanipals', *Orientalische Literaturzeitung* 22 (1919), 55 f.
M. Lidzbarski, 'Altaramäische Urkunden aus Assur', *Wissenschaftliche Veröffentlichungen der Deutschen Orient-Gesellschaft* 38 (1921), 5–15.
R. A. Bowman, 'An interpretation of the Ashur Ostracon', in Waterman, op. cit. 273 f.
A. Dupont-Sommer, 'L'Ostracon araméen d'Assur', *Syria* 24 (1944–5), 24–61.
Koopmans, *Chrest.* no. 14.
KAI no. 233.

Plates and figures

Lidzbarski, loc. cit. (1921); Dupont-Sommer, loc. cit.; Driver, *Writing*, pl. 55; *KAI* Taf. XXVI.

Note: in making the transcription below I have used Lidzbarski's photograph as well as the sketch by Dupont-Sommer reproduced on plate V.

---

1. To my brother Pir'i-Amurri, your brother Bel-etir, greetings . . . .
2. . . . . you were with me in Akkad; and I and Arbai and . . . . .
3. . . . . . you [departed] from Uruk with Ger-Ṣaphon and with WGMR . . . .
4. I . . . . Bit-Amukkani. They were four in number. A letter of the king of Babylon . . . .
5. in their hands, [which began, To those of] Bit-Amukkani. At Hafiru in the desert we captured them . . . .
6. them . . . . I dispatched to my lord, the king. Then we captured [Abai] . . . .
7. and I came . . . . before my [lord], the king. Our . . . . . had been put with the dogs. My lord, the king, gave them to me . . . .
8. for this, yes this, is what my lord, the king, said to me, They [belong to you]. So they did not (any longer) grind (grain) for him. Let this decision be accepted! You have seen . . . . [With those]

9 בית אוכן המו ידיהם כתבת וקימת קדמי קרק קרקו הלו
בבית אוכןהמו מנידהי[הם].............

10 אבי יאמר לאמר מן שמהיקר [נ]בוזרכן אחש[י] וולול
נבוזרכן ואחשי אפקנרביל שם............

11 וולול שמהיקר ואבי הלו ה---- כזי יאתה אפקנרביל אשור
מן עקב יהתב המו לאפק[נרביל והן]

12 פלסר [יש]אל הצדא הני מליא אלה ב[לטר] שמי כתב על
ידה[י]הם וקרא המו שאלהמו הצד[א הני]

13 [מלי]א אלה הל[ו] עבדןהמו זלי קרקו הלו [עם] זיבית
אוכןהמו הלו נדמרדך עזרך שלחתקדמ[יך]

14 [----] המו אחזא המו הושרלן אזי ברנמ-[--]בן ובר
ב---זבן זבנאדן ונבושלם זי בית עדן אזי

15 [-----]ע שבי שבה תכלתפלסרמן ביתאוכן [ושבי] שבה
אללי מנבית עדן ושבי שבה שרכן מנדרסן

16 ושב[י שבה סנ]חרב מנכשו--[מלכי] אשור-יג.... *c.* 8 ....
מן שנה יקרקרן ויכסאןהמו וכימןמלכי א[שור]

17 .... *c.* 14 .... לאמר קרקי אל תחזו מ .... *c.* 13 ......
אשור אשה אכלתהם ומראי מלכא פקד [איתי]

18 למ-נדא א----- קרקי אשור יכסאן

19 לנבוזרש[בש]----ארה מלאכתי אשלח לך וה........ *c.* 16
.... הלבתי מלא את לבת אלהא זי -טי.....

20 למה לבתי מלא [את] וכעת------אפיאס--ק...... *c.* 12
......[א]פיא כזי תחזה ו---- שנה שלחנה........

21 בביתדבלא ל---ן ש[וד]ן ה-- זי המרתך זי את....... *c.* 13
......שודן זי בית דבלא

9. of Bit-Amukkani they were. Their own hands have written and established (it) before my eyes. They had indeed defected. I tell you, they were in Bit-Amukkani. From [their] hands . . . . (a letter to)

10. Abai, which began, From Shemehyaqar, Nabu-zer-ukin, Aheshai and WLWL. As for Nabu-zer-ukin and Aheshai, Upaqa-ana-Arbaili has put . . . .

11. As for WLWL, Shemehyaqar and Abai, they . . . . When Upaqa-ana-Arbaili arrives at Ashur, let him immediately return them to Upaqa[-ana-Arbaili. And if]

12. Pileser asks, Are these words true?, Bel-etir, my name, is written on their hands. Call them (and) ask them, Are these

13. [words] true? I tell you, they are slaves who belong to me. They had defected. I tell you, they were [with] those of Bit-Amukkani. Note that I have sent Naid-Marduk, your assistant, to [you]

14. (to fetch) them. I would like to see them. Dispatch to us also the son of NM——BN and the son of B——ZBN, Zaban-iddina and Nabu-ushallim of Bit-Adini. Furthermore,

15. (you will know) that Tiglathpileser deported prisoners from Bit-Amukkani, and Ululai deported [prisoners] from Bit-Adini, and Sargon deported prisoners from Dur-Sin,

16. and Sennacherib [deported] prisoners from Kish. And . . . . [the kings of] Assyria . . . . (who) defect from here, and let them pursue them! And down the years the kings of [Assyria]

17. saying, Have no regard for defectors from my service! (If any defect from) Ashur, fire will consume them. Now, my lord, the king, commanded [me]

18. to . . . ., Let those who defect from Assyria be pursued!

19. To Nabu-zer-ushabshi . . . . I shall send my report to you . . . . Is it against me that you are filled with anger (or) against the god who . . . .

20. Why are you filled with anger against me? And now . . . . when you see . . . . we sent (them) here . . . .

21. At Bit-Dibla . . . . Shum-iddin . . . . who made you feel bitter . . . . Shum-iddin of Bit-Dibla.

NOTES

1. פרור is equivalent to Akkad. *Pir'i-Amurri*, 'offspring of Amurru' (Tallqvist, *Names*, 181) or possibly *Pir'i-Mēr*; cp. אלור (no. **5** Zakir A 1); the medial ['] seems to have lapsed in pronunciation; for the equation between [m] and [w] see also the note to Zakir A 1. בלטר; Akkad. *Bēl-ēṭir*, 'Bel is saviour' (Tallqvist, 56). אחוך = ['ḥūk] with internal *mater lectionis*. With the formula cp. Cowley xl 1; no. **28** Padua i; here the correspondents were prob. not related, but being of roughly equal rank, avoid using the term 'servant'.
2. את; see at no. **18** Nerab i 5. מתכדי; in Akkad. writing the name appears as (*māt*)*Akkadi*, with the determinative unpronounced. Apparently the scribe was accustomed to writing Akkadian as well as Aram., and transfers the convention from one orthography to the other. The northern region of Babylonia is meant, though Uruk seems to be included. ערבי; Akkad. *Ar-ba-a-a* (Tallqvist, 28), a gentilic; for a tribe called Arbai see *ARAB* II, 447. Another name follows; Bel-etir and his companions presumably proceeded southwards to Bit-Amukkani.
3. אזלת = ['zalt]; the restoration is Lidzbarski's, although he took the verb as 1 pers., referring to Bel-etir; but his movements seem to be dealt with in the previous line. Pir'i-Amurri returned to Ashur; at any rate he was there when the letter was sent. ארך is the modern Warka; Gen. x 10. גרצפן; the name is of Phoen. origin, meaning 'client of the god Ṣaphon'; cp. the names צפנבעל on a Punic inscr. from Carthage and גרמלקרת on a Phoen. inscr. from Kition; references in *KAI*, index. A person of this name (Akkad. *Gir-ṣa-pu-nu*) was eponym for the year 660; see introduction. וגמר can hardly be an Anatolian name (see at no. **14** Panammu 2); it is prob. Iranian; for Iranian names beginning with [w] see Driver x 1.
4. בית אוכן; Akkad. *Bīt-Amukkāni*, a region in southern Babylonia; see *ARAB* (index). The lacunas at the end of 3 and the beginning of this line contain a reference to a meeting with the four men, the circumstances of whose capture is now related. The numeral is indicated by four short strokes. On the vocalization of the pronoun see at no. **5** Zakir A 9 ([hōmū] or less likely [himmō]). אגרת = ['iggrat] (constr.); a loan-word from Akkad., found also in Hebr. and Syriac. בבל; Akkad. *Bābilu*.
5. ידהיהם = [ydāhay/ēhōm]. The reading is Dupont-Sommer's; he justifies it by the text in 12, where only the י is lacking, and compares the plur. form in Syriac [īdahātā], 'hands', and the general Aram. ['bāhātā], 'fathers', though these both have the fem. [t]. Lidzbarski reads ידהום in both cases, but there is no other example so early of the *mater lectionis* ו used in writing this suffix. With the restoration cp. 10 (יאמר לאמר) and 13 (זי); there is room for ten or eleven letters. חפירו; Lidzbarski mentions Arab. [ḥafīr] in southern Babylonia, the first station after Basra on the route to Mecca. אחזן = ['ḥaḏn]; on the ending see at no. **7** Sefire i C 1.
6. איתהם possible = ['ītēhōm], 'they were'; Egyp. Aram. (י)אית; cp. ליש (no. **15** Barrakkab i 16). This vocalization gives a case of the shift [ṯ] to [t], attested already at Sefire and in this text (11), and would supply proof of a reduced diphthong [ē] from [ay]. The form is, however, more easily explained as the object-marker אית = ['iyyāt] with suffix; see at no. **5** Zakir B 5; note that the isogloss here is with Arpad, a Syrian dialect, not with later imperial texts, which have ית or ות. In the lacuna supply 'Them and the letter of the king of Babylon I dispatched . . . .', or similar. הושרת = [haw/ōšrēt]; a

common verb in the papyri. מרי = [mārī]; Dan. iv 16 (Qere); possibly here a scribal slip, since the full form מראי is found in 7, 8, 17. אזי = [’d̲ay]; cp. later Aram. אדין; Hebr. אזי in Ps. cxxiv 3. There is just room in the following lacuna for three letters, and on the basis of 10, 11 Dupont-Sommer very plausibly suggests the insertion of the name אבי. The letter (two letters?) following the verb are illegible; we may have ו plus מן or another 1 plur. verbal form.

7. אתית = [’tayt] or as in biblical Aram. [’tēt]. Afterwards supply ‘to Nineveh’? In the lacuna before עם we may restore קרקין, ‘our fugitives’ or similar noun. שמן = [śīmīn]; passive partic. The phrase ‘put with the dogs’ is apparently metaphorical for some kind of confinement to which deportees and prisoners of war were subjected; cp. the similar references in Ashurbanipal’s annals to captives being chained like dogs at the gates of Nineveh; *ANET*, 298. Note that לי is written above מראי, having been carelessly omitted by the scribe.

8. זא = [d̲ā] is repeated for emphasis. לאמר; the infin. form without the מ prefix is attested in Old Aram. (e.g. no. **7** Sefire i A 24) and is retained in this conventional phrase even as late as the papyri, where it is a frequent alternative to למ(א)מר; the phrase should not therefore be regarded as a Canaanitism. זלך = [d̲ī lāk]; the restoration is made by Dupont-Sommer on the basis of זלי in 13. לטחנו = [lā ṭ̣ḥánū]; with the nuance of servitude, here as state prisoners, לה referring to the king, cp. Judg. xvi 21; Isa. xlvii 2 (of Babylon); Job xxxi 10. יטעם prob. = [yuṭʿam]; jussive pass., lit. ‘let it be so tasted’; cp. Syriac [ṭʿīm], ‘palatable’, ‘acceptable’ and the use of the noun טעם in Ezra vi 14; Dan. iii 10, etc. כא; see note to no. **7** Sefire i C 1. חזית = [ḥzayt], ‘you saw’; the implication of this reading is that Pir’i-Amurri had been present or had seen a record of the proceedings, and should not now be questioning the decision. Alternatively the verb could be 1 pers.; the following word is illegible, except for the first letter, which is ב; might this go with חזית, ‘I saw my desire upon’? (cp. Cowley xxx 17; Hebr. ראה with ב; vol. I no. **16** Mesha 7). The reading ח is suggested by Lidzbarski, although he and Dupont-Sommer prefer ב; but no hook on the right vertical is visible. Lidzbarski interprets as the prepos. plus זית, ‘olives’. Dupont-Sommer thinks of the base BZY, ‘to despise’ or of Palest. Aram. BZY (BZ’?), ‘to split, break’; Pael ‘to divide’; cp. BZʿ; thus, e.g., ‘You have despised (this decision)’, ‘I divided (the prisoners)’.

9. At the end of 8 I restore עם זי as in 13 (q.v. note). ידיהם = [yday/ēhōm]; the dual is used against the plur. forms in 5, 12, and later in this line. כתבת = [kitbat]. A 3 fem. sing. verb accompanying a dual or plur. subject (inanimate) is regular in Arab., common in Ugar. (Driver, *Canaanite Myths and Legends*, 130) and not infrequent in Hebr. (e.g. 1 Sam. iv 15; Jerem. iv 14), but is not otherwise found in Aram. קימת = [qayymat]; Pael. The faded word after קדמי I read as קרק = [ġrāq]; infin. absol.; the second letter is usually taken as ב. קרקו = [ġráqū] (so Baneth); this verb occurs several times on no. **9** Sefire iii (4, 19), describing fugitives from one realm to another. Dupont-Sommer follows Lidzbarski in regarding such a sense as unsuitable, and connects the base with Arab. [qaraḍa], ‘cut, gnaw’; II ‘censure, blame’; i.e. here presumably Pael [qārēġū]. But this base is otherwise unknown outside Arab., and seems awkwardly used without an object; cp., however, the similar ranges of meaning in the related bases (1) QRʿ; Arab. ‘knock, strike’; II ‘upbraid’; Hebr. ‘tear’, and in Ps. xxxv 15 ‘rail, malign’ (2) QRṢ; Arab., Hebr., Aram., Akkad. ‘pinch, nip off’; Akkad. also ‘gnaw’ and in the phrase

ākil qarṣi, 'calumniator, slanderer', whence Aram. ['kal qarṣē], 'accuse maliciously', lit. 'eat the pieces of'. הלו; cp. אלו (Dan. ii 31).

10. אבי = ['bay/ī] or the like, a shortened form of a name beginning with the element, 'the father (god)'. יאמר = [yi'mar] or as later [yēmar]. שמהיקר is perplexing; it makes an acceptable Aram. phrase [šmēh yqar], 'His (the god's) name is honourable'; but there are no parallels among known Syrian Semitic names; cp., however, in Akkad. *La-bar-šumšu* (Tallqvist, 119), 'venerable is his name'; perhaps, as Lidzbarski suggests, it is an Aram. form of an Akkad. name. נבוזרכן; Akkad. *Nabū-zēr-ukīn*, 'Nabu (Nebo) has established a seed'; for similar names see Tallqvist, 319. אחשי; Akkad. *Aḫē-ša-a* (Tallqvist, 14), shortened form of a name, 'His brothers . . . . .'. ולול; see on וגמר (3). Of the 5 prisoners, one at least seems to be Aramaean, and one Iranian by race; the others have Akkad. names, but this does not preclude a foreign origin. אפקנרביל; Akkad. *Upāqa-ana-Arbaili* (Tallqvist, 242), 'I wait for (the goddess) of Arbela', i.e. Ishtar. Though it is not explicitly stated, this person seems to have been entrusted with the prisoners while Bel-etir returned to Babylonia. Two of them he 'put' (שם) separate from the other 3, but although he himself was not in Ashur when the letter arrived (11), it is not certain whether he took the second group with him or merely arranged separate places of confinement for both groups in Ashur. The Pileser mentioned in 12 may have been involved in the arrangements.

11. The first letter of the word following הלו is doubtful, and could be ש or ע instead of ה. Possibly the short phrase contained המו followed or preceded by an adverb (? 'there', i.e. in Ashur) or a prepositional phrase (? 'with him', i.e. Upaqa-ana-Arbaili; 'with you', i.e. Pir'i-Amurri). יאתה = [yi'tē] or [yētē]; for another example of a direct object after a verb of coming, going, etc., see no. **9** Sefire iii 5; alternatively, supply ל, which may have dropped out through haplography. מן עקב; lit. 'from a heel', thus perhaps 'thereafter', 'immediately', or the like (Lidzbarski). Bowman prefers to read a place-name, and cites a town Akaba from Ashurbanipal's annals; *ARAB* II, 301. יהתב = [yahtēb] or [yhātēb], either 'let him (Pileser) return them' or impersonally, 'let one return them'; note ת for earlier שׁ, and on the form see at no. **7** Sefire i C 18.

12. פלסר is a short form of a name like Tiglathpileser (see at no. **14** Panammu 13). The few lines (12–16) which are complete or nearly so seem to finish with a full word, so a first part of the name should not be supplied in the previous line. If Pileser is the subject of יהתב in 11, he may have been in charge of the prisoners during Upaqa-ana-Arbaili's absence; but he was more than a temporary gaoler, for he was clearly unwilling for them to be handed over. For all we know, he may have entered a counterclaim for possession of them; this would explain Pir'i-Amurri's hesitation to accord immediately with Bel-etir's request, even although he knew something (end of 8) about its background. ישאל; see the end of the line. הצדא; a strong interrogative particle, occurring also in Dan. iii 14; the derivation is unknown. הני = [hinnī]; fem. plur. pronoun used as an enclitic; cp. אנין in Dan. vii 17. אלה = ['ēllē]; Jerem. x 11; Ezra v 15 (Kethibh) and commonly in the papyri. כתב = [ktīb]. ידהיהם; see at 5. קרא = [qrā] or possibly [qrē]; cp. [śē] (Ezra v 15) and אחזא (14). The addition of הני at the end makes the phrase an exact replica of that earlier in the line; it also regularizes the left-hand margin, which (as restored) finishes after eight extra spaces in the previous line, after four in this and after two in the following line; lines 14 and 15 are already complete. Thereafter

the margin moves outward again, since 3 letters have to be supplied at the end of 16.

13. For the small lacuna after the second הלו I suggest עם, though there may be room for a third letter; cp. Peshitta, Matt. xxii 16. נדמרדך; Akkad. *Nā'id-Marduk*, 'Exalted is Marduk' (Tallqvist, 166). עזרך = [ʿāḏrāk]; if the second letter is a faded ב, a possible reading is עבדך. At the end Dupont-Sommer restores י instead of ך', i.e. 'I have sent ahead (lit. before me)', sc. to give more details about the situation. Naid-Marduk prob. carried the letter with him.

14. Restore perhaps ל plus the infin. of a verb meaning 'to fetch' or the like; there is scarcely room for להתבת, 'to bring back'. Alternatively, with Dupont-Sommer read הושר and begin a new sentence. אחזא = ['iḥzē]; note the א, suggesting that bases final ['] and [w, y] have partly merged, as they generally have in biblical and Egyp. Aram.; contrast תחזה (20). Note the position of אזי after the verb, and cp. the usage of [dēn] in Syriac, which may therefore not be entirely explained by the analogy of Greek δε. נמ - - - - בן; a deity Nawar is known from names at Mari (*Archives royales* XV, 1954, 163); the base NMR, 'to shine', is common in Akkad. names (Tallqvist, 297); for names ending in *ibni*, 'he created' see no. **18** Nerab i 1 and Tallqvist, 275. זבנאדן; cp. Akkad. *Za-ban-Iddina* (Tallqvist, 245); the meaning of the first element, whether divine or a noun as object of the verb, is unknown; it seems to occur at the end of the previous name as well. נבושלם; Akkad. *Nabū-ušallim*, 'Nabu has kept safe' (Tallqvist, 163). The names belong to other slaves of Bel-etir, but it is not certain what connection they had with the previous events, or even whether there are four or two of them (there is no ו after זבן). בית עדן; Akkad. *Bīt-Adini*; see *ARAB* (index).

15. A new argument is introduced by אזי at the end of 14; for opinions of its purpose see the introduction. The ע suggests a part of the verb YDʿ, e.g. 'You (את) will know (that)'. שבי = [šbī]; collective; Judg. v 12; Ps. lxviii 19. תכלתפלסר; see on פלסר (12). אללי; Akkad. *U-lu-la-a-a*, 'born in the month of Elul', the Babylonian name of Shalmaneser V. שרכן; Akkad. *Šarru-kīnu*, 'the king is true'. דרסן; Akkad. *Dūr-Sin*, on the lower Tigris. Of the three campaigns mentioned in this line only one (the first) is definitely recorded in the Assyrian annals; see *ARAB* I, 281. A campaign of Sargon in the lower Tigris region is known (II, 14 f.), although Dur-Sin is not mentioned; but we have no information of the campaign of Shalmaneser in Bīt-Adini.

16. סנחרב; Akkad. *Sin-aḫḫē-erība*, 'Sin has rewarded the brothers'. כש; although there is no space between ש and the following letter, this is the best reading, since we know that Sennacherib did deport people from Kish; see *ARAB* II, 116. Where I read ו Bowman has ר and Dupont-Sommer נ; but they can suggest no suitable place-names. After ו it is tempting to restore כימן as later in the line, but there is hardly room. There follow spoken instructions of the kings of Assyria about the pursuit and punishment of defectors. After אשור Lidzbarski and Bowman read יגז[לו], 'they rob, plunder'; but no ז is visible on the photograph, and there may be a further letter before the י. מן שנה = [min ṯnā] (so Baneth); cp. Egyp. Aram. תנה; Syriac [tnān]. יקרקן = [yiġrqūn]. ויכסאן; the ו could begin the apodosis of a conditional sentence; see at no. **9** Sefire iii 10. The ס is clearer in 18; Dupont-Sommer connects the base with Akkad. *kasū*, 'to bind, catch', and Arab. [kasa'a], 'to follow, pursue'; he adopts the Akkad. meaning, but the Arab. fits better with ĠRQ, 'to flee, defect'. The א precludes any link with KSW; Arab. 'to clothe'; Hebr. and Aram. (Piel, Pael), 'to cover, hide'. כימן = [kyōmīn] with reduced

diphthong, lit. 'according to days'; cp. מימים ימימה, 'from year to year' (Exod. xiii 10) and other biblical phrases where 'days' is to be rendered 'years'. A similar phrase כימם is found in vol. I no. **10** Yavneh-yam 5, but the context there demands a different interpretation.

17. There are some faded letters at the beginning of the line, variously read by the commentators, thus Lidzbarski בעריג; Bowman רבעי בל; Dupont-Sommer ב–דיב. תחזו = [tiḥzū]; jussive; syntactically קרקי could be the subject rather than the object, or it could be *casus pendens* with ב̊[הם] following. אשה; fem. as normally in Aram., against the masc. form of no. **7** Sefire i A 25. אכלתהם = ['aklat hōm]; הם is not a suffix, but a shorter form of the pronoun, which is found occasionally in the papyri as an alternative to המו. The phrase is either the apodosis of a conditional sentence, whose protasis contained the verb יקרקן (cp. 16) or it follows the *casus pendens* קרקי אשור (cp. 18); in the first case the perf., like the biblical 'prophetic' perf., may be used for emphasis. איתי = ['iyyātī]; no. **9** Sefire iii 11; this restoration makes the line roughly the same length as the previous one.

18. The verb here seems to be passive, i.e. [yuks'ūn]; imperf. for jussive, as occasionally at Sefire. However we interpret the details in 15 f., it is clear that Ashurbanipal's action on this occasion is being justified by citing precedents from the reigns of former kings, although there does not seem to be any mention of prisoners being made over to their captors.

19. נבוזרשבש; Akkad. *Nabū-zēr-ušabši*, 'Nabu has called seed into being' (Tallqvist, 164). The link with Nabu-ushabshi, governor of Uruk (see introduction), is attractive, since it offers a reason for his anger. ארה; Lidzbarski compares biblical Aram. ארו; Mishnaic Hebr. הרי, 'behold, see'. מלאכתי = [mal'kūtī]; so Syriac [malakūtā], which also has the meaning 'embassy'; Hebr. מלאכה is 'work'. הלבתי מלא את = [hlibbātī mlē 'at]; cp. Cowley xli 4 ('how I am filled with anger against you (לבתך)'); Ezek. xvi 30. If ML' has not yet been assimilated to MLY, the passive partic. should be vocalized [mlī]. The noun is not a fem. form of לב, but a borrowing from Akkad. *libbāti*, plur., 'anger, passion'.

20. After מלא there are two faded letters, which look like מל repeated and may be dittography. אפיא; Lidzbarski, 'the people of Opis' on the lower Tigris; *ARAB* I, 99; II, 145; or = ['appayyā], dual, 'face' or even ['āpayyā], 'the bakers' (cp. nos. **3**, **4** Dan, Ein Gev; Gen. xl 16). שנה; see at 16 above. If after שלחן we restore המו, there is a link with the main letter; but ה could be a sing. suffix and refer to מלאכתי (19) or to the person mentioned in 21. Note that reading המו would give a further instance of omission of a space.

21. בית דבלא; the location is unknown. שודן; Akkad. *Šum-iddin*, '(The god) has given a name' (Tallqvist, 125). המרתך = [hammartāk] or the like; 2 masc. Haph. from MRR. There is the trace of a letter after כ, but this could go with the next word (כזי ?). The final phrase is very faint.

21. Saqqara: The Adon papyrus Pl. VI, 1

The fragment of papyrus was discovered in 1942 during an Egyptian excavation at Saqqara (Memphis), and is now in the Cairo Museum; its measurements were not reported by the first editor. On the relation of the script to other early examples of Aram. cursive writing see the introduction to no. **20** Ashur ostracon. Words are separated by spaces; the larger ones after פרעה (1); אמין (3); and לחצלתי (7) clearly indicate sense-divisions. There do not seem to be any true ligatures, though occasionally letters touch. One internal *mater lectionis* occurs, in אמין (3).

Historical circumstances

The papyrus comprises part of a letter addressed to the Egyptian Pharaoh by a ruler with the Syrian Semitic name Adon, requesting assistance against the army of the king of Babylon who had invaded his land. Historically, it has to belong to the period following 609 B.C. when, after 4 years or so of Egyptian domination, control of the Syrian area was for two or three decades disputed between the Pharaoh and Nebuchadnezzar. Cp. in particular the Babylonian Chronicle (see under Wiseman in the bibliography below), which records campaigns by Nebuchadnezzar in the west, not necessarily always successful, in nearly every year from 604 until it breaks off in 593; cp. also the several times the situation described is paralleled in the history of Judah after the death of Josiah at Megiddo; 2 Kgs. xxiii 33 f. (609); xxiv 1 f. (603–602); xxiv 7 (this statement should be taken with a pinch of salt in the light of the evidence of the Babylonian Chronicle, but by its present position it at least suggests that Jehoiachin during his brief reign made advances to Egypt); xxiv 10 f. (597); vol. I no. **12** Lachish iii 13 f.; Jerem. xxvii 3 f.; xxviii 1–4; 2 Kgs. xxv 1 f. (588–586); Jerem. xxxvii 5 f.; xlii 7 f.; lii 30 (581). Unfortunately, the name of Adon's kingdom is not preserved; but a place Aphek is mentioned (4) as having already been reached by the Babylonian forces (cp. vol. I no. **12** Lachish iv 12). If this is the Aphek (Akkad. *Apqu*) in the plain of Sharon astride the coastal route to Egypt (Josh. xii 18; 1 Sam. iv 1), Adon can only have been ruler of one of the Philistine city-states, most likely Ashdod or Gaza. Ashkelon, which fell to Nebuchadnezzar in 604 B.C., is excluded from consideration, unless we assume that an Adon who sent the letter died or was assassinated very soon afterwards; for Babylonian sources inform us that the king of Ashkelon at the time of its destruction had the name Aga; see bibliography under Weidner, 928; Vogt, 85 f. However, there are at least two other towns called Aphek which can be brought into the reckoning, both pointing to southern Phoenicia as the site of Adon's kingdom. The first of these was situated about 14 miles east of Byblos (Josh. xiii 4; the modern Afqā) in one of the less important passes through the Lebanon range; if on one of his campaigns Nebuchadnezzar came that way with his army, Adon must have been king of Byblos or of Sidon further to the south. The second lay in the plain of Acco some 6 miles SE. of that town (Josh. xix 30; Judg. i 31), and would have been on Nebuchadnezzar's route if we suppose that he left the main southern highway at Megiddo and turned north to attack Phoenician territory; this would make Adon ruler of Acco, if it constituted a separate kingdom at the time, or of Tyre. So far most commentators, while admitting there is no certain solution, have preferred to place Adon's kingdom in Philistia. But, though the Philistine city-states may by 600 B.C. have succumbed in many ways to Canaanite influence in culture and language, there is no definite proof from elsewhere of a Philistine king calling himself by a Semitic name or invoking a Semitic deity (2). Over and above this there is one small but positive indication in the letter of a Phoenician connection, namely the title 'lord of kings' in the address to Pharaoh in 1, a rather rare title, which does not occur in Egyptian sources, but is found occasionally in Akkad. texts and significantly a number of times on Phoen. inscriptions. For these reasons I incline with a minority towards locating Adon's territory in southern Phoenicia. As to date, the contents of the letter may suggest that Egypt is still Adon's actual as opposed to nominal overlord, and that we should therefore bring it as close as we can to Necho's major defeat at Carchemish in 605. But it can be read more generally, so that theoretically Adon's appeal could have been presented during any of the expeditions mentioned in the Babylonian Chronicle or even during a later expedition; for events in Judah, as we have seen, and in Tyre which, according to Josephus, finally fell to Nebuchadnezzar only after a 13 years' siege about 572, shows that his campaigns did not cease in 593.

Language

The dialect, though to be classed as official or imperial since it is not native to the writer, scarcely differs from the Old Aram. of Damascus, and to that extent lends support to my view that the imperial dialect originated in an extended currency of the dialect of the major Aramaean power; see further in the introduction to nos. **7–9** Sefire. Thus there is no evidence of the lapse of ['], of diphthongal reduction, of a merging of verbs final ['] and final [w, y], or of any of the phonological features in official Aram. that derive from Akkad. There is, however, one case of a non-Aram. construction, the use of כי after ידע (6); this must be due to the influence of Adon's native Canaanite, i.e. of Hebrew, if he ruled in Philistia, or of Phoenician. In 8 נגווא and in 9 פחה and מתא are Akkad. loan-words.

Bibliography

First publication: A. Dupont-Sommer, 'Un Papyrus araméen d'époque saïte découverte à Saqqarah', *Semitica* 1 (1948), 43–68.

See further:

E. F. Weidner, 'Jojachim, König von Juda, in babylonischen Keilschrifttexten', *Mélanges syriens offerts à M. René Dussaud* (Paris, 1939), II, 923 f.

H. L. Ginsberg, 'King of kings and Lord of kingdoms', *AJSL* 57 (1940), 71 f.

H. L. Ginsberg, 'An Aramaic contemporary of the Lachish Letters', *BASOR* 111 (1948), 24 f.

D. Winton Thomas, 'The age of Jeremiah in the light of recent archaeological discovery', *PEQ* (1950), 8–13.

R. Meyer, 'Ein aramäischer Papyrus aus den ersten Jahren Nebukadnezars II', *Festschrift für F. Zucker* (Berlin, 1954), 251–62.

D. J. Wiseman, *Chronicles of Chaldaean Kings* (*626–556* B.C.) *in the British Museum* (London, 1956).

E. Vogt, 'Die neu-babylonische Chronik über die Schlacht bei Karkemisch und die Einnahme von Jerusalem', *VT Supplements* 4 (1957), 67 f.

Koopmans, *Chrest.* no. 16.

KAI no. 266.

K. Galling, 'Eschmunazar und der Herr der Könige', *ZDPV* 79 (1963), 140 f.

J. A. Fitzmyer, 'The Aramaic letter of King Adon to the Egyptian Pharaoh', *Biblica* 46 (1965), 41–55.

F. Vattioni, 'Il papiro di Saqqarah', *Studia Papyrologica* 5 (1966), 101–17.

S. H. Horn, 'Where and when was the Aramaic Saqqara papyrus written?', *Andrews University Seminary Studies* 6 (1968), 29–45.

Translation

DOTT, 251 f.

Plates

Dupont-Sommer, loc. cit.; *KAI* Taf. XXXIII.

No. **21**

1 אל מרא מלכן פרעה עבדך אדן מלך [----שלם מרא מלכן פרעה ---- וכל אלהי]

2 שמיא וארקא ובעׄלשמין אלהׄ[א רבא ישאלו בכל עדן וישמו כרסא מרא מלכן]

3 פרעה כיומי שמין אמין זי .... [חילא]

4 זי מלך בבל אתו מטׄאׄוׄ אפק ושׄ ....

5 ----אחזו----ו ..... c. 9 .... כ-...............

6 כי מרא מלכן פרעה ידע כי עבד[ך] ....

7 למשלח חיל לחׄצלתי אל יׄשבקנ[י] ....

8 וטבתה עבדך נצר ונגוׄא זנהׄ ....

9 פחה במתא וספר שניוהׄ ספ[ר] ....

1. To lord of kings, Pharaoh, your servant Adon, king of [. . . . . . The welfare of lord of kings, Pharaoh, may . . . . . . and all the gods]
2. of heaven and earth and Baalshamayn, the [great] god, [seek at all times; and may they make the throne of lord of kings,]
3. Pharaoh, enduring like the days of heaven. What . . . . [the forces]
4. of the king of Babylon have come; they have reached Aphek and (encamped) . . . .
5. . . . . . . they have taken . . . .
6. For lord of kings, Pharaoh, knows that your servant . . . .
7. to send an army to deliver me. Let him not abandon me . . . .
8. and your servant has kept in mind his kindness. But this territory . . . .
9. a governor in the land, and as a border they have replaced it with the border . . . .

NOTES

1. מרא מלכן = [māri' malkīn] is best regarded as an Aram. translation of the Phoen. title אדן מלכם; *KAI* no. 14 Eshmunazar 18; *KAI* no. 19 Maʿṣub 5; *KAI* no. 42 Larnaka (Lapethos) i 2, etc. In the later inscrs. it is applied to Ptolemaic monarchs, but in Eshmunazar (5 cent.), it can only refer to the Persian king. Whether it was derived from the Akkad. title *bēl šarrāni*, found occasionally in letters and other sources belonging to late Assyrian and neo-Babylonian times (e.g. Waterman, *Royal Correspondence of the Assyrian Empire*, Chicago, 1930–6, nos. 256, 1, 2; 281, 3, 16, 32; 992, 2) or vice versa, or whether the two are unconnected, is uncertain. The occurrence in Dan. ii 47 (in Nebuchadnezzar's confession of Daniel's god) doubtless depends on the Akkad. usage. The title is not found in Egyptian sources, and should be distinguished from the Greek title *κυριος βασιλειων* (Rosetta stone, 1), which prob. reflects one or other of the indigenous Egyptian epithets 'lord of the crowns' or 'king of upper and lower Egypt'. Some have tried to link the two, comparing Phoen. and Ugar. *mlk*, 'kingdom'; but Aram. only has [malkūtā]. The title should also be distinguished from the Achaemenid 'king of kings' (Ezra vii 12; Dan. ii 37). See further on the problem Ginsberg (1940); Galling. פרעה = [parʿō] as in Hebr.; Pharaoh Necho II (609–594) or his successor is meant. אדן; the Canaanite equivalent of מרא and a component in many names; cp. in the Bible אדניצדק; אדניהו, etc. The restoration in 1 and 2 (down to עדן) is based on the formula in Cowley xxx 1–2. At the end Dupont-Sommer proposes עשתרת בעלת = [ʿaṯtart baʿlat], 'Astarte, mistress of heaven and earth'. He cites a hymn to Ishtar (*ANET*, 384), where a similar epithet appears as one in a list of conventional descriptive phrases; but since several of these are elsewhere predicated of other deities, we cannot regard this one as specifically belonging to Astarte; thus in the title in Jerem. vii 18, which is usually held to refer to Astarte, 'earth' is not mentioned. More attractive is Ginsberg's relating of the expression to Gen. xiv 19, 22; i.e. here אל (עלין) מרא (cp. IQ ap Gn xxii 16,

21); but again one wonders whether the fuller title is original; in *KAI* no. 26 Karatepe iii 18 and in the Palmyrene inscrs. אלק(ו)נרע (references in Jean-Hoftijzer, *Dictionnaire*, 260; cp. *KAI* no. 244 Hatra xxiii 3), 'heaven' is omitted; see further at no. 7 Sefire i A 11. The restoration in the text plays safe; a similar phrase occurs in the middle of the list of gods in the treaty of Esarhaddon with the king of Tyre (*ANET*, 534a; cp. 535a). If the lacuna in 2 is correctly restored and if, as is likely with a papyrus document, both margins were straight, there is room in front for another god's name, perhaps a dynastic or civic deity like Rakkabel at Zenjirli or Melcarth of Tyre and Eshmun of Sidon; the progression thus given, from local god to pantheon to high god, seems not unfitting. See further on this lacuna Milik, *Biblica* 48 (1967), 561 f.

2. בעלשמין; see at no. 5 Zakir A 3. For רבא as his epithet see *KAI* no. 245 Hatra xxiv 1; below no. 34 Guzneh 3. ישאלו = [yiš'ălū]; jussive and therefore lacking [n]. עדן = [ʿiddān]. ישמו = [yśímū]; with the restoration cp. Ps. lxxxix 30; Deut. xi 21.

3. יומי = [yawmay]; constr. אמין = ['ammīn] with internal *mater lectionis*. זי; restore, 'What I have written to lord of kings, Pharaoh, is to inform him that . . . . .' or similar. Instead of חילא (= [ḥayla']; cp. 7), which has to be construed as a collective with the following verbs, we may supply עבדיא, 'the servants of'; cp. 2 Kgs. xxiv 10.

4. מלך בבל; Nebuchadnezzar II (605–562). אתו = ['taw]. מטאו = [mṭá'ū]; the base is MṬ'; contrast at a later stage מטו (Cowley xxxvii 15). The two verbs are joined by asyndeton. In Egyp. Aram. MṬ' is followed by a direct object as often as by a prepos. אפק; see the introduction. Another plur. verb prob. follows; e.g. Ginsberg שריו = [šarrīw], 'they have begun (to besiege or the like)'; Fitzmyer שרו = [šraw], 'they have encamped'.

6. כי, 'for, because' can be paralleled from no. 5 Zakir A 13; no. 9 Sefire iii 22; but כי, '(knows) that' is not found in Aram. In the lacuna supply, 'is not able to resist them. So may lord of kings, Pharaoh, be pleased . . .' or similar.

7. לחצלתי = [lḥaṣṣlūtī]; Pael infin.; on the verb see at no. 5 Zakir A 14 and with the suffix cp. המתתי (no. 9 Sefire iii 11). The sense may be filled out, 'Let not lord of kings, Pharaoh, forsake me; for your servant has been loyal to lord of kings, Pharaoh, . . .'; cp. no. 16 Barrakkab ii 3–5.

8. טבתה = [ṭābtēh]. נצר = [nṭar]; no. 7 Sefire i C 15; with the sense cp. Dan. vii 28. This seems the simplest way to take the phrase; alternatively Dupont-Sommer, 'has safeguarded his property'; Fitzmyer, 'has guarded his good relations' (see note to no. 7 Sefire i C 4). Dupont-Sommer reads the next word as נגרא = [nāgra'], 'prefect'; also possible is נגדא; see at no. 9 Sefire iii 10. But זנה is on these readings very awkward, there being no obvious place in preceding lacunas where the officer in question could have been mentioned. Ginsberg's reading נגוא = [nigwa'] or the like, from Akkad. *nagū*, 'region, territory' is preferable, although the letter slopes slightly to the right; Palest. Aram. only plur. (fem.) [ngāwān]. He completes the sense, 'This territory is my lord's possession, but if the king of Babylon takes it, he will appoint . . . .'; cp. Isa. xx 6. The perf. verb in 9 suggests, however, that the lost half of this line also refers to actions already taken by the Babylonians; they seem to include (cp. 9) the annexation of part of Adon's country and the appointment of a governor. זנה; Dupont-Sommer reads זכם = [d̲ikkēm] or the like, a pronominal form found a few times in the Egyp. papyri; cp. biblical דכן; but though the final letter is smudged, the נ is reasonably clear.

9. פחה; see at no. 14 Panammu 12. מתא; from Akkad. *mātu*, 'land'; cp. מתכדי (no.

20 Ashur ostracon 2). The syntax of the next phrase is very difficult. ספר could mean 'letter' ([spar]) or 'scribe, secretary' ([sāpēr]) or, with Meyer, 'boundary, border' ([spār]); the latter fits well with נגוא in 8, and is well attested in Palest. Aram. and Syriac. שניוה = [šannyūh]; Pael plur. with suffix, lit. 'they have changed, exchanged it'; the suffix presumably refers back to נגוא or to another noun in the previous lacuna. However the final two lines are interpreted, they patently emphasize the urgency of Adon's request; if Judah's experience is anything to go by, it was likely to have gone unheeded; cp. Isa. xxx 1 f.; xxxi 1 f.; xxxvi 6; Jerem. ii 18; xxxvii 6 f.; xlvi 17 f.

22. Sefire: clay tablet (571–570 B.C.) Pl. VI, 2

The clay tablet (5×7 cm.) was published with a photograph by Starcky in *Syria* 37 (1960), 99 f., having been obtained by purchase shortly before; it is now in the Louvre. It seems to have originated from Sefire. A small piece is missing from the top which, since the writing on the reverse begins at the opposite end, is there the bottom. The tablet records a transaction between two men, in which some unknown merchandise (mentioned in the missing piece) was exchanged for a sum of money. The date is given along with the names of four witnesses and (on the missing piece) that of the scribe.

Although the tablet is precisely dated (and is one of very few Aram. texts from the 6 cent.), its script can be used for comparative purposes only with caution. It belongs to a style adapted by cuneiform scribes for writing on clay, and tends to mix features which elsewhere at this time are limited to either the lapidary or the cursive medium; thus cp. the lapidary א and כ with the open-headed ב; ד; ע; and ר, which do not appear on stone inscriptions before the Persian era. There are many further examples of the style on Aramaic endorsements appended to cuneiform tablets belonging to late Assyrian, neo-Babylonian, and Persian times; see further in the Table of scripts and the Bibliographical Notes (p. 159), and in particular the article by Lieberman in *BASOR* 192 (1968), 25 f., and Naveh, 'Script', 16 f. Words are occasionally but by no means always separated by spaces.

Bibliography

KAI no. 227; Naveh, 'Inscrs.', 23 f.

. . . .

[- -]ן̊ ב̊יתאלעשני̊ 1 Obverse

[ל]ביתאלידע בכסף 2

שקלן *20 3 3 1* 3

4 בשנת *20 10 3 1*

5 [נ]בוכדרצר מלך

6 [בב]ל שהד געלא

Reverse 1 [בר] סוה שהד

2 [ב]ית̊אלדלני בר

3 [-]יזכה שהד

4 ב̊יתאלדלני בר

5 [-]ד̊יחוט שהד

6 [--]י̊לא ספרא

. . . .

NOTES

Obverse 1. The bottom of נ is visible at the beginning; the best restoration is נתן, i.e. '(Such and such goods) gave B. to B. in exchange for (ב) 27 shekels of silver'; cp. Akkad. *nadānu ana kaspi*, 'to sell', and Gen. xxiii 9; so Kutscher in Naveh, 'Inscrs.', 24. On the theophoric element ביתאל, common at Elephantine, see at no. **8** Sefire ii C 3; it occurs as a divine name in the treaty of Esarhaddon with the king of Tyre (*ANET*, 534) and in a personal name in Zech. vii 2. That four of the names contain this element may indicate that their bearers were related. The second element here means 'has made me' (base ʿŚY) or 'has helped me' (base ʿWṮ = Hebr. ʿWŠ; Joel iv 11); cp. Biblical אלעשה; יעוש.

3. The numeral is made up of the sign for 20 followed by seven strokes, arranged in two groups of three and a single. That in the next line comprises the signs for 20 and 10, followed by three strokes, then a single, i.e. 34.

5. Cp. biblical נבוכדראצר; Akkad. *Nabū-kudur-uṣur*, 'Nebo, protect the boundary!' His regnal years were 605 to 562.

6. שחד = [śāhēd]. געלא; cp. Hebr. געל (Judg. ix 26); Arab. (juʿalun], 'beetle'.

Reverse 1. Cp. Hebr. מסוה, 'veil' (Exod. xxxiv 33)?

2. The second element means 'has drawn me up', sc. from death to life or the like; cp. biblical דליהו (also at Elephantine), and with the metaphorical meaning of the verb Ps. xxx 2, 4.

3. Hardly from the base ḎKW, 'be clean, pure', since there is only room for one letter at the beginning.

5. The base ḤWṬ, 'to sew', does not seem suitable.

6. Starcky compares Akkad. *Zir-'i-ila* (Tallqvist, *Neubabylonisches Namenbuch*, 1905, 232); the father's name is not given in the case of this witness.

IV

INSCRIPTIONS FROM PERSIAN TIMES

THE chief representatives of the official Aram. dialect of the Persian empire are on the literary level, the biblical book of Ezra and the romance of Ahiqar (text in Cowley, pp. 204 f.), and on the non-literary, the collections of papyri from Egypt published by Cowley and Kraeling, and the leather documents of Driver. It is regrettable that, apart from occasional photographs in works like Driver, *Writing* (pl. 56 = xiv) and *DOTT* (pl. 16 = xxx 1–17), reference has to be made for plates of the Cowley documents to the older volumes of Sayce and Cowley, *Aramaic Papyri Discovered at Assuan* (London, 1906), and Sachau, *Aramäische Papyrus und Ostraka* (Leipzig, 1911). The selection of stone inscriptions, ostraca, and papyri given in the present chapter supplements these sources, with which it is assumed students will already have some familiarity. Texts not included are listed in the Bibliographical Notes (pp. 159–60).

Both in its scripts and in its grammar the dialect remained remarkably uniform from the stage reached in the late 6 cent. down to the end of the Persian empire, and even for a time beyond that (cp. the book of Daniel). Although it was widely used outside original Aramaean territory, foreign influence is by and large restricted to the sphere of vocabulary, where there are many loan-words, at first from Persian and Egyptian, later from Greek, and also, carried over from the period of Mesopotamian dominance (see chap. III), from Akkadian. The links with earlier writing may be studied from *CIS* ii 123 and no. **23** Saqqara (lapidary), and from the Bauer and Meißner and Hermopolis (no. **27**) papyri (cursive), those with later writing, particularly Jewish, from no. **32** the Nebi Yunis ostracon and the Papyrus Luparensis; see Table of scripts. The points especially to notice are: (*a*) the influence of the cursive style on the lapidary, the beginning of which may be traced back through the Nerab stelae (nos. **18**, **19**) as far as the Hamath graffiti (no. **6**), is now very pervasive; (*b*) within the cursive formal and vulgar sub-styles can be detected. Though it is neat, Naveh ('Script', 18) classifies the script of Hermopolis papyri i–vi as vulgar, since the peculiar forms of certain letters (notably ז and ס) suggest to him that they were not written by a professional scribe; most of the other papyri and ostraca represented here show the formal style, though not necessarily the highly skilled hands used on the official documents from Elephantine. See further on the writing Naveh, op. cit. 15 f., 21 f., 43 f. Grammars and studies on the language are mentioned in the Bibliographical Notes (p. 162). On my view of the origin of the dialect see the introductions to nos. **7–9** Sefire and nos. **15–17** Barrakkab.

In most of the texts given below words are separated by spaces, though frequently on no. **36** Bahadirli and occasionally on nos. **26** Dream ostracon and **30** Tema they are run together. The dots and strokes widely used as word-dividers on the Old Aram. inscrs. seem to have been abandoned, though cp. no. **27** Hermopolis iii 4; no. **37** Daskyleion 2.

23. Saqqara (482 B.C.)

The inscr. (*CIS* ii 122), found in a grave in the necropolis of ancient Memphis in 1877 and now in the Staatliche Museen, Berlin, is written across the fourth register of a tablet, on the first three panels of which is carved an Egyp. funeral scene. On the uppermost panel Osiris sits in judgement in the afterworld, attended by Isis and Nephthys; the father and mother of the donor approach the deity with outstretched hands; their clipped hair betrays the foreign, prob. Aramaean, origin of the family. An inscr. in hieroglyphics is interspersed among the figures of this panel. On the second panel the jackal-headed Anubis prepares the mummies of the deceased, while their son, the donor, looks on. The third panel represents mourning relatives. The family had clearly adopted Egyp. religious practices, but this should not be taken as evidence of a general surrender of native beliefs on the part of immigrants from Asia; see further in the introduction to no. **27** Hermopolis papyri.

The transcription below is made from the plate in *CIS*, q.v. for bibliography; see also *NSE* p. 448; *NSI* no. 71; Koopmans, *Chrest.* no. 21; *KAI* no. 267. There is a sketch in *NSE* Taf. XXVIII, 1.

A 1 בריך אבה בר חור ואחתבו ברת עדיה כל *2* [זי] חסתמח
קרבתא

2 קדם אוסרי אלהא אבסלי בר אבה אמה אחתבו

3 כן אמר בשנת *4* ירח מחיר חשיארש מלכא זי מ[לכיא]

4 ביד פמנ- - -

B חכנא

C מ

1. Blessed be Aba, son of ḤWR and 'ḤTBW, daughter of Adiya, both of whom were favoured, faithful. The approach
2. before the god Osiris. 'BSLY, son of Aba, his mother being 'ḤTBW,

3. said this in the 4th year, the month Mehir, of Xerxes, king of [kings].
4. By the hand of PMN . . . .

NOTES

A 1. אבה and עדיה are short forms of Semitic names; cp. Eleph. אבה and Hebr. עדיאל; חור is Egyp. (Horus); אחתבו recalls the Akkad. *Aḫāt-abiša*, 'sister of her father' (Tallqvist, *Names*, 14). חסתמח is thought to be compounded of two Egyp. words, חסת meaning 'favoured (by a god)' and מח, 'faithful'; cp. חסיהו (no. **24** Carpentras 4). קרבתא = [qarrībūtā] or the like; doubtless of the appearance of the dead before Osiris for judgement; cp. *ANET*, 36 (from the 'Book of the dead').

2. אבסלי is Semitic; with the second part cp. Hebr. סלי; סלו; the base is SLY = SL', 'to weigh'; Arab. 'pay promptly, repay'.

3. מחיר; the 6th month in the Egyp. calendar. חשיארש; biblical אחשורוש; Xerxes reigned from 485 to 465 B.C. On the title see at no. **21** Adon 1.

4. The name of the Egyp. mason.

B Apparently an Egyp. name used by 'BSLY; it is carved beside his figure on the second panel.

C A mason's mark? It is written at the right of the third panel.

24. The Carpentras stele — Fig. 13

The famous funerary stele (*CIS* ii 141) was the first Syrian Semitic inscr. to become known in Europe, being discovered in the early 18 cent.; it measures 0·35 m. high by 0·33 m. broad and is housed in a museum at Carpentras in southern France; its original site in Egypt is unrecorded. It is considerably later than the previous inscr., with developed cursive forms, and prob. belongs to the early 4 cent. B.C. Above the inscr. is a relief picturing the embalmed body of the deceased on a lion-shaped bier, attended by the jackal-headed Anubis at the feet and by the hawk-headed Horus at the head. The two figures kneeling in mourning at the head and feet are respectively Isis and Nephthys.

Bibliography

Early bibliography in *CIS*; *NSE* p. 448; *NSI* no. 75. See further:
S. R. Driver, *Notes on Samuel* (2 edn., 1913), pp. xii f.
C. C. Torrey, 'A specimen of Old Aramaic verse', *JAOS* 46 (1926), 24 f.
Koopmans, *Chrest.* no. 49.
KAI no. 269.
P. Grelot, 'Sur la stèle de Carpentras', *Semitica* 17 (1967), 73 f.
Rosenthal, *Handbook*, sect. II (C), 2.
B. Couroyer, 'A propos de la stèle de Carpentras', *Semitica* 20 (1970), 17–20, with Postscriptum by Grelot, 21–2.

Photographs

CIS; *NSE* Taf. XXVIII, 3; Driver, op. cit.; *KAI* Taf. XXXIV.

Note: the verse arrangement in the transcription is not visible on the original.

תמנחא זי אוסרי אלהא	בריכה תבא ברת תחפי	1
וכרצי איש לא אמרת תמה	מנדעם באיש לא עבדת	2
מן קדם אוסרי מין קחי	קדם אוסרי בריכה הוי	3
ובין חסיה̊[י חיי לעלם]	הוי פלחה נמעתי	4

1. Blessed be TB', daughter of TḤPY, devotee of the god Osiris.
2. Naught of evil did she do, nor calumny against any man did she utter up there.
3. Before Osiris be you blessed; from Osiris receive water.
4. Serve the lord of the Two Justices; and among his favoured ones [live for ever].

NOTES

1. תחפי; the ת is the Egyp. fem. definite article, seen also in תבא and several of the female names on the Hermopolis papyri (no. **27**); there follows the divine name Apis, i.e. 'she who belongs to Apis'. The second element in the first name is unknown. תמנחא; article plus an Egyp. adjective meaning 'perfect' or 'pious'. The א represents the vowel of the Egyp. fem. ending, the original [t] being by this time unpronounced, although still written in the demotic script. In Egyp. belief each man at his death re-enacted the experience of Osiris, slaughtered by Seth and brought to life again by his son Horus; his entry to the afterworld was dependent on his son or other relative playing the role of Horus and performing the proper ritual at burial, but also on a favourable verdict upon his earthly life being pronounced at a process of judgement in the presence of Osiris. It is likely that 2 is TB''s defence at this process, and 3 and 4 such a verdict, which by writing down her relative hoped to bring about.
2. מנדעם = [mindʿam] with nasalization; Cowley xxi 7, etc.; contrast מדעם (Cowley xlix 3, 4); Syriac [meddem]. באיש; Ezra iv 12 (Kethibh). כרצי; on the dissimilation of [q] to [k] see at no. **15** Barrakkab i 19, and on the idiom at no. **20** Ashur ostracon 9. תמה; Ezra v 17. With the statement cp. the more detailed protestations of innocence in the Egyp. 'Book of the dead'; *ANET*, 34 f.
3. מין; the bestowal of water upon the dead is a common motif on Egyp. monuments.
4. פלחה = [pālḥā]; partic. fem.; on the compound imper. tense see no. **27** Hermopolis, introd., language par. (d). נמעתי is explained by Grelot as the Egyp. prepos. [n], followed by the word for the bark or boat, in which Re, the sun-god, traverses the celestial ocean during the day and the netherworld sea during the night; i.e. 'become an attendant of the divine bark'; the word is fem., the ending being by this late date vocalic, and in this example seemingly denoted by י (for [ē]?) instead of the א used in 1. Couroyer in his subsequent study criticizes this suggestion on two grounds, the use in an Aram. text of an Egyp. prepos. (as opposed to Egyp. nouns), and the suspect explanation

of the ending, and proposes an alternative solution, which is accepted by Grelot in his postscriptum and adopted in the translation above. He cites an example of the title from the 'Book of the dead' (*ANET*, 34), where it is given to Osiris. The first word is Egyp. *nb*, the [b] here having coalesced with [m]. The second is the difficult term *maʿat*, 'justice, order, truth' or the like; here presumably, since the dual is used, we have to think of the two opposing verdicts open to Osiris as judge; the י then more appropriately represents the Egyp. dual ending. The older interpretation of the word, as a mistake for נעמתי = [nʿīmtī], 'my pleasant one, darling' is by comparison very weak. חסיהי is prob. an Egyp. word meaning 'praised, favoured' with the Aram. suffix [ōhī], which replaces the older [awh] in the Persian period; a good example of the word's usage is cited by Grelot; 'he fell into the river and became a favoured one.' An etymological link between this word and Syriac [ḥasyā], 'saint', which is with difficulty derived from a Semitic base, is not, however, to be excluded. At the end the usual restoration is הוי שלמה, 'be you perfect' or better, 'safe, at peace'; Couroyer improves on this with חיי לעלם, 'live for ever'; an equivalent Egyp. phrase occurs often in demotic funerary texts.

25. Tell el Maskhuta — Fig. 9

The inscr. is written round the inside rim of one of a number of silver bowls acquired in the 1950s by the Brooklyn Museum, and reported to have been found at Tell el Maskhuta near Ismailia in Lower Egypt. The writing is as much cursive as lapidary, and may have been engraved from a copy previously made on papyrus; the date is around 400 B.C. The bowls witness to the presence in the Delta region of a community of north Arabs, who belonged to the tribal confederacy of Kedar (Gen. xxv 13; Jerem. xlix 28; Isa. lx 7) and worshipped the pre-Islamic goddess Han-ilat. This particular bowl was donated by the chief of the confederacy on a visit to the community; his name shows him to have been the son of the Geshem who opposed Nehemiah (Neh. ii 19; vi 1 f.). The community was prob. established at the time of Cambyses' invasion of Egypt in 525, which according to Herodotus was carried through with Arab assistance. For a further example of the use of Aram. among the people of north Arabia see the inscr. from Tema, below no. **30**.

Bibliography

I. Rabinowitz, 'Aramaic inscriptions of the fifth century B.C.E. from a North-Arab shrine in Egypt', *JNES* 15 (1956), 1–9 (three inscriptions including the above).

I. Rabinowitz, 'Another Aramaic record of the North-Arabian goddess Han-Ilat', *JNES* 18 (1959), 155 f.

A. M. Honeyman, 'Two votaries of Han-Ilat', *JNES* 19 (1960), 40 f.

Koopmans, *Chrest.* no. 44.

W. J. Dumbrell, 'The Tell el-Maskhuta bowls and the kingdom of Qedar in the Persian period', *BASOR* 203 (1971), 33–44.

Translation

ANET, 657.

Photograph

Rabinowitz, loc. cit. (1956).

זי קינו בר גשם מלך קדר קרב להנאלת

That which Qaynu son of Geshem, king of Kedar, offered to Han-ilat.

NOTES

קינו and גשם are both found as proper names in Nabataean, Safaitic, Liḥyanite, and Thamudic inscrs.; the first is related to Hebr. Cain, which is thought to mean 'spear'; cp. Kenan (Gen. v 9 f.); with the second cp. Arab. [jasuma], 'to be stout, big'. קרב; Pael. הנאלת means 'the goddess', the אלת of the Nabataean and Palmyrene inscrs. (see *NSI*, 222) and the ['al-Lāt] of the Koran (Sura liii 19). The element [han] is the definite article, a form found in Liḥyanite instead of the usual [ha] before the consonants ['] and [ʿ], and long claimed as the original form of the Hebr. article. Since it occurs in Liḥyanite only in a restricted environment, however, it may merely indicate nasalization taking the place of gemination; on this feature in Aram. see at no. **18** Nerab i 12; no. **24** Carpentras 2.

26. Elephantine: The Dream ostracon — Pl. VIII, 2

The small ostracon from Elephantine (*CIS* ii 137), fully inscribed on each side, belongs to the late 5 cent. B.C. It was acquired by purchase in 1886 and is now in the Staatliche Museen, Berlin. The fem. verb in B 2 suggests that it was written to his wife by a man who was at the time away from home; he refers to an earlier dream which had perturbed him greatly, but informs her that he had now been granted a vision, and this had assured him that all was well. No doubt he had consulted the appropriate experts about these experiences. As on the Ashur ostracon (no. **20**), the language is disjointed and cryptic, but hardly so much so as to lend conviction to Dupont-Sommer's reinterpretation (see below), which excises all reference to dream and vision, and makes the text concerned solely with a transaction in vegetables. The traditions on which the biblical book of Daniel is based may well be contemporary with this ostracon, and show in a different cultural milieu a similar belief in the power of dreams to shape human destiny.

Bibliography

NSI no. 73.

A. Dupont-Sommer in *Annales du Service des antiquités de l'Égypte*, 1948, 109–30.

Koopmans, *Chrest.*, no. 51.
KAI no. 270.
J. A. Levine, 'Notes on an Aramaic dream text from Egypt', *JAOS* 84 (1964), 18–22.

Photographs

CIS; *KAI* Taf. XXV; Levine, loc. cit.

A 1	כען הלו חלם	B 1	כען הן צבתי
2	*1* חזית ומן	2	כ̊ל תזבני המו
3	עדנא הו אנה	3	יאכלו ינקיא
4	חמם שגא	4	הלו לא
5	[א]תחזי חז[ו]	5	שאר
6	מלו̊הי	6	קטין
7	שלם		

Now, in the matter of the first dream I saw—since that time I have been exceedingly feverish. (But) a vision has appeared. Its words, All is well. So if you will sell all my valuables, the children may eat. There should be not a few left.

NOTES

A 1. Lit., 'Now, behold, a dream, one, I saw'. The numeral is explained from the Egyp. practice of employing a number as a shorthand for a cardinal; see *KAI*, where references are given. Presumably the writer had already informed his wife about this dream. כען; Dan. ii 23, etc. הלו; no. **20** Ashur ostracon 9. חלם חזית; Dan. ii 26, etc.

3. הו; so regularly in the papyri.

4. חמם = [ḥammīm]. שגא; Dan. ii 12, etc.

5. There being nothing to suggest that the sherd has been damaged, we must assume that the missing letters were crushed in at the beginning and end, and have subsequently disappeared; cp. the ה at the end of A 3; the י at the end of A 6; the א at the end of B 3; and the faded כ at the beginning of B 2. The verb is restored as Ithpe., which replaces the old Hithpe. in the papyri, though not generally in the biblical dialect. חזו; Dan. ii 19, etc.

7. The greeting seems more than conventional here, since on the strength of the vision, the writer counsels his wife to sell his valuables. This suggests that the family troubles were financial, and that he may have left home to try to alleviate the situation; his earlier dream had only served to increase his disquiet. Alternatively, like the writers of the Hermopolis papyri, he may have been a soldier on service elsewhere in Egypt.

B 1. צבתי; cp. Syriac [ṣebtā], 'ornament'; base ṢBT. The meaning 'bundles, swathes' (of grain) has also been proposed; cp. Ruth ii 16.

2. כל unusually follows the noun, perhaps a spoken idiom. תזבני; fem.; the form appears to be jussive, unless the [n] was dropped before the pronoun 'them'.
3. יאכלו; jussive.
5. שאר = [š'ār], lit. 'behold, there is not a small remainder', perhaps an idiom. לא in a nominal phrase may be spoken usage, though it is not uncommon in the Hebr. Bible.
6. קטין = [qaṭṭīn]. Levine takes it as a plur. noun meaning 'pieces' or 'coins' (base QṬṬ, 'to cut'); the fact that the family had no money left would supply an excellent reason for selling valuables or produce, but such a noun is not otherwise attested.

Dupont-Sommer's translation of the ostracon reads:

Maintenant, voici, une bourrache j'ai vu, et dès à présent (elle est) cuite, toute chaude. (Si) tu vois Yaḥmoliah, paye(-le). Maintenant, si tu veux (ces choses-ci), ne les vends pas; que les enfants (les) mangent! Voici, il ne reste pas de concombres.

He understands חלם (A 1) and קטין (B 6) as kinds of vegetable, comparing with the first Peshitta [ḥlamtā] in Job vi 6 (which is fem., however) and with the second Syriac [qṭūtā]; plur. [qṭayyā], 'cucumber'. His proposed readings, where they differ from the above, are in A 3 אפה; in A 5, 6 יחמליה; in A 7 שלמי (lowering י from 6); and in B 2 אל. Only in A 6, where the sense as much as the photograph suggests ו, does his reading seem to me to merit consideration.

27. The Hermopolis papyri (i–vii) Pl. VII, 1 (iv)

The eight papyri, now in a museum at Cairo University and dating from around 500 B.C. (see Naveh, 'Script', 16), were discovered at Hermopolis in 1945, although not published till 20 years later. They were not written in Hermopolis, however, but in Memphis (ii 3), and comprise private letters addressed to people resident in either Syene (i–iv) or Ofi (v–vii; Greek ὦφις), a sector of ancient Thebes. Perhaps the carrier was not 'trustworthy' (iv 9) or died *en route*; but whatever the reason, they were never delivered. On viii the address has disappeared; this papyrus is very fragmentary, and is not given below. Papyrus vi is also imperfect, having a piece missing down the middle, but enough survives to make restoration possible. The measurements of the complete papyri are i. 27 cm. broad by 11 deep; ii. 33·5 by 27; iii. 27 by 11·5; iv. 27 by 16; v. 27 by 11·5; vii. 27·5 by 12·5. The two halves of vi are at their broadest respectively 11·5 and 13 cm.; the length is 8 cm. From the restoration in line 10, which is certain, I calculate the original width to have been around 32 or 33 cm. Possibly papyri were available at Memphis in two roughly standard widths, one around 27 cm., the other some 6 cm. more. The papyri were rolled up so that the address, which is sometimes written upside down, came out on top; a seal was affixed to the rolls after the word אל, 'to'. Letters i–vi and viii were by the same scribe; vii is in a different hand and is unconnected with the others. The writing throughout is exceptionally clear, and only a few signs are doubtful.

Background

In the view of most (but not all) commentators, the writers and recipients of i–vi (and viii) and a majority of the people referred to were related to each other in two main families, having their homes in the two towns to which the letters were sent. Several other names may belong to members of families connected with one or other of these by marriage. Various means of linking the families genealogically have been proposed; the difficulty is that we cannot always be sure that the titles 'brother', 'sister', 'father', etc., are employed literally; cp. no. **20** Ashur ostracon 1; for my reconstruction see the Table of Relationships (p. 186). The senders were prob. soldiers from a small detachment stationed temporarily at Memphis. Government salary is mentioned (i 8). It is less likely that they were merchants arranging business transactions, since the amounts of money and commodities they send or request (ii 6, 8, 13; iii 8, 12; iv 4 f.; v 4) are not usually large; nor would merchants require to look for a boat (vi 9) nor, for that matter, a messenger (ii 12; iii 11; iv 9). See, however, the notes to ii 14; iii 9; v 6.

The ethnic affiliation of the families in i–vi is Semitic and almost certainly native Aramaean. Most of the personal names are Semitic, many being Syrian Semitic but many also going back to an Akkadian structure, suggesting that some of their ancestors originated from Mesopotamia or at least northern Syria. The reasons why the original group or groups came to Egypt in the first place were doubtless similar to those that brought the Jews of the Cowley and Kraeling documents to Elephantine. 'Aramaeans of Syene' are mentioned a number of times in these documents, and the first family of the Hermopolis papyri must belong among them. Prob. the second family had also lived earlier at Syene and now formed part of a very small Aramaean community at Ofi since, in contradistinction to i–iv, the letters addressed to Ofi include no mention of places of worship. Letter iv is addressed to Syene, but was written by a member of the Ofi family. From the greeting in line 1 we can deduce that the Syrian deities Bethel and the Queen of heaven were especially revered in that family. The favourite deities of the Syene family were the Babylonian Nebo (i 1) and Banit (ii 1; iii 1). The large minority of Egyp. names can be explained through intermarriage after emigration; it need not imply wide acceptance of Egyp. beliefs; contrast no. **23** Saqqara grave. Likewise the mention in the opening felicitations of each letter of the deity Ptah, who was the god of Memphis, is prob. conventional. On letter vii Egyp. names predominate.

On a personal level the letters evince much charm and warmth of feeling, but they give no historical information, nor do they add greatly to our knowledge of economic life in Persian Egypt. Their chief significance undoubtedly lies in the spheres of orthography and grammar where, in a number of particulars, they present a divergent picture from the Elephantine and Driver documents.

Orthography

The following differences in orthography are noteworthy (where second forms are cited, they represent the practice in the other collections):

(*a*) Defective spellings like אחכי (i 1) for אחוכי; את (i 9) for אית; עבר (ii 14) for עבור; גשר (ii 14) for גשור. These do not occur in letter vii; thus אחוכי (1); יובל (5).

(*b*) Phonetic spellings consequent on the reduction of diphthongs; thus בת (ii 12, 15) for בית (cp. also i 12); יהתו (v 4) for יהיתו (base 'TY); עלהי (vi 5; restoration) for עלוהי; cp. תשרי (i 10) from YŠR. In letter vii, by contrast, we have עליכי (2) and בניה (3).

(*c*) Random substitution of א for ה in perfs. of the causative verbal theme, and random omission and insertion of ה in imperfs. of the same theme; thus אושרתי (iv 4) but הושרתן (v 7); יתו (v 5, etc.) but יהתו (v 4). In the other collections such inconsistency is rare.

(*d*) ה for א in the emph. ending of nouns; here also letter vii is exceptional, having the usual א.

(*e*) The negative is לה except for i 8, where the normal spelling לא occurs.

(*f*) Less frequent representation of the sub-phonemic feature of nasalization; thus מדעם (*passim*) against only מנדעם (v 4). On this feature see further at no. **18** Nerab i 12.

Such fluid practice was prob. due to lack of expertise on the part of the scribe responsible for letters i–vi; it suggests that he sometimes copied standard spelling, but often forgot and wrote what he heard. This scribe is also guilty of a fair number of mis-spellings and careless mistakes, showing again that he was not a professional; see the notes to i 2, 3, 6, 12; ii 4, 5, 7, 16; iv 7; v 1, 5. The scribe of vii makes one mistake of dittography; see note to 4.

(*g*) What has been claimed as a unique grammatical feature of the letters is the ת ending, which frequently replaces the expected ה with fem. sing. nouns in the abs. state, fem. adjects. and partics. and (H)aphel infins.; thus נקיה (ii 8); תקבת (ii 11) but תקבה (iv 5); מטאה (iii 4); שלחת (i 11); שפרת (ii 12); מתיה and מיתית (both iii 11); מחתה (v 6). There is one case of ת in vii; חזית (3). On the face of it, this ambivalence implies that a change [at] to [ā] had only recently taken place in this ending. But an ending [at] is unknown in official Aram. and is moreover not found in any Old Aram. dialect. Since a borrowing from Phoen. is highly unlikely, one wonders whether the forms with ת might not have resulted from the scribes' acquaintance with Egyptian where, in the contemporary demotic script, the fem. ending was still written, although the consonant [t] had ceased to be pronounced in the spoken language. The fact that תקבה(ת) from the above list is an Egyp. loan-word lends support to this supposition; note also the unknown noun ופרת in ii 5; see further at no. **24** Carpentras 1.

Language

Setting aside the last feature, therefore, as belonging essentially to the sphere of orthography, we are left with the following differences in grammar:

(*a*) 3 and 2 masc. plur. suffixes end either in [m] or in [n] as in biblical Aram.; שלמהן (i 3); להן (i 8); מושרתהם (ii 13); לכן (iii 11). The other collections have the older forms הם and כם consistently.

(*b*) Aphel infins. are prefixed by מ as in later Palest. Aram. and Syriac; for examples see the list in par. (*g*) above; these are the earliest known occurrences of this feature.

(*c*) 3 masc. plur. partics. from verbs final weak end in ן = [an], again as in the later dialects; בען (vi 9). The earlier ending is ין = [ayn].

(*d*) There is a compound imper. tense formed with הוי and a partic. (i 11; ii 14; iii 9; vii 3), recalling the frequent compounds of parts of the verb 'to be' and partics. in later dialects, notably Syriac; cp. also no. **24** Carpentras 4.

Since the Hermopolis papyri are contemporary with the other collections, these differences cannot be put down to changes within imperial or official Aram., but must reflect changes in the living dialect of the two families. While official Aram. remained by its nature ossified, dialects such as this, spoken in the areas of Syria and Mesopotamia where native Aramaeans still formed a substantial proportion of the population and continuously transferred to Aramaean communities in Egypt through migration, went on developing and at a later date emerged from obscurity to contribute to the break-up of the official language and the rise of the new dialects of the Christian era such as Palest. Aram., Syriac, and Mandaic. The Hermopolis letters give us our first significant glimpse of this process at work in the Persian period itself.

In vocabulary, finally, there are a number of words, prob. of Egyp. origin, which are so far unknown or very doubtfully identified. As long as we are unsure of their meaning the interpretation of certain passages in the papyri must remain provisional.

Bibliography

E. Bresciani and M. Kamil, 'Le lettere aramaiche di Hermopoli', *AANL, Memorie*, ser. VIII, vol. XII, fasc. 5 (1966), 357–428.

P. Grelot, 'Le Papyrus pascal d'Éléphantine et les lettres d'Hermopolis', *VT* 17 (1967), 481 f.

J. T. Milik, 'Les Papyrus araméens d'Hermopolis et les cultes syro-phéniciens en Égypte perse', *Biblica* 48 (1967), 546–622.

E. Hammershaimb, 'Some remarks on the Aramaic letters from Hermopolis', *VT* 18 (1968), 265 f.

B. Porten, *Archives from Elephantine* (Berkeley, Los Angeles, 1968) (background).

B. Porten and J. C. Greenfield, 'The Aramaic papyri from Hermopolis', *ZAW* 80 (1968), 216–31.

J. P. Hayes and J. Hoftijzer, 'Notae Hermopolitanae', *VT* 20 (1970), 98 f.

On the non-Aramaean personal names consult Tallqvist, *Names*, and his earlier volume, *Neubabylonisches Namenbuch* (1905); H. Ranke, *Die ägyptischen Personennamen* (2 vols., 1935, 1953).

Plates

Bresciani and Kamil, loc. cit.

i

1 שלם בית נבו אל אחתי רעיה מן אחכי מכבנת Obverse

2 ברכתכי לפתח זי יחזני אפיך בשלם שלם בנתסרל וארג

3 ואסרשת ושרדר חרוץ שאל שלמהן וכעת שלם ל

4 לחרוץ תנה אל תצפי לה כדי תכלן תעבדן לה עבד אנה

5 לה ותפמת ואחתסן מסבלן לה וכעת ארה ספר לה שלחת֯י

6 בשמה וכעת זי מלתי לבתי לאמר לה שאל על חרוץ כעת

7 ה֯לו כזי עבד אנה לחרוץ כות תעבד בנת עלי

8 א֯ר֯ה לא אחי הו חרוץ וכעת הלו יהב להן פרס Reverse

9 תנה ויתלקח קדמתהן בסון וכעת הן את ערב עליכי

10 אתיה לתפמת וכעת מדעם אל תזבני בכסת ותשרי לה

11 ש֯ל֯ם יקיה הוי שלחת לה וכעת הוי חזית על תשי ועל

12 ברה ושלחי כל טעם זי הוה בביתי לשלמכי שלחת ספר

13 ה זנה

Address 14 אל אבי פסמי בר נבונתן מן מכבנת סון יבל

1. Greetings to the temple of Nebo. To my sister Rʿ YH from your brother Makkibanit.
2. I have blessed you by Ptah, that he may let me see your face in peace. Greetings to BNTSRL and ’RG
3. and ’SRŠT and ŠRDR. ḤRWṢ asks after their welfare. Now it is well with
4. ḤRWṢ here. Do not worry about him. As you would be able to do for him, I am doing
5. for him; and TPMT and ’ḤTSN are supporting him. Now look, you have not sent a letter addressed
6. to him. Now, because you were filled with anger against me and said, He is not caring for ḤRWṢ, now
7. look, as much as I am doing for ḤRWṢ, so may Banit do to me!
8. Look, is not ḤRWṢ my ‘brother’? Now look, salary has been given to them
9. here, and it will be received ahead of them at Syene. Now if you have (something to serve as) a pledge,
10. send it to TPMT. Now do not buy anything as clothing and send it to him.
11. Include the greetings of YQYH when you write to him. Now look after TŠY and
12. her son; and write a report about all that has been happening in my house. For your welfare I have written this
13. letter.
14. To my father PSMY, son of Nabunathan, from Makkibanit. For delivery to Syene.

NOTES

1. Nebo; no. 7 Sefire i A 8. רעיה (Eleph. רעיא) is a shorter form of a name meaning ‘friend of . . . .’, i.e. [rʿī]; cp. Hebr. רעואל. מכבנת is compounded with Aram. [man], ‘who?’ and the prepos. כ; cp. Hebr. מיכאל; Eleph. מיכא; Akkad. *Mannu-kī-ilu*. בנת; Akkad. *Bānītu*, the goddess of birth.
2. ברכתכי = [bāriktēkī] or the like; Pael. יחזני = [yaḥzēnī]; Aph. jussive, therefore lacking [inn] before the suffix. A different verb (יחוני) is used in iv 2; vi 2. אפיך; a mistake for אפיכי (ii 2). בנתסרל; the second element is unknown; an Akkad. verbal phrase? ארג; ‘weaver’?
3. אסרשת is Egyp.; Eleph. אסרשות (fem.). שרדר recalls the common Akkad.

structure . . . . . -*dūrī*, 'Such and such a god is my defence (wall).' Is it a mixed name, the first element being the West Sem. שר = Hebr. [šōr]; Aram. [ṯōr], [tōr], 'the bull (god)'? The four names prob. belong to children of RʿYH, the younger brothers and sister of ḤRWṢ. RʿYH's husband seems to be dead, since he is not mentioned, and the address in 14 makes it clear that she lived in her father's house; his name, however, may occur in v 6. חרוץ is Egyp. and occurs also at Eleph. שאל; partic.; cp. שאלן (vi 7). שלמהן; masc. suffix. Note the superfluous ל at the end; an attempt seems to have been made to erase it.

4. תצפי = [tēṣápī] (cp. Syriac); 2 fem. jussive from YṢP, therefore lacking [n]. כדי; contrast כזי in 7. תכלן = [tikklīn]; 2 fem. imperf. from YKL.

5. תפמת is Egyp. (fem.); cp. Eleph. פמת; תתפמת. אחתסן; Akkad., 'daughter of Sin'. מסבלן = [msabblān]; fem. plur. partic. Pael. ארה = [ʾrē]; biblical Aram. ארו; Mishnaic Hebr. הרי.

6. בשמה does not seem to have here the legal sense it carries in the Eleph. papyri (Cowley vi 14; viii 12, etc.). מלתי = [mlētī] as with verbs final [w, y]. לבתי is written above the line, having been carelessly omitted; see on this idiom at no. **20** Ashur ostracon 19. שאל; lit. 'ask concerning'.

7. הלו; so Milik. The editors read מלו from MLL and render, 'Now in as much as you spoke to BTY (iii 3) and said, He is not caring for ḤRWṢ, now do you speak (and say), As much as . . . . .'. Hayes and Hoftijzer propose, 'Now as to the fact that you said to BTY, He does not show concern for ḤRWṢ, now then people say that . . . . .'. But Pael forms from this base ought to be מללת and מללו. Porten and Greenfield link מלו with Akkad. *mala*, 'whatsoever', and regard it as a particle strengthening כזי, 'fully as much'. לאמר; no. **20** Ashur ostracon 8, 10 and frequently in the Eleph. papyri.

8. לא; only here with א. הן; no. **26** Dream ostracon A 3. The next sentence is very cryptic. As I interpret it (partially following Milik), יהב is Peil (impersonal) as in ii 8; פרס is official government salary as in Cowley ii 16; xi 6; להן is masc. ([lhōn]), referring to ḤRWṢ and other members of his detachment; and קדמת has temporal meaning as in Dan. vi 11; Cowley xxx 17; Ahiqar 2. Makkibanit informs his sister that her son and his fellow soldiers have been given their pay, and that it is to be sent on immediately to Syene so as to be available for their families. In the opinion both of Porten and Greenfield and of Hayes and Hoftijzer, the payment is made to TPMT and ʾḤTSN (5), i.e. להן = [lhēn]; but there is no other mention in the letters of the presence of women with the soldiers, who seem to have been at Memphis only on a temporary tour of duty. I prefer to locate TPMT and ʾḤTSN at Ofi; they were prob. relatives of ḤRWṢ on his father's side; see also at v 6. Cp. further no. **28** Migdol papyrus (Padua i), obverse, 3 f.

9. את = [ʾīt]; in the other papyri איתי or אית. ערב = [ʿa(r)rāb] as in Syriac and earlier, *CIS* ii 65, line 1 (an endorsement on a cuneiform tablet); the form in Cowley is the more familiar ערבן. With the use of על for ל cp. Cowley xxx 23 and above, 7. Makkibanit asks his sister to forward a suitable article to TPMT as a pledge, presumably against repayment of the money she had sent to ḤRWṢ at Memphis (5). Alternatively על could have the sense 'owed by', 'promised by', as frequently in the Eleph. papyri (e.g. Cowley xxxv 3; lxix 2) and below ii 9; but though this would usefully connect letters i and ii, it would imply that RʿYH knew of the two women's support of her son, and detract from the force of the statement in 5. For another interpretation of this

sentence, in which ערב means 'guarantor', again as in Syriac, see Porten and Greenfield.

10. אתיה = [ʾētīh] with internal *mater lectionis* in the second syllable; Aph. imper. fem. with suffix. With the meaning 'send' rather than 'bring' cp. iv 10; v 5. מדעם; see at no. **24** Carpentras 2 and contrast מנדעם (v 4). כסת = [ksūt]; so Palest. Aram. and possibly Ahiqar 205. ב in this sense is not uncommon in the papyri; Cowley xxiv 35; Ahiqar 173; cp. in Hebr. Deut. i 13; Josh. xiii 6, 7. תשרי = [tōšērī]; Aph. jussive fem. The negative אל is to be construed with this verb also. לה; in view of the next request, the suffix is more likely to refer to ḤRWṢ than to TPMT.

11. יקיה = [yqīh], 'heard, answered'; cp. South Arab. WQH in proper names; the same name occurs in ii 4 without the internal *mater lectionis*; he is prob. Makkibanit's son. הוי שלחת = [hwī šālḥā]; on the ת see the introduction, par. (g). חזית = [ḥāzyā]. תשי is an Egyp. name; Makkibanit's wife and the addressee in ii.

12. ברה; i.e. YQYH. טעם; lit., 'Send any report of what was . . . . .'; Ezra v 5. בביתי; the middle י has been inserted above the line.

13. זנה = [dnā]; historical spelling; cp. כדי and כזי (4, 7).

14. פסמי is Egyp.; it occurs at Eleph., as do compounds like פסמשכחסי. נבותתן; West Sem., but compounded with an Akkad. divine element. יבל = [yūbal]; Peil imperf. or jussive; cp. יובל (vii 5). With the omission of the prepos. after this verb cp. no. **14** Panammu 14.

ii

Obverse

1 שלם בית בנת בסון א̊ל אחתי תשי מן אחכי מכבנת
2 ברכתכי לפתח זי יחזנ̊י אפיכי בשלם שלם נבושה
3 תנה אל תצפו לה לה מנס אנה לה מן מפי שלם
4 פסמי יקה שלם נניחם ו̊כעת הלו מסת כספה זי
5 הוה בידי נתתן ופרת לבנתסר בר תבי אחת
6 נבושה כסף ש 3 3 וזוז כסף זוז וכעת שלחי
7 על תבי ותושר לכי עמר מן קצתה זי כסף ש 1
8 וכעת הן יהב לכי נקיה וגזתה שלחי לי
9 והן יהב לכי עמרה זי על מכי שלחי לי
10 והלה יהב לכי שלחי לי ואקבל עליהן תנה
11 וכעת זבנת משח זית ליקה וכתן ואף לכי תקבת
12 1 שפרת ואף משח בשם לבת בנת ולעד אשכח
13 אש למושרתהם לכן וכעת הושרי לי תקם חפנן
14 3 2 והוי יהבת עב̊ר לוחפרע ויהוי זבן גשרן

15 ושבק בבתה אל תקמי קדמתה כל גשר זי ישכח

16 יזבן והן יהב לכי רעיה עמר שלחי לי שלם

17 תטסרי אזדהרי בה לשלמכן שלחת ספרה זנה

18 אל תשי מן מכבנ̊ת בר פסמי סון יבל Reverse (Address)

1. Greetings to the temple of Banit at Syene. To my 'sister' TŠY from your 'brother' Makkibanit.
2. I have blessed you by Ptah, that he may let me see your face in peace. It is well with Nabusha
3. here. None of you worry about him. I will not let him leave Memphis. Greetings
4. to PSMY (and) YQH. Greetings to NNYḤM. Now look, a due amount of the money that
5. was in my control I have given as . . . . . to BNTSR, son of TBY, sister of
6. Nabusha, 6 silver shekels and one zuz, in silver zuzes. Now write
7. to TBY that she send wool to you from her share, which is one silver shekel.
8. Now if a lamb and its fleece are given to you, write to me;
9. and if the wool that is owed by MKY is given to you, write to me;
10. but if nothing is given to you, write to me, and I will lodge a complaint against them here.
11. Now I have bought olive-oil for YQH and a tunic, and also for you a . . . . . ,
12. a pretty one, and also perfumed oil for the temple of Banit; but I cannot so far find
13. a man to deliver them to you. Now, send to me 5 measures of castor oil,
14. and give grain to WḤPR', that he may buy beams
15. and leave them in his house. Do not stand in his way; every beam that he finds,
16. let him buy. If R'YH gives you wool, write to me. Greetings
17. to TṬSRY; be attentive to her. For the welfare of you all I have written this letter.
18. To TŠY from Makkibanit, son of PSMY. For delivery to Syene.

NOTES

1. **בנת**; see at i 1. תשי; the writer's wife; i 11.
2. Contrast שלם ל in i 3. נבושה is a short form of the full name נבושזב, which occurs in iv 15; Akkad. *Nabū-ušēzib*; the verb has been accommodated

to Aram. [šēzēb], itself an Akkad. loan-word (Shaphel); cp. ביתאלשזב (v 6). He is the brother-in-law of Makkibanit and TŠY.

3. תצפו = [tēṣápū]; jussive; i 4. מנס = [mnīs]; Aph. partic., lit. 'making to flee' (NWS); the verb is not found elsewhere in Aram. in this sense. מפי; Eleph. מנפי.

4. 'And' has been carelessly omitted between the two names; father and son of the writer. יקה; i 11. נניחם; Akkad.; compounded with Nanaia, a Babylonian goddess; Nabusha's wife and TŠY's sister and the addressee in iv. מסת = [missat]; constr.; in Palest. Aram. and Syriac in various phrases with meanings like 'quantity, sufficiency, enough'; in Hebr. only in Deut. xvi 10; the derivation is obscure.

5. ידי; sing.; cp. ידה (vi 7). נתתן; comparison with vi 3–4 suggests that this is a mistake for נתנת = [nitnēt]; a 2 plur. perf. does not make good sense ('you will have given'?). ופרת; an unknown Egyp. technical term, prob. like פרס (i 8) to do with government payments; Makkibanit may have been in a position of command and responsible for seeing that these were properly made and forwarded to relatives. בנתסר is perhaps an abbreviated form of an Akkad. name like *Ea-šar-ibni*, 'Ea has created the king.' תבי is Egyp.; cp. תבא (no. **24** Carpentras 1); the sister of Nabusha and the addressee in letters v and vi; she lived at Ofi.

6. כסף זוז may distinguish a silver zuz (half-shekel) from some other kind or indicate (Milik) that the money was paid out in zuzes.

7. עמר = ['mar]; Eleph. also קמר; Hebr. צמר. תושר is prob. a mistake for תושרי; jussive; cp. תשרי (i 10). Similar careless uses of masc. for fem. are found in i 2 (אפיך) and below 16 (יהב); could they reflect spoken practice? קצתה = [qṣātah]; Dan. ii 42; Cowley xxxv 4.

8. יהב; Peil, used impersonally, 'if there has been given'; cp. in Hebr. Josh. vii 15, etc. In 16 יהב seems to be a mistake for the fem., perhaps induced by its use here. נקיה = [niqyā]; fem. absol. גזתה = [gizztēh], lit., 'its shearing'. Presumably the money was to be sent to Ofi, and would enable TBY and MKY (9) to repay debts to TŠY.

9. על; see note to i 9. מכי occurs at Eleph., and is prob. Egyp.; a relative of TBY and of the writer of vi (q.v. line 5).

10. הלה; הן and לא (לה) are not elsewhere found joined in official Aram. אקבל; Peal; cp. Cowley x 12; Kraeling i 4 f. The fact that in the case of default proceedings are to be instituted at Memphis supports the view taken above of ופרת (5).

11. כתן = [kittūn] (Palest. Aram.); Eleph. כתון. It is fem. in Syriac ([kuttīn]); cp. iv 4. תקבת; in iv 5 תקבה; according to Porten and Greenfield an Egyp. word with the fem. article, meaning 'vessel'.

12. שפרת = [šappīrā]. בשם = [baśśīm]. לעד = [lā 'ōd]; Cowley xxviii 13; Kraeling xi 8. אשכח = ['aškaḥ]; Aph. imperf.

13. מושרתהם = [mōšārathōm] or [mōšārūthōm]; Aph. infin. constr.; see further at no. **8** Sefire ii C 1. Note the suffix ending in [m], masc., since two of the four articles mentioned are masc.; contrast להן (i 8). לכן is prob. fem., since the writer is addressing his wife, although YQH, the other person mentioned, is male. תקם; an Egyp. loan-word; Cowley xv 16; Kraeling ii 6. Castor oil seems to have been scarce at Memphis; cp. iii 12; iv 7. חפן meant originally 'handful' (cp. Exod. ix 8), but here and in the other papyri it signifies a measure (in Cowley xv 16 it is abbreviated as ח).

14. עבר = [ʿbūr]; cp. עבור (Cowley xiv 4; Kraeling xi 11). The editors wrongly read עבד, 'slave'; cp. iii 9. וחפרע is Egyp. and occurs at Eleph.; he is the brother of Makkibanit and seems to be responsible for a transaction between PSMY's household and Makkibanit's; cp. iii 9, 10; TŠY acts for Makkibanit in his absence. Note, however, that the commodities are exchanged in Syene; only in v 6 is there a possible question of large quantities of goods being transported to Memphis. יהוי = [yihway/ē]; jussive. גשר; Akkad. *gušūru*; cp. גשור (Kraeling iv 8, etc.).

15. תקמי; jussive; in the other collections this verb is usually written plene. קדמת; here in a local sense as in Ahiqar 101; contrast i 9.

16. יהב; partic. (active); see at 7 and 8 above. RʿYH is the writer's sister; cp. i 1.

17. תטסרי (an Egyp. name) may be an older daughter, who had married and left home and was not therefore mentioned in i 11, 12 or in 4 above. אזדהרי = ['izdhárī] or the like; Ithpe. imper. fem. from ZHR; the nuance is 'protect, take care of', as often in Syriac. לשלמכן; as in 13 the suffix is prob. fem., though PSMY and YQH are doubtless included.

iii

Obverse

1 שלם בית בנת בסון על מראי פסמי עבדך מכבנת ברכתך̊

2 לפתח זי יחזני אפיך בשלם שלם אמי ממה שלם

3 אחי בתי ואנשתה ובנוהי שלם רעיה אל תצף לחרוץ

4 לה שבק אנה לה' כדי מטאה ידי וכעת עבד אנה לה

5 אל אחי וחפרע מן אחך מכבנת שלם וחין שלחת לך וכעת

6 הן מטאך סרחלצה שלח לי ביד עקבה בר וחפרע

7 וכעת כל זי תצבה שלח לי הושר לי משכן

8 מסת לבש משך *1*

Reverse

9 והוי לקח שערן מן תשי ויהב בגשרן

10 ושבק כל גשר זי תשכח לממה זבנת חטבת ומשח

11 בשם למתיה לכן ולה אשכחת אש למיתית לכן וכעת

12 תקם יתו לי חפנן *3* *2* אל תצפו לי לכן אנה יצף

13 לשלמכן שלחת ל[כן] ספרה זנה

Address

14 אל אבי פסמי מן מ̊כב̊נ̊ת̊ בר פסמי סון יבל

1. Greetings to the temple of Banit at Syene. To my lord PSMY from your servant Makkibanit. I have blessed you

2. by Ptah, that he may let me see your face in peace. Greetings to my mother MMH. Greetings
3. to my brother BTY and his wife and children. Greetings to R'YH. Do not worry about ḤRWṢ.
4. I shall not leave him, as far as it lies in my power. Now I am taking care of him.
5. To my brother WḤPR' from your brother Makkibanit. Prosperity and long life I have written wishing you. Now
6. if SRḤLṢH has reached you, write to me through 'QBH, son of WḤPR'.
7. Now if you want anything, write to me. Send to me skins
8. sufficient to make one leather garment.
9. Acquire barley from TŠY and pay in beams,
10. and leave any beam that you find. For MMH I have bought coloured cloth and perfumed
11. oil; (they were) to be brought to you, but I have not found a man to bring them to you. Now
12. let castor oil be brought to me, 5 measures. None of you worry about me, (though) I worry about you.
13. For the welfare of you all I have written this letter to you.
14. To my father PSMY from Makkibanit, son of PSMY. For delivery to Syene.

NOTES

1. The same opening as in ii 1. The letter is addressed to the writer's father, but includes within it instructions for his brother WḤPR'. Note **על** for **אל**.
2. **ממה**; unknown; perhaps not a proper name, but a term of endearment like 'mum', 'mummy', etc.
3. **בתי** is prob. Egyp.; it occurs at Elephantine. **אנשתה** prob. = ['anttēh] with nasalization and retention of the older spelling; so iv 14; in the Eleph. papyri the form (constr.) is always **אנתת** or **אתת**. **בנוהי** = [bnōhī]; on the suffix see at no. **24** Carpentras 4. **תצף** = [tēṣap]; jussive; masc., since the letter is addressed to PSMY, but cp. i 3 f.
4. **כדי**; i 4. **מטאה** = [māṭ'ā]; fem. partic.; cp. 1 Sam. xxv 8. Note the stroke.
5. **חין** = [ḥayyīn].
6. **סרחלצה** is perhaps an Aram. form of an Akkad. name, 'The king is his fortress', i.e. *Šarru-ḫalṣušu* (unattested). **עקבה**; cp. Eleph. **נבועקב**; **עקבן**. Prob. this request is addressed to PSMY, and 'QBH is his grandson and the writer's nephew. He and SRḤLṢH are presumably soldiers on leave from Memphis.
7. **תצבה** = [tiṣbē]; imperf.; contrast **יהוי** (ii 14), which is jussive. **משך**; Akkad. *mašku*; Ahiqar 118.
8. **מסת**; ii 4.
9. **שערן** = [ś'ārīn]; this request is addressed to WḤPR'; cp. ii 14 f. **יהב**; partic. following **הוי**.

10. חטבת = [ḥṭībā]; passive partic. as noun; Kraeling vii 7; cp. Prov. vii 16.
11. בשם; ii 12. מתיה and מיתית both = [mētāyā]; Aph. infin. לכן is prob. masc. since the addressee is PSMY; so 12, 13.
12. תקם and חפן; ii 13. יתו = [yētō]; Aph. jussive plur.

iv

Obverse
1 שלם בית בתאל ובית מלכת שמין אל אחתי נניחם
2 מן אחכי נבושה ברכתכי לפתח זי יחוני אפיך בשלם
3 שלם ביתאלנתן שלם נכי ועשה ותשי וענתי ואט̊י ו̊רע[יה]
4 וכעת מטתני כתנה זי אושרתי לי ואשכחתה שנטת כלה
5 ולבבי לה דבק לה הן חזית מה אתרתן אתננה בתקבה̊
6 *I* לאטי וכעת כתנה זי התתי לי ס̊ון הי מלבש
7 אנה וכעת תקם יתו לן ונתנהי במשח וכעת אל
8 תצפי לן לי ולמכבנת לכן אנחן יצפן אזדהרי
9 בביתאלנתן מן חבב וכעת אן אשכחת אש מהימן
10 אתה לכן מדעם שלם שבתי בר שוג שלם פסי

Reverse
11 שלם עדר בר פסי שלם שאל בר פטחרטיס ואשה
12 בר פטחנם שלם סחתה כלה לשלמכן שלחת ספרה
13 זנה שלם אבי פסמי מן עבדך נבושה שלם אמי
14 ממה שלם אחי בתי ואנשתה שלם וחפרע

Address
15 אל נניחם מן נבו̊ש̊זב בר פטחנם סון

1. Greetings to the temple of Bethel and the temple of the Queen of heaven. To my 'sister' NNYḤM
2. from your 'brother' Nabusha. I have blessed you by Ptah, that he may show me your face in peace.
3. Greetings to Bethelnathan. Greetings to NKY and 'ŚH and TŠY and 'NTY and 'ṬY and R'[YH].
4. Now the tunic which you sent me has reached me, but I found it all . . . . . ,
5. and I have no liking for it. If I knew what you folk had plenty of, I would exchange it for a . . . . .
6. for 'ṬY. Now the tunic which you brought to me at Syene—I am wearing

7. it. Now let castor oil be brought to us, that we may exchange it for (other) oil. Now do not
8. worry about us, myself and Makkibanit, (though) we worry about you folk. Be attentive
9. to Bethelnathan on account of ḤBB. Now if I could find a trustworthy man,
10. I would have something brought to you. Greetings to Shabbethai, son of ŠWG. Greetings to PSY.
11. Greetings to ʿDR, son of PSY. Greetings to Š'L, son of PṬḤRṬYS, and to 'ŠH,
12. son of PṬḤNM. Greetings to all the . . . . . For the welfare of you all I have written this
13. letter. Greetings to my 'father' PSMY from your servant Nabusha. Greetings to my 'mother'
14. MMH. Greetings to my 'brother' BTY and his wife. Greetings to WḤPRʿ.
15. To NNYḤM from Nabushezeb, son of PṬḤNM. To Syene.

NOTES

1. Bethel; see at no. **8** Sefire ii C 3 and no. **22** Clay tablet, 1. מלכת שמין; Astarte; see at no. **21** Adon 1. נניחם; the writer's wife (ii 4).
2. יחוני = [yḥawwṓnī]; jussive Pael from ḤWY, therefore lacking [(i)nn] before the suffix.
3. ביתאלנתן may be a son still at home; cp. 8–9. נכי is unknown and prob. Egyp.; perhaps an older daughter and wife of BNTSR (ii 5; vi 3, 8). עשה; possibly from the base ʿŚY, 'to make', although this verb is absent from the Aram. dialects; cp. the name in no. **22** Clay tablet, 1; he may be an older son of the writer, who has left home, or his grandson and younger son of BNTSR and NKY. תשי; the writer's sister-in-law and wife of Makkibanit; cp. ii 1 f. ענתי occurs at Eleph.; short form of a name compounded with the divine element Anath; cp. the deity ענתביתאל in Cowley xxii 125; he is perhaps a brother-in-law. אטי; unknown; perhaps wife or daughter of ʿNTY; the allusion in 6 suggests she was a near relative of the writer and his wife; cp. ii 11. רע[יה]; there is hardly room for two letters to have faded, but this is prob. the writer's sister, who is not mentioned in 13 f., but who was a close friend of TŠY (i 11).
4. מטתני = [mṭātánī]; fem. agreeing with כתן (ii 11). אשכחתה = ['aškaḥtah]. שנטת; a fem. adject.; cp. the plur. noun שטטן in Cowley xlii 8, also with reference to a tunic. The meaning 'striped', suggested by Cowley, and adopted by some commentators here, is based on a supposed link with Mishnaic Hebr. [šiṭṭā], 'row, line'. שנטא in Kraeling vii 11 may also be connected. כלה; 'all of it' (no. **7** Sefire i A 5) or an adverb 'entirely'; Eleph. כלא.
5. דבק; partic.; with the idiom cp. Gen. xxxiv 3. חזית = [ḥzay/ēt]. אתרתן = ['ōtartān]; prob. fem., the subject being NNYḤM and her family; Aph. perf. from YTR; cp. Deut. xxviii 54; Peshitta Joel i 4. אתננה = ['ittninnah]; the suffix refers to the tunic. תקבה; ii 11.
6. התתי = [h(')ētītī]; (H)aph. perf.; perhaps from Ofi after a visit to her husband's family. הי; so regularly in the Eleph. papyri. מלבש; Aph. partic.

7. תקם יתו; iii 12. נתנהי is an anomalous form; it should be נתננה = [nittninnēh]; cp. אתננה (5). Perhaps following the jussive יתו the writer had in mind יתנהי = [yittnūhī], where both the absence of [inn] and the suffix form הי (after [ū]) would be correct.

8. תצפי; i 4. אזדהרי; ii 17.

9. מן; the phrase seems almost to mean 'protect from'. חבב; cp. Hebr., Num. x 29. Note אן for הן. מהימן; Dan. vi 5; the [h] is always retained in this verb in the official and later dialects.

10. אתה = [ʾētē]; i 10. The names in 10–12 prob. belong to more distant relatives and friends of NNYḤM than those in 3. שבתי; perhaps a Jew, 'one born on the Sabbath'; Cowley lviii 3; Kraeling viii 10; Ezra x 15; but cp. Akkad. *Ša-ba-ta-ai*, 'one born on the day of the full moon'. שוג is unknown. פסי is prob. Egyp.; cp. Eleph. פסן.

11. עדר; cp. Eleph. עדרי and Hebr. names with עזר. שאל = [šʾīl]; cp. Hebr. Saul; he is prob. the same as in v 3. פטחרטיס is Egyp.; cp. Eleph. אחרטיס. אשה; cp. אשא (vol. I no. 2 Samaria ostracon xxix).

12. פטחנם is Egyp. and occurs at Eleph.; it is compounded with the name of the god Khnum or Khnub, worshipped by the Egyp. population there; Cowley xxx 5. He is a different person from the writer's father (15). סחתה; fem. sing.?; the editors compare an Egyp. word meaning 'neighbours, friends'. כלה; 4.

13, 14. Relatives of Makkibanit, who was mentioned in 8, are included in the greetings. אנשתה; iii 3. The wife of WHPRʿ is not mentioned, and was therefore prob. dead; iii 6.

15. נבושזב; the writer's full name; see at ii 2. פטחנם; 12 above.

v

1 Obverse אל אחתי ת֯ר֯ו֯ ותבי מן אחוכן נבושה ו֯מ֯כבנת ברכנכן

2 לפתח זי יחזני אפיכן בשלם וכעת תדען זי מדעם

3 לה מפקן לן מן סון ואף מן זי נפקת [מ]ן סו֯ן שאל

4 לה הושר לי ספר ומנדעם וכעת יהתו לן ארון

5 ובינבן והן תכלן תהיתן לן תקם י֯תו ביד חרוץ

6 בר ביתאלשזב זי אתה למחתה לבמ֯רשרי אתריה

7 ומהי דה זי ספר לה הושרתן

8 Reverse לי ואנה נכתני חויה והות מית ולה שלחתן

9 הן חי אנה וה֯ן מת אנה לשלמכן שלחת ספרה זנה

10 Address אל תרו מן נבוש֯ה בר פטחנם אפי יבל

1. To my sister(s) TRW and TBY from your brother(s) Nabusha and Makkibanit. We have blessed you

2. by Ptah, that he may let me see your face in peace. Now you know that nothing

3. is being sent out to us from Syene. Moreover, since I left Syene, Š'L
4. has not sent me a letter or anything else. Now let a chest be brought to us
5. and . . . . . , and if you are able to send us castor oil, let it be brought through ḤRWṢ,
6. son of Bethelshezeb, who is coming to fetch down . . . . for BMRŠRY.
7. And what is the reason that you did not send a letter
8. to me, when the snake had bitten me and I was dying? Yet you did not write to ask
9. whether I was alive or dead. For the welfare of you both I have written this letter.
10. To TRW from Nabusha, son of PṬḤNM. For delivery to Ofi.

NOTES

1. תרו is prob. Egyp. תבי; ii 5. The sisters of Nabusha and sisters-in-law of Makkibanit. Note the confusion between sing. and plur. in this and the next line. ברכנכן = [bāriknākēn] or the like.
2. תדען = [tiddʿān].
3. מפקן = [mappqīn]; Aph. partic. masc. plur. (indefinite) from NPQ. שאל; iv 11.
4. הושר = [h(')ōšar]; (H)aph. perf. מנדעם; only here with nasalization. יהתו; a historical spelling; cp. יתו (iii 12; iv 7). ארון = ['rūn]; so Syriac.
5. בינבן is unknown. תכלן = [tikklān]; i 4; here plur. (cp. 7). תהיתן seems to be a mistake for תהתין = [tētyān]. ביד; no. 5 Zakir A 12.
6. ביתאלשזב; ii 2; if his son ḤRWṢ is the same as in i 3, he is the dead husband of RʿYH. Perhaps TPMT and 'ḤTSN (i 5 f.), who I suggested lived at Ofi, were relatives of his. אתה; partic.; a perf. does not make sense. מחתה = [ma(ḥ)ḥātā]; Aph. infin. from NḤT; sc. from Memphis to Ofi or from Ofi to Memphis or, possibly, to Syene (cp. i 9). אתריה; plur. emph.; the editors render 'logs, planks' and compare אשרנא (Ezra v 3; Kraeling iii 23; Cowley xxvi 5), but the meaning of this much-discussed word is still unsettled; see Jean-Hoftijzer, *Dictionnaire*. If their interpretation is accepted, the argument that Nabusha and his companions at Memphis were merchants rather than soldiers is strengthened; for the transportation of such products would be a major undertaking, and not the kind of personal favour a soldier visiting relatives could perform. Contrast the rather different situation in ii 14. במרשרי; unknown; perhaps he was TRW's husband.
7. מהי דה; lit., 'what is this?' Note דה followed by זי (= [dī]).
8. חויה; masc. emph.; the absol. occurs at no. 7 Sefire i A 31. מית = [māyēt]; active partic.; in 9 מת = [mīt] (passive).

vi

1 Obverse אל אחתי תבי מן [אחכי ---]ר ברכתכי לפתח זי

2 יחוני אפיכי בשׁ[לם ---- ב]ר̊י שאל שלמכי

3 וכעת יהב מ[כבנת לבנתסר] חתנה זי נבשה כסף

4 ש *3 3* וזוז [כסף זוז ו---] ואפקני אנה וברי

5 וכתבת לה ע[להי וכעת ---י] וזבני עמר כזי תמט

6 ה ידכי ואו[שרי לתשי בס]ו̊ן הלו כספה זי הוה

7 בידה יהב [לה נבשה ומכ]בנת שאלן שלמכי

8 ושלם תרו [ו------ וכ]עת שלם בנתסר תנה Reverse

9 וברה אל ת[צפו להן וכעת] אנחן בען אלף

10 ויתונה לכן ל̊[שלמכי שלחת ספ]רה זנה

11 אל אמי [תבי מן ---ר בר] סרה אפי יבל Address

1. To my 'sister' TBY from [your 'brother' . . . .]R. I have blessed you by Ptah that
2. he may show me your face in peace. [. . . . .], my son, asks after your welfare.
3. Now M[akkibanit] has given [to BNTSR], son-in-law of Nabusha,
4. 6 silver shekels and one zuz, [in silver zuzes; and he has . . . . .] and released me and my son,
5. and I have written him (sc. a receipt) for [it. Now . . . . .] and buy as much wool as you can
6. lay hands on, and send [it to TŠY at Sye]ne. Look, the money that was
7. in his control he has given [to him. Nabusha and Makki]banit are asking after your welfare
8. and the welfare of TRW [. . . . . N]ow it is well with BNTSR here
9. and with his son. None of [you worry about them. Now] we are looking for a boat
10. that it may be brought to you. For [your welfare I have written] this letter.
11. To my 'mother' [TBY from . . . . . R, son of] SRH. For delivery to Ofi.

NOTES

1. The writer is a younger relative of TBY (ii 5), prob. on her (dead) husband's side. He is not her son, since he refers to BNTSR by his relationship to Nabusha. MKY in ii 9 may be his mother and the husband of SRH (11); see at 5. The restoration in 10, which is certain, and those in 3 and 6, which from comparison with ii 4 f. are reasonably so, suggest that the missing middle portion from line 3 onwards contained room for between nine and eleven letters; the lacunas in 1 and 2 are about two spaces shorter.

2. יחוני; iv 2. ברי; cp. 4.
3. חתנה = [ḥatnā] (masc. emph.) or perhaps [ḥatnēh] with suffix. נבשה; ii 2; note the defective spelling.
4. אפקני = [’appqánī]; Aph. from NPQ, lit. ‘to bring out’; possibly here ‘to release’ from a debt, or simply ‘to pay’ (?). The subject may be either BNTSR or Makkibanit.
5. כתבת; cp. Cowley ix 4; xiii 9. עלהי = [‘lōhī]; contrast the fuller spelling in בנוהי (iii 3), for which there is no room here. כזי; i 4, 7. תמטה = [timṭē], accommodated like מטתני (iv 4) to verbs final [w, y] in contrast with מטאה (iii 4); note that the word is split between the two lines and cp. i 3. The money would soon (9–10) be on its way to Ofi, so TBY could meanwhile pay off her own and MKY’s debt to TŠY. Makkibanit had already (ii 4 f.) written to his wife about this matter, and had been concerned to see it settled (ii 10). TBY also seemed anxious about it; note the repetition in 6–7, prob. meant to reassure her.
6. אושרי; Aph. imper.
7. לה; possibly restore לי, the reference in that case being more directly to MKY’s family’s share; cp. ii 7, where TBY’s share is mentioned.
8. After תרו perhaps insert ובמרשרי; see at v 6.
9. תצפו; cp. ii 3; a sing. verb as in i 4 is also possible. אנחן; so sometimes Eleph.; biblical אנחנא. בען = [bā‘an]; partic. plur. with [a] as in the later dialects; in the biblical dialect and the other collections (Driver x 2) the earlier [ayn] is usually retained. אלף; Akkad. *elippu*.
10. יתונה = [yētōnnēh]; Aph. imperf. plur. (indef.) with [(i)nn] and suffix (referring to the money).
11. סרה; unknown; there is not room for a longer name.

vii

1 Obverse א֯ל אמי עתררמרי מן אחוכי אמי [שלם וח]י֯ן שלחת לכי
2 שלם אחתי אסורי וזבבו וככי וכען עליכי מתכל אנה הוי
3 חזית על ינקיא אלכי שלם וסרו ושפנית ובניה ופטמון שלם
4 הריוטא ואחתהה֯ לשלמכי שלחת ספרא זנה
5 Reverse (Address) אל אחתי ע֯ת֯ררי מן א֯[חוכי א]מ֯י אפי יובל

1. To my ‘mother’ ‘TRRMRY from your ‘brother’ ’MY. [Prosperity and long] life I have written wishing you.
2. Greetings to my sister(s) ’SWRY and ZBBW and KKY. Now I am relying on you. Look

3. after these little ones. Greetings to WSRW and to ŠPNYT and her children and to PṬMWN. Greetings
4. to HRYWṬ' and his sister. For your welfare I have written this letter.
5. To my 'sister' 'TRRY from your ['brother'] 'MY. For delivery to Ofi.

NOTES

1. עתררמרי; the first element recalls the divine name Athtar; see at no. 7 Sefire i A 1; the second element (apparently shortened in 5) is unknown. She is an aunt or other older relative of the writer. אמי is prob. Egyp.; cp. אמון (Driver v 3); he was doubtless a soldier on service in Memphis, who made use of the same messenger as the writers of letters i–vi, although he had no family connection with them. The three females in 2 may have been his younger sisters, for whose upbringing he was responsible after the death of their parents; while he was in Memphis they were left in the charge of the addressee.
2. אחתי, though sing., prob. applies to all three names; cp. v 1. אסורי is Egyp. and occurs at Elephantine. זבבו may be a short form of a name compounded with the Babylonian divine element Zababa (a goddess). ככי is prob. Egyp. עליכי; the editors wrongly print עלכי. מתכל = [mittkēl]; Ithpe. partic. from TKL (cp. Syriac).
3. חזית; i 11. ינקיא; no. 26 Dream ostracon B 3; note א against ה of i–vi. אלכי; Cowley xiv 8; biblical ['illēk]. The names in this line and that in 4 are all Egyp.; with the divine element נית in the second cp. Eleph. פסמסנית; פטמון occurs on a graffito from Abydos (*CIS* ii 126).
4. אחתהה; the ה of the suffix is carelessly written twice; the editors read אחתהי.

28. Padua i (the Migdol papyrus) Pl. VIII, 1

The partially complete papyrus (22 by 10·8 cm.) was found in Egypt at the beginning of the 19 cent., but was not published until 1960 after it had come into the possession of the civic museum at Padua from a private source. At least one line has disappeared at the top of the reverse side; and from the restorations proposed for obverse 1–3, it appears that a strip containing about four letter-spaces is missing from the right of the papyrus, and one containing about eight to ten from the left, except in the case of obverse line 5 (= reverse 4) where, due to a piece being cut out, the lacuna is some ten spaces larger. The contents comprise a letter written by a Jew resident at Migdol in the eastern Delta (cp. Jerem. xliv 1) to his son in Elephantine, where he was prob. on military service. A mention of the temple of Yahu dates the papyrus prior to its destruction in 410 B.C. The writer informs his son that a difficulty over his unit's salaries had been cleared up (cp. the not dissimilar situation described in no. 27 Hermopolis papyrus i 8 f.), encourages him to be brave, and apologizes that he had not been able to bring him some articles of clothing he had requested before he left. There are one or two suggestive parallels in language with the Hermopolis letters, which were also written in Lower Egypt.

The papyrus was published along with two other fragmentary papyri from the same museum by Bresciani in *RSO* 35 (1960), 11–24. There are further studies by Fitzmyer, *JNES* 21 (1962), 15–24 and Naveh, 'Inscrs.', 25 f. The transcription below is made from the very clear plates in Bresciani, loc. cit.

Obverse

1 [שלמ ב]ית יהו ביב אל ברי שלמם [מ]ן֯ אחוך אושע שלם ושררת [שגיא הושרת לך]

2 [כעת מ]ן יום זי אזלת בא֯רחא֯ זך֯ ב[רי] לי טיב אף אמך כעת ברך אנת֯ [ליהו אלהא]

3 [זי יח]ונ֯י אנפיך בשלם כעת מן יום [ז]י֯ נפקתם מן מצרין פרס לא י֯[היב לכן תנה]

4 [כעת] ק֯בלן לפחותא על פרסכן תנה ב[מ]גדל כן אמיר לן לאמר על זנה֯ ....

5 [---] ס֯פריא ויתיהב לכן כעת כזי תא֯תון מצרין על ....

6 [---פ]רסכן זי כלי כלה כעת איך בי֯תא עביד ואיך נפקת הן יהו ....

7 [------ ש]לם ומחבל לא איתי גב[ר] הוי אל תתאשד עד תאתה ....

Reverse

1 ....

2 [-------] ב֯אגרתא זילך על כתון ול֯בש כתונך ולבשך עבידן ....

3 [---] לאמך עבדת אל תמלי לבת[י] בז֯י לא איתית המו מנפי כזי ת[אתה מצרין]

4 [איתה] ה֯מו קדמתך כעת זבנת לי אנה [כ]ת֯ן *I* זי כתן כעת֯ ....

5 [---]ר֯ן ולבש עד תאתה שלם אמך וינקיא כלא כעת תנה הוין [יצפן לך]

6 [ב---] למחר כתבת אגרתא זא כעׄ[ת] כן שמיע לן לאמר תתפטרן ....

Address

7 (upside down) אל אחי שלׄמם בר [או]שע אחוך אושע בר פט....

Obverse.

1. [Greetings] to the temple of Yahu in Elephantine. To my son Shelomam from your 'brother' Osea. Health and prosperity [in abundance I have sent wishing you.
2. Now] from the day when you went on that way, my son, it has been well with me, also (with) your mother. Now be you blessed by [the god Yahu,
3. that he may] show me your face in peace. Now from the day when you (men) left Egypt, salary has not [been paid to you here.
4. Now] we have complained to the officials about your salary here in Migdol. We were told as follows, About this matter, (it has been taken to Memphis
5. before) the clerks, and it will be given to you. Now when you come to Egypt . . . . (the clerks will pay
6. you) in its entirety your salary, which has been withheld. Now how is the family faring, and how (are you faring since) you left? If Yahu . . . .
7. . . . . it will be well, and there will be no harm done. Be a man (and) do not be troubled until you come (back) . . . . . .

Reverse.

1. . . . . (Now concerning what
2. you wrote) in your letter about a tunic and clothing—your tunic and clothing have been made . . . .
3. . . . . I have made for your mother. Do not be angry with me because I did not bring them to Memphis. When you [come back to Egypt,
4. I shall bring] them before you. Now I have bought for myself a tunic of linen. Now . . . .
5. . . . . and clothing until you come. It is well with your mother and all the children. Now here we have been [worrying about you.
6. On the . . . . day] of Mehir I have written this letter. Now we have heard a report that you (men) will be allowed home (soon).
7. To my 'brother' Shelomam, son of [O]sea, your 'brother' Osea, son of PṬ . . .

NOTES

Obverse.

1. With the initial greeting cp. the first words of no. **27** Hermopolis i–iv. שלמם is compounded with Hebr. [šalōm] and the ending [ām]; cp. שלומם (Cowley i 2, etc.). אושע is a shortened form of אושעיה; both occur in the Eleph. papyri; cp. Hebr. הושע(יה). Note that the grandfather's name is Egyp. (rev. 7). With the restoration at the end cp. Driver iii 1, etc. שררת is hardly constr. before שגיא, but must be a similar form to אגרת = ['iggart], which alternates with אגרה as an absol. in the papyri; cp. Hebr. קוטלה and קוטלת. שגיא; adverb; שגא would perhaps be better on grounds of space.
2. ארחא; fem.; no. **9** Sefire iii 9. זך = [dāk]; historical spelling. טיב = [ṭyēb]; biblical [ṭ'ēb]. Note the omission of ל before אמך. ברך; passive partic., written defectively. With the following formula cp. no. **27** Hermopolis iv 2; vi 1, 2.
3. נפקתם = [npaqtōm] with [m]; cp. המו (rev. 3, 4) and contrast פרסכן (4, 6); לכן (5); forms with [n] predominate on the Hermopolis papyri, even for the 3 masc. plur. Shelomam and his fellow soldiers are meant; cp. no. **27** Hermopolis i 8. מצרין; Elephantine is apparently regarded as outside Egypt proper.
4. קבלן; cp. no. **27** Hermopolis ii 10. פחותא = [paḥ(ḥ)wātā]; hardly here governors of a province. The restorations in the translation at the end of this and the following lines are guesses; the lacunas are too large to be completed with any certainty. Cp., however, rev. 3 f., where Shelomam's arrival back at Memphis seems to be expected.
5. ספריא; Cowley ii 12. תאתון = [tētōn]; with the omission of the prepos. cp. no. **20** Ashur ostracon 11.
6. כלי; passive partic.; cp. Cowley xxxvii 13 f. כלה prob. goes with the previous noun rather than with כלי. With the form cp. כלה in no. **27** Hermopolis iv 4, 12 and כלא (rev. 5). ביתא must refer to members of the family at Elephantine. נפקת; cp. 3 above. יהו; alternatively we may have a part of the verb 'to be'.
7. מחבל is prob. Pael passive partic., used as a noun, 'ruin, hurt, damage'. The word occurs in Cowley xxvii 2, where it means injury caused by the writers, '(nothing) disloyal' or the like. If that is the sense here, there may be an allusion to some misdemeanour, which had led to the soldiers' salaries being withheld. Or the writer is simply assuring his son that there is no danger; cp. חבל in Dan. iii 25. תתאשד; Ithpe. from 'ŠD, 'to pour out'; cp. the metaphorical use of Hebr. ŠPK in Job xxx 16 (Hithpa.).

Reverse.

1. A few marks of writing are visible; none is detectable beneath obv. 7.
2. The son's letter had obviously been received before his departure for Elephantine; it had been written from Memphis (3 below), where presumably his unit was usually stationed. כתון; no. **27** Hermopolis ii 11. Prob. an outer cloak and inner garments are meant.
3. תמלי; jussive. On the idiom see at no. **20** Ashur ostracon 19; no. **27** Hermopolis i 6. איתית = ['ētīt]; with א as in the Hermopolis papyri against the forms with ה of the other collections. המו; see at no. **5** Zakir A 9.
4. איתה; Aph. imperf. קדמתך; no. **27** Hermopolis ii 15. The second כתן = [kittān], 'linen'.
5. The first letter could also be ד or כ, but is hardly ו; not therefore כתון. שלם; with the omission of ל cp. no. **27** Hermopolis ii 2; a translation 'Greetings to' is not possible. ינקיא; no. **27** Hermopolis vii 3. יצפן; no. **27** Hermopolis iv 8.

6. A numeral in figures followed ב; cp. Cowley xxvi 28; Kraeling xiii 8. תתפטרן; Ithpe. as in Palest. Aram. Though their salary had been withheld (obv. 6), there is no mention of Shelomam and his companions being under confinement, so the meaning here is prob. simply 'be given leave'; cp. Syriac Peal, 'to return home'. A final adverb or a phrase indicating the time is missing.
7. —פט; part of an Egyp. name.

29. The Abydos papyrus (417 B.C.) Fig. 14

The well-preserved papyrus (17 cm. broad by 8 cm. deep) was acquired by the National Archaeological Museum in Madrid in 1964 and published by Teixidor in the same year (*Syria* 41, 285–90); see also Naveh, 'Inscrs.', 30 f.; idem, *JNES* 27 (1968), 321 f. It concerns two Sidonian brothers who made a pilgrimage to the temple of Osiris at Abydos, in Egypt. Many graffiti in both Phoen. and Aram. scripts have been found in this temple; see Lidzbarski, *Ephem.* III, 93 f. The Phoen. graffiti were usually written in the 1 person by the pilgrims themselves; that the papyrus is in Aram. suggests it was composed for the brothers by a temple scribe, who was naturally more familiar with the lingua franca; cp. also the Nebi Yunis ostracon (no. **32** below). Photograph: Teixidor, loc. cit.

1 ב *3* לכסלו שנת *3 3 1* הו יום *10 1* לתחות
2 שנת *3 3 1* דריוהוש מלכא עבדבעל
3 צידני ב̊ר עבדצדק אתה עם אחוה[י]
4 עזרבעל ל̊אבוד זי מצרין קדם אוסי[רי]
5 אלהא רבא

1. On the 3rd of Kislev, the 7th year, that is the 11th day of Thoth,
2. the 7th year of Darius, the king, ʿBDBʿL
3. the Sidonian, the son of ʿBDṢDQ, came with his brother
4. ʿZRBʿL to Abydos of Egypt before Osiris,
5. the great god.

NOTES

With the date formula cp. Cowley vi 1; viii 1, etc. Kislev is the 9th month of the Mesopotamian calendar, equivalent in this particular year to Thoth in the Egyp. calendar. דריוהוש; so Cowley xx 1, etc.; in some papyri the first ו is not written; biblical דריוש (so also Cowley i 1). Darius II (423–404) is meant. The name עזרבעל is common on Phoen. inscrs., as are names beginning with עבד; see *KAI* III, 50–1. With the theophorous element in the second name cp. צדקמלך (*KAI* no. 28, 2). אחוהי; the usual form in the papyri; a piece broken off in the bottom left corner took in one letter from this line and two from the next; the form אחוה occurs only in Cowley xxv 3. אבוד; the Cowley papyri have אבוט. אוסירי; the first י is not usually written; cp. the Saqqara and Carpentras inscrs. (nos. **23**, **24**).

30. Tema (i) Pl. IX

The inscr. (*CIS* ii 113), belonging to the mid 5 cent., was found in 1880 and covers the face of a stele about 1 m. in height and 0·42 m. in width. On the narrow left side of the stone (0·11 m. broad) there are two panels in relief; the top one depicts the god ṢLM, bearded in the Assyrian manner, with above his head a carving of the winged sun disc; on the lower panel the priest responsible for setting up the stele makes an offering at a horned altar; his name is written underneath. On the circumstances surrounding the discovery of the stele see Doughty, *Travels in Arabia Deserta* I, 531; Dougherty, *American Journal of Archaeology* 34 (1930), 296 f.; it is now in the Louvre.

The inscr. records the introduction of a new cult from a place called HGM into Tema, the oasis city in north Arabia, and describes arrangements for the endowment and service of its sanctuary. The deity, named as ṢLM, was prob. Mesopotamian in origin, as the relief of him suggests. He was already (16) worshipped in Tema under the designation ṢLM of MḤRM, a locality near by. Two other deities, who seem to be respectively Mesopotamian and Syrian, are mentioned (16). Such a cosmopolitan religious situation accords with the position of the oasis at the juncture of trade-routes north-west to Egypt and Syria, east to Mesopotamia, and south to the Yemen; but the particularly strong Mesopotamian influence prob. also reflects the prominence that had been enjoyed by Tema in the previous century, when Nabonidus, the last monarch of the neo-Babylonian dynasty, captured it and made it his residence for several years in his despairing retreat from imperial affairs. That in the 5 cent. the population also was very mixed is suggested by the Akkad. name of the priest of the new cult and the Egyp. name of his father. The dialect is imperial, but shows one or two unusual forms; see on שת (1); זן (4); יהבן (15). For further evidence of the use of Aram. in northern Arabia see above, Tell el Maskhuta (no. **25**).

Bibliography

Two other small inscriptions (ii, iii) were published at the same time as the stele by Th. Nöldeke, *Sitzungsberichte der Preußischen Akademie der Wissenschaften*, 1884, 813 f.; for further early bibliography see *CIS* ii 113–15. See also *NSE* p. 447; *NSI* nos. 69, 70; Gevirtz, 'Curses', 145; Koopmans, *Chrest.* nos. 45,

50; *KAI* nos. 228–30. Several inscrs. have been found since, all fragmentary; see Altheim and Stiehl, *Die Araber in der Alten Welt*, vol. 5, 1 (Berlin, 1968), 74 f.; idem, *Geschichte Mittelasiens im Altertum* (Berlin, 1970), 141 f.

Plates

CIS; *NSE* Taf. XXVII.

1 A ... *c.* 6 ... בשת *20 2* .... *c.* 7 ...

2 [- - בתימ]א צלם [זי מחרם ושנגלא]

3 [ואש]יר֯א אלהי תימ֯א לצ֯לם זי

4 [הגם להן] ש֯מ֯ה ביומא זן [בתי]מא

5 .... 19–20 .... זי

6, 7 illegible

8 - - - -א לה֯ן֯ .... 7–8 .... [סותא ז]א

9 זי֯ [הקי]ם֯ צל֯מ֯ש֯זב בר פטסרי

10 [בבית צ]לם֯ זי הגם להן אלהי

11 תימא צ[דק]ו לצל֯משזב בר פטסרי

12 ולזרעה בבית צלם זי הגם וגב֯ר

13 זי יחבל סותא זא אלהי תימא

14 ינסחוהי וזרעה ו֯שמה מן אנפי

15 תימא והא זא צדקתא זי י[הבן]

16 צלם זי מחרם ושנגלא ו֯אשיר֯א

17 אלהי תימא לצלם זי֯ הגם א[ו]

18 מן חקלא דקלן *10* *3 3* ומן שימתא

19 זי מלכא דקלן *3 2* כל דקלן

20 *20 1* [הא] ש֯נה בשנה ואלהן ואנש

21 לא יהנ[פק] צלמשזב בר פטסרי֯

22 מן בי֯תא זנה ול[זר]עה ושמה

23 כמר֯י֯א֯ ב֯[ב]יתא זנ֯ה ל֯ע֯ל[מא]

צלמשזב B
כמרא

A 1. (On the . . . .) in the 22nd year of . . . . . (the king),
2. ṢLM [of MḤRM and ŚNGL'
3. and 'Š]YR', the gods of Tema (gave entrance into Tema) to ṢLM of
4. [HGM. Therefore] they have appointed him this day (a place) in Tema
5. . . . . which
6–7. Missing
8. . . . . Therefore . . . . [this monument],
9. which ṢLMŠZB, son of PṬSRY, [has set] up
10. [in the temple of] ṢLM of HGM. Therefore the gods
11. of Tema have dealt generously with ṢLMŠZB, son of PṬSRY,
12. and with his seed, in the temple of ṢLM of HGM. If any man
13. harms this monument, let the gods of Tema
14. remove him and his seed and his posterity from
15. Tema. This is the grant which
16. ṢLM of MḤRM and ŚNGL' and 'ŠYR',
17. the gods of Tema, shall [give] to ṢLM of HGM, namely
18. from the (temple) estates 16 palms and from the property
19. of the king 5 palms, making
20. 21 palms in all, year by year. Neither gods nor men
21. shall eject ṢLMŠZB, son of PṬSRY,
22. from this temple, or his seed or his posterity,
23. priests in this temple for ever.

B ṢLMŠZB, the priest.

NOTES

1. The lacuna at the beginning of the line prob. indicated the day of the month and that at the end the name of a king (cp. 19). שת is as in Phoen. and Moabite against שנת of no. **14** Panamu 1; Cowley i 1, etc.
2. Corpus suggests at the beginning צדקו as in 11, but 'in Tema' is then awkward. A verb meaning 'accept' or the like is more likely; there is just room for three letters, but not for four. תימא; Isa. xxi 14; Jerem. xxv 23; Job vi 19. The names of the deities in 2, 3 are restored from 16. צלם is generally connected with Akkad. *ṣalmu*, 'black, dark'; cp. *kakkabu ṣalmu*, 'the dark star', an epithet of Saturn, and the name *Ṣalmu-ma-lik*, 'Ṣalmu is counsellor'. An astral deity is indicated, perhaps the sun-god himself, who in Mesopotamian belief was a special patron of astrological rites; note also the solar disc on the relief. מחרם is prob. to be identified with Maḥramat in the area of Jebel Selma to the east of Tema. שנגלא may be compounded with the name of the Mesopotamian moon-god, Sin; cp. the Palmyrene fem. name שגל (*NSI* no. 143, 12).

3. אשירא is almost certainly the Canaanite goddess Ashera (1 Kgs. xviii 19; Ugar. *'ṯrt*); the spelling here and in 2 Kgs. xvii 16 and some other biblical passages suggests that the original form was a passive partic., 'the chosen one'; cp. Arab. ['aṯara]. The ל is the object-marker, found in biblical Aram. and occasionally in the papyri (Cowley vii 5), but not previously.
4. הגם is unidentified. להן; so Corpus (cp. 8, 10); Dan. ii 6; in Hebr. Ruth i 13 and perhaps Job xxx 24. שמה = [śāmūh], written defectively; cp. for the sense no. **19** Nerab ii 3. Alternatively the verb may be singular with the priest's name following, i.e. 'ṢLMŠZB has set, placed him'. זן is as in the Byblian dialect of Phoen. and the Zenjirli dialect; the regular spelling זנה (historical?) occurs in 22.
8. להן; see the previous note. סותא is restored from 13; Akkad. *asūmātu*, variant *sumētu* (sing. *asūmu*), a plur. form meaning 'relief' or 'stele'; on the sound-change [m] to [w] see at no. **5** Zakir A 1; no. **20** Ashur ostracon 1.
9. צלמשזב; see at no. **27** Hermopolis ii 2. פטסרי is Egyp., compounded with the divine name Osiris. The priest's family was prob. native Aramaean and, like those of the Hermopolis papyri, had apparently lived in Egypt for a time.
11. צדקו; Pael; cp. the noun צדקתא (15); Syriac [zedqtā] in Matt. vi 2; cp. also Dan. iv 24 ('charity'). On a rather different meaning of the base see at no. **14** Panammu 1.
13. יחבל; Pael; Cowley xxx 14.
14. ינסחוהי = [yinsḥūhī]; jussive with nasalization and suffix; see at no. **18** Nerab i 9, 12; no. **27** Hermopolis iv 7. שמה; Nerab i 10. אנפי; Cowley xv 19; contrast אפי (no. **7** Sefire i A 28).
15. הא זא; cp. Palest. Aram. הדין, fem. הדא; Syriac [hādē/ā]. יהבן = [yĕhbūn]; the Corpus restores a perf. יהבו, but the phrase 'year by year' in 20 makes an imperf. more appropriate; the imperf. of this verb occurs at Zenjirli (no. **13** Hadad 12) and Arpad (*KAI* no. 222 Sefire i B 38), though elsewhere in the imperial dialect it is replaced by the imperf. of NTN. יתנן is, of course, possible, though the damaged letter after י is more like ה than ת.
17. או; so Corpus, citing Gen. xxiv 55, i.e. 'viz.', 'say', or the like.
18. חקלא; *CIS* ii 24 (an Aram. endorsement); lit. 'field', but here prob. cultic or priestly land as opposed to royal (19). דקלן; the staple of oasis economy; Doughty, *Arabia Deserta* I, 293, 543, etc.; Targum Exod. xv 27. שימתא is prob. a loan-word from Akkad. *šimtu*, 'purchase', 'property so obtained' (base *šâmu*, 'to buy') rather than connected with Palest. Aram. and Syriac [sīmtā], 'treasure, treasury' (base ŚYM, 'to place').
20. הא; so Corpus. אלהן; plur. אנש; collective. They are construed in the next line with a sing. verb, i.e. 'As for gods and men, let one not . . . . .'.
22. יהנפק; cp. *NSI* no. 90, 7 (Nabataean). Note the object-marker ל with the second noun.
23. כמריא; no. **18** Nerab i 1.

31, 32. Two ostraca from Palestine (Tell Arad and Nebi Yunis)

Fig. 10 (no. 32)

The two tiny ostraca given here were unearthed in Israeli excavations in the early 1960s, and are welcome additions to the meagre written remains from post-Exilic Judah. Until the Samaria papyri (as yet unpublished) were discovered, we had little beyond some fragmentary potsherds from Samaria and Elath; see Bibliographical Notes (p. 160). Both the ostraca were published with plates in *IEJ* for 1964, that from Tell Arad (no. by Aharoni and Amiran (141), that from Nebi Yunis (no. **32**; in modern Ashdod) by Cross (185 f.); see further Naveh, 'Inscrs.', 31–2. The Tell Arad script belongs to about 400 B.C., the Nebi Yunis script to a generation or so later, being similar to the cursive writing of the Papyrus Luparensis from Egypt (*CIS* ii 146); see Table of scripts. The Tell Arad ostracon is now in the Israel Museum, the Nebi Yunis in the Department of Antiquities in Jerusalem.

No. **31**

מערת ענני
ומתבנה
ובית תו̊ר̊ה

The cave of Anani,
and his straw-shed,
and his ox-stable.

NOTES

מערת = [mʿārat]. The personal name occurs in 1 Chron. iii 24 and at Elephantine. מתבן = [matbēn]; so Talmud. תורה; so Naveh, citing Talmudic lists, in which straw-shed and ox-stable figure together. The ו is carelessly formed, and was read by the editors as נ; no word תנב is known, but they proposed a link with נוב, 'fruit' (Targum Hosea viii 7), i.e. 'fruit-store'. The 'and' after his name suggests that Anani himself lived in the cave, and supplies an illustration of the poverty of the times. The ostracon prob. served for purposes of registration or taxation.

No. **32**

בעלצד תק[לן ......]
דשנא

BʿLṢD; . . . shekels.
Donation.

NOTES

בעלצד is a Phoen. name, occurring on a graffito from Abydos; Lidzbarski, *Ephem.* III, 93 f., no. 67; cp. צדיתן, 'Ṣid has given', ibid., no. 34; the god's name may be connected with the base 'to hunt'. A number is prob. missing after 'shekels' (note with ת). דשנא = [dāšnā], a Persian loan-word, also found in Palest. Aram. and Syriac; the donation was prob. made to the local shrine. The former Philistine territory comprised in Persian times the province of Ashdod, except for the coastal city of Ashkelon, which was a Tyrian possession. It is likely therefore that the Phoen. element in the population was considerable, but the scribe who recorded the donation naturally used the lingua franca; cp. the Abydos papyrus (above no. **29**).

Inscriptions from Asia Minor (Nos. 33–7).

The stone inscrs. given below date to the 5 or 4 cents. B.C. and witness to the use of the imperial dialect in Persian Asia Minor. This had not previously been an Aram.-speaking area, and a number of solecisms show that the masons were not completely at home with the language; see on פתכר (no. 33 Nanasht 1); נוה (Nanasht 2); יבעה (Nanasht 5) and יבעון (no. 34 Guzneh 2); מהחסן (no. 36 Bahadirli 3); יחגה (Bahadirli 5); ארחא (no. 37 Daskyleion 3).

33. Nanasht

The stone (30·5 cm. high by 45·7 broad) was discovered near the town of Kesecek Köyü in Cilicia, and is now in the museum of Yale University.

The first publication was by Torrey, *JAOS* 35 (1915), 370 f.; see also Gevirtz, 'Curses', and Hanson, 'Inscrs.'; Cross, *BASOR* 184 (1966), 10; Koopmans, *Chrest.*, no. 48; *KAI* no. 258.

Photographs

Torrey and Hanson, loc. cit.

1 פתכר זנה הקם ננשת
2 קדם אדרסו֯ן ונוה
3 נפש֯י זילה֯ ומן ביש
4 יעבד עם פתכר֯ זנה
5 ויבעה לה שהר֯ ושמש

1. Nanasht erected this relief
2. before 'DRSWN, because he gave rest (?) to
3. my soul, which belongs to him. If anyone
4. does damage to this relief,
5. then may Sahar and Shamash seek him out!

NOTES

1. פתכר is from a Persian word meaning 'relief' or 'picture'; cp. Syriac and Palest. Aram. [ptakrā], 'idol'. The relief described has not been found, and must have been destroyed or removed. Note that, though followed by זנה, the noun lacks the emph. ending. נגשת is Anatolian in origin, perhaps compounded with the name of the Mesopotamian goddess Nana or Nanai, who was worshipped in Asia Minor into Greek times.

2. אדרסון; an Anatolian deity, appearing in names like Ἄδραστος from the Greek period. נוה; the reading is certain in Hanson's photo, and must supersede Torrey's reading לגננה, an infin. or nominal form from GNN, 'to protect'. Hanson suggests the Pael of NWH, 'to beautify, adorn', taking נפש as 'funeral monument' (cp. no. **37** Daskyleion 2); but this base is not known in Aram. Could it be a mistake for נוח, Pael, 'to give rest to, refresh', or a mishearing due to an inability on the part of the inhabitants of Cilicia to pronounce the pharyngal [ḥ] properly? For another possible example of this inability see at יהגה (no. **36** Bahadirli 5). For ו in the sense 'because' see no. **1** Barhadad 4, also a votive text. (See now Addenda, p. 166.)
3. ביש = [bīš] as in the later dialects against באיש in the papyri; no. **24** Carpentras 2.
5. יבעה; imperf. where we expect the jussive; cp. no. **34** Guzneh 2. The ו does not begin a main clause after a subordinate, but picks up the reference earlier to מן; cp. no. **8** Sefire ii C 10. With the imprecation cp. the next inscr. and no. **5** Zakir B 23 f.

34. Guzneh

The boundary-stone, still *in situ*, was discovered in 1905 at Guzneh or Gözne in Cilicia.

The inscr. was published by Montgomery, *JAOS* 28 (1907), 164 f.; see further Halévy, *Revue sémitique* 16 (1908), 434 f. and the studies of Gevirtz, 'Curses', and Hanson 'Inscrs.'; Koopmans, *Chrest.*, no. 42; *KAI* no. 259.

Photographs

Montgomery and Hanson, loc. cit.

1 עד תנה תחום ד̊ - - [-]
2 ומ̊ן זי א תתב ויב[ע]
3 ון לה בעלשמין
4 רבא שהר ושמש
5 ולזרעא זילה

1. To here (extends) the boundary of D . . . .
2. If any of you turn (it) back, then may
3. great Baalshamayn,
4. Sahar, and Shamash seek him out,
5. and his seed!

NOTES

1. תחום; Cowley viii 5, etc. The place-name is more or less illegible.
2. את is written א through haplography of ת; note the following space. תתב =

[ttīb]; imperf. (H)aph.; not a common meaning, but cp. in Hebr. Ps. xliv 11; lxxxix 44. ויבעון; so Hanson, surely correctly, on the basis of no. **33** Nanasht 3 f.; note again ו following מן and imperf. replacing jussive.

3 f. Cp. no. **5** Zakir B 23 f.

35. Saraïdin

The stone bearing the inscr. was discovered in 1892 at Saraïdin near Tarsus in Cilicia, and is still *in situ*.

See *NSE* p. 446; *NSI* no. 68; Koopmans, *Chrest.* no. 47; *KAI* no. 261.

Sketches

NSE Taf. XXVI, 3; Diringer, *Alphabet*, fig. 127; *KAI* Taf. XXI.

1 אנה ושונש בר
2 אפושי בר ברה זי
3 ושונש ואמי
4 אשולכרתי וכזי
5 צידא עבד אנה תנה
6 ובאתרא זנה משתרה אנה

1. I am WŠWNŠ, son of
2. ’PWŠY, grandson of
3. WŠWNŠ, and my mother is
4. ’ŠWLKRTY. While
5. I was hunting here,
6. it was in this place I made my meal.

NOTES

1. ושונש; this and the other names are prob. Persian or Anatolian.
2. Lit., ‘son of his son of’.
4. כרתי may be a gentilic (Cretan?) referring to WŠWNŠ rather than part of the mother’s name.
5. צידא = [ṣaydā]. עבד; partic.
6. The ו here seems to open the main clause. משתרה; Ithpa. partic. from ŠRY, ‘to encamp, dwell’; cp. Syriac Ethpa., ‘break one’s fast, dine’ (Peshitta John xxi 12, 15).

36. Bahadirli

Pl. VII, 2

The inscr. is carved on a stone discovered in 1957 at Bahadirli, near Karatepe in Cilicia, and still *in situ.*

Bibliography

A. Dupont-Sommer, *CRAIBL*, 1961, 19–22; idem and L. Robert, *La Déesse de Hiérapolis Castabala* (Paris, 1964), 7 f.; G. Garbini, *RSO* 40 (1965), 135 f.; G. Levi della Vida, *RSO* 40 (1965), 203 f.; G. Ryckmans, *Muséon* 78 (1965), 468 f.; Naveh, 'Inscrs.', 32 f.; *KAI* (2 edit.).

Photographs

Dupont-Sommer, loc. cit. (1961 and 1964).

1 זנה תחום כרביל
2 וכרשי קריתא
3 זי מהחסן כבבה
4 זי פושר זי בכשתבל֯י֯
5 ואיש זי יחגה
6 לתחומא זנה קדם
7 כבבה זי פושר
8 או איש אחרא֯
. . . .

1. This is the boundary of
2. the cities of KRBYL and KRŠY,
3. which belong to Kubaba
4. of PWŠR, which is in KŚTBLY.
5. Any person who effaces
6. this boundary (stone) before
7. Kubaba of PWŠR,
8. or any person thereafter

. . . .

NOTES

1. **תחום**; no. **34** Guzneh 1. The names of the cities both contain the Hittite element **כר** as in Carchemish; neither is known.
2. **קריתא** = [qiryātā]; plur.
3. **מהחסן** = [mhaḥsēn], lit., 'which Kubaba possesses'. **כבבה** is the name of a goddess, a prototype of the Cybele or Cybebe of Greek times; the masc. partic. is therefore a mistake.

4. פושר is unidentified, but כשתבלי (Castabala) was known in classical times; Strabo mentions it as famous for a temple of Artemis. Prob. Castabala was a district or capital of a district containing the other towns.
5. יחגה = יהגע with confusion of the pharyngal and laryngal sounds; see no. **5** Zakir B 16; cp. נוה = נוח (no. **33** Nanasht 2). This suggestion is made by Kutscher in a note in Naveh, 'Inscrs.', 33, and seems to render unnecessary the forced derivations of other commentators.
8. אחרא is perhaps an adverb 'afterwards'; see at no. **18** Nerab i 13. Dupont-Sommer's reading אחרן, 'other', is unlikely. The final lines of the inscr. are missing.

37. Daskyleion

Fig. 12

The stele with the inscr. is one of three discovered in 1965 at ancient Daskyleion, on the southern side of the sea of Marmara; they are now housed in the archaeological museum at Istanbul. Each is decorated with motifs in relief, for instance, a stylized palm-tree, a horse-drawn wagon, and a banquet scene, which the comparative studies of Hanfmann, *BASOR* 184 (1966), 10 f. and Delcor, *Muséon* 80 (1967), 301 f. show belong to the funerary art of the Near East in the Persian era.

The inscr. was published, with plates of the stelae, by Dupont-Sommer, *CRAIBL*, 1966, 44–57, who wrongly took it as votive in purpose; see the revised treatments of Cross, *BASOR* 184 (1966), 7–10, and Delcor. The transcription below is made from the excellent plate given by the last-named.

1 אלה צלמה זי אלנף בר אשי
2 הו עבד לנפשה 'הומיתך
3 בל ונבו זי ארחא זנה
4 יהוה עדה איש אל יעמל

1. These (pictures) represent Elnaf, son of Ishai.
2. He made (them) as his funeral monument. I adjure you
3. (by) Bel and Nebo that whoever passes
4. this way, let no man disturb (me).

NOTES

1. אלה; 'these', referring to the scenes on the stele. צלמה = [ṣalmēh], lit. 'his image'; cp. the Nerab inscrs. (nos. **18**, **19**). אלנף = ['ilnāp], 'El is exalted'; cp. Hebr. נוף in Ps. xlviii 3; the base, to be distinguished from NWP, 'to move to and fro, wave', occurs in South Arab. personal names, but is not found in Aram.; perhaps, as Cross suggests, he was an Aramaized Arab.

2. נפש in this meaning is common on Nabataean and Palmyrene inscrs.; see Jean-Hoftijzer, *Dictionnaire*, 183. Note the stroke after לנפשה, suggesting a break in the sense at this point. הומיתך = [haw/ōmaytāk] or the like; Haph. perf. from YMY, 'to swear'.
3. בל; from Akkad. *Bēl*, not בעל. The prepos. ב is omitted by haplography. ארחא = ['urḥā]; this word is usually fem. in Aram.; the mistake, if it is one, will be due to the mason rather than Elnaf.
4. יהוה עדה = [yihwē 'ādē]; cp. the compound imperatives in the Hermopolis papyri. יעמל is prob. Aph.; so Syriac 'to weary or trouble (someone)'; cp. *KAI* no. 13 Tabnit 4 (תרגזן).

(For a new reading of 1, 2 see Addenda, p. 166.)

BIBLIOGRAPHICAL NOTES

1. Texts not included in the present volume may be studied as follows:

Ordek-Burnu (Cilicia; 9 cent.) in J. Friedrich, *Kleinasiatische Sprachdenkmäler* (Berlin, 1932), 38 f.; Koopmans, *Chrest.* no. 6.

Deir-Alla (Jordan; 8 cent.) in J. Naveh, *IEJ* 17 (1967), 256 f.; Naveh, 'Script', 67 note.

(Only the writing of these two inscrs. is Aramaic.)

Arslan Tash and Nimrud (9 and 8 cents.); short inscriptions and single letters (fitters' marks) on ivories; bibliography in F. Vattioni, *Augustinianum* 11 (1971), 82 f.; see also A. R. Millard, *Iraq* 24 (1962), 41 f.

Tell Sifr (Syria; 8 cent.) in F. M. Tocci, *Oriens Antiquus* 1 (1962), 21 f.; fragment of a relief.

Nineveh (late 8 cent.) in *CIS* ii 1–14; brief inscrs. on lion-weights; see also *NSI* no. 66; Koopmans, *Chrest.* no. 13; Naveh, 'Script', 11.

Nimrud (*c.* 700) in J. B. Segal, *Iraq* 19 (1957), 139 f.; ostracon with list of names; see also W. F. Albright, *BASOR* 149 (1958), 33 f.; G. Garbini, *AION* 17 (1967), 94 f.; Naveh, 'Script', 14.

Assyria (7 cent.), Nerab (6 cent.), and Babylonia (6 and 5 cents.); brief endorsements for identification on cuneiform tablets, in

CIS ii 15–71.

A. T. Clay, *Business Documents of Murashu Sons of Nippur Dated in the Reign of Darius II 424–404 B.C.*, The Babylonian Expedition of the University of Pennsylvania, Series A, Cuneiform Texts, vol. 10 (1912).

L. Delaporte, *Épigraphes araméens; Étude des textes araméens gravés ou écrits sur les tablettes cunéiformes* (Paris, 1912).

E. Dhorme, 'Les Tablettes babyloniennnes de Neirab', *RA* 25 (1928), 53–82.

Koopmans, *Chrest.* no. 41.

S. J. Lieberman, 'The Aramaic argillary script in the seventh century', *BASOR* 192 (1968), 25–31.

Naveh, 'Script', 16 f.

F. Vattioni, *Augustinianum* 10 (1970), 493 f. (bibliography on 154 examples).

Assyria (*c.* 600) in M. Lidzbarski, *Wissenschaftliche Veröffentlichungen der Deutschen Orient-Gesellschaft* 38 (1921), 5–15; short inscrs. on clay tablets; see also *KAI* nos. 234–6.

Send-Qaleh (Persia; 6 cent.) in *CIS* ii 111; prob. only the script is Aramaic.

Aramaic seals (mainly 8–6 cents.) in *CIS* ii 73–107; see further Rosenthal, *Forschung*, 297 f.; K. Galling in *ZDPV* 64 (1941), 121 f.; Naveh, 'Inscrs.', 22 f.; F. Vattioni, *Augustinianum* 11 (1971), 47 f. (bibliography on 178 seals and stamps). On the *Yhwd* and *Mwṣh* seal-impressions from post-Exilic Judah see Naveh, 'Script', 58 f.

Papyrus (Egypt; 515 B.C.) in Bauer and Meißner, *Sitzungsberichte der Preußischen Akademie der Wissenschaften*, 1936, 414 f.; a very difficult text; see also Dupont-Sommer, *Mémoires présentés par divers savants à l'Académie*, etc., 14, 2 (1944), 51 f.; Koopmans, *Chrest.* no. 19.

Scheich-Fadl (Egypt; 6 cent.?) in Aimé-Giron, *Ancient Egypt*, 1923, 38 f.; very fragmentary tomb inscrs.; see also Naveh, 'Script', 40 f.

Stone inscrs. from Egypt in *CIS* ii 123 (*c.* 500) and 142 (4 cent.); *NSE* p. 448; *NSI* no. 72; *KAI* nos. 268, 272.

Asswan (5 cent.) in W. Kornfeld, *WZKM* 61 (1967), 9 f.; names on sarcophagi.

Wadi Hammamat (5 cent.) in G. Goyon, *Nouvelles Inscriptions rupestres du Wadi Hammamat* (Paris, 1957); alphabet; see also Dupont-Sommer, *RA* 41 (1947), 105 f.

Abydos (5 and 4 cents.) in *CIS* ii 125 f.; Lidzbarski, *Ephem.* III, 93 f.; graffiti; see also N. Aimé-Giron, *Textes araméens d'Égypte* (Cairo, 1931); Koopmans, *Chrest.* no. 40.

Ostraca from Persian times. An edition of the Clermont-Ganneau collection from Elephantine is still awaited. Bibliography to 1939 in Rosenthal, *Forschung*, 296. See further:

E. L. Sukenik, 'Inscribed Hebrew and Aramaic potsherds from Samaria', *PEQ*, 1933, 152–6.

N. Glueck, 'Ostraca from Elath', *BASOR* 80 (1940), 2–10.

A. Dupont-Sommer, 'Un Ostracon araméen inédit de Larsa', *RA* 39 (1942–4), 143–7.

Idem, 'l'Ostracon araméen du Sabbat', *Semitica* 2 (1949), 29–39.

L. H. Vincent, 'Les Épigraphes judéo-araméennes postexiliques', *Revue Biblique* 56 (1949), 274–94.

S. A. Birnbaum in *Samaria Sebaste, The Objects from Samaria* (London, 1957), 9 f.

A. Dupont-Sommer, 'Un Ostracon araméen inédit de l'Éléphantine', *RSO* 32 (1957), 403–9.

Koopmans, *Chrest.* nos. 33–9.

A. Dupont-Sommer in *Hebrew and Semitic Studies presented to G. R. Driver* (Oxford, 1963), 53–8.

Naveh, 'Script', 37 f., 43 f.

Papyri from Persian times; see foreword to chap. IV; Koopmans, *Chrest.* nos. 23–30; Rosenthal, *Handbook*, sect. II; J. Naveh, *JAOS* 91 (1971), 379 f.; Naveh, 'Script', 31 f., 43 f. On the 4-cent. papyri from Samaria, not yet published, see F. M. Cross, *BA* 26 (1963), 110 f.; most seem to be very fragmentary.

Persepolis (*c.* 400) in R. A. Bowman, *Ritual Objects with Aramaic Inscriptions from the Persepolis Treasury* (Chicago, 1970); a large collection of difficult cultic texts.

Asia Minor (5 and 4 cents.) in *CIS* ii 108; *NSE* p. 446; *NSI* no. 67; Koopmans, *Chrest.* no. 20; *KAI* nos. 260, 262, 263. See further in Hanson, 'Inscrs.'

Additional texts from the period covered by this volume are noted in the introductions to nos. **11**, **12** Luristan; no. **25** Tell el Maskhuta; no. **28** Padua i; no. **30** Tema (i).

Later inscriptions. On the important 3-cent. Aram. text in cuneiform characters from Uruk see *ANET*, 658 and bibliography cited there. A 3-cent. papyrus from Egypt with a list of transliterated Greek names was published by E. Bresciani, *AANL, Rendiconti* 17 (1962), 258 f.; see further Naveh, 'Inscrs.', 35 f. A list of inscrs. from Parthian territories (3 cent. B.C. to 3 cent. A.D.) with bibliography is given in Altheim and Stiehl, *Sprache*, 262 f.; see also *KAI* nos. 273–6. For selections of inscrs. in Palmyrene and Nabataean see *NSE* pp. 449 f.; *NSI* nos. 78–147; Rosenthal, *Handbook* I, 40 f., 47 f. On the texts from Hatra (1–2 cents. A.D.) see *KAI* nos. 237–57; Rosenthal, *Handbook* I, 44 f. For inscrs. in Palest. or Jewish Aram. see J.-B. Frey, *Corpus Inscriptionum Iudaicarum* (Rome, 1952); Rosenthal, *Handbook* I, 52 f., 69 f.; Naveh, 'Script', 62 f. (the Tobiah inscr.). A short selection of Syriac inscrs. is given in H. J. W. Drijvers, *Old Syriac (Edessan) Inscriptions* (Leiden, 1972).

Note: for full and up-to-date bibliographies see Degen, *Grammatik* (Old Aramaic); F. Vattioni, 'Preliminari alle iscrizioni aramaiche', *Augustinianum* 9 (1969), 305–61 (1253 items, excluding Nabataean, Palmyrene, and Syriac, but including 12 pages on the Elephantine papyri). For continuing bibliography consult the 'Bulletin d'épigraphie sémitique' of J. Teixidor in *Syria* 44 (1967) and succeeding vols.

2. On the history and civilization of the Aramaeans consult:

E. G. H. Kraeling, *Aram and Israel* (New York, 1918).

A. Alt, 'Die syrische Staatenwelt vor dem Einbruch der Assyrer', *ZDMG* 13 (1934), 233–58. Reprinted in *Kleine Schriften* (Munich, 1959), III, 214 f.

A. T. Olmstead, *History of Palestine and Syria* (New York, 1941).

R. A. Bowman, 'Aramaeans, Aramaic and the Bible', *JNES* 7 (1948), 65–90.

R. T. O'Callaghan, *Aram Naharaim: A Contribution to the History of Upper Mesopotamia in the Second Millennium B.C.* (Rome, 1948).

Dupont-Sommer, *Araméens*.

P. K. Hitti, *History of Syria*, 2 edit. (London, 1957).

M. F. Unger, *Israel and the Aramaeans of Damascus* (London, 1957).

A. Malamat, 'The kingdom of David and Solomon in its contact with Aram Naharaim', *BA* 21 (1958), 96 f.

J. C. L. Gibson, 'Observations on some important ethnic terms in the Pentateuch', *JNES* 20 (1961), 217–38.

B. Mazar, 'The Aramaean empire in its relations with Israel', *BA* 25 (1962), 98 f.

B. Porten, *Archives from Elephantine: The Life of an Ancient Jewish Military Colony* (Berkeley, 1968).

A. Malamat, 'Aramaeans' in D. J. Wiseman, *Peoples of Old Testament Times* (Oxford, 1973), 134 f.

See further the relevant chapters of the forthcoming revised edition of the *Cambridge Ancient History*, vols. 1 and 2; some of the chapters have already been published in fascicle form.

On geography consult:

R. Dussaud, *Topographie historique de la Syrie antique et médiévale* (Paris, 1927).

M. A. Beek, *Atlas of Mesopotamia* (Edinburgh, 1962).

L. H. Grollenberg, *Atlas of the Bible* (Edinburgh, 1963).

Y. Aharoni and M. Avi-Yonah, *The Macmillan Bible Atlas* (New York and London, 1968).

3. Grammars of Old and Imperial (including biblical) Aramaic:

Garbini, 'Antico', supplemented by G. Garbini, 'Nuovo materiale per la grammatica dell'aramaico antico', *RSO* 34 (1959), 41–54.

Degen, *Grammatik* (with a full bibliography).

Leander, *Ägyptisch.*

H. Bauer and P. Leander, *Grammatik des Biblisch-Aramäischen* (Halle, 1927).

Rosenthal, *Grammatik.*

Other studies on the problems of the early Aramaic dialects are:

H. H. Rowley, *The Aramaic of the Old Testament: A Grammatical and Lexical Study of the Relations with Other Early Aramaic Dialects* (Oxford, 1929).

Ginsberg, 'Problems'.

H. L. Ginsberg, 'Aramaic studies today', *JAOS* 62 (1942), 229–38.

Bowman, loc. cit. (above 2), 65 f.

E. Y. Kutscher, 'The language of the Genesis Apocryphon', *Scripta Hierosolymitana*, vol. 4 (Jerusalem, 1958), 1–36.

S. Segert, 'Zum Problem der altaramäischen Dialekte', *Archiv Orientální* 26 (1958), 561–72.

Altheim and Stiehl, *Sprache*, passim.

K. A. Kitchen, 'The Aramaic of Daniel', *Notes on Some Problems in the Book of Daniel* (London, 1965), 31 f.

K. Beyer, 'Der reichsaramäische Einschlag in der ältesten syrischen Literatur', *ZDMG* 116 (1966), 242–54.

J. C. Greenfield, 'Dialect traits in early Aramaic' (in Hebrew with English summary), *Leshonenu* 32 (1968), 359–68.

J. A. Fitzmyer, *The Genesis Apocryphon of Qumran Cave I* (Rome, 1971), 19 f.

On the dialect of Zenjirli see the introduction to no. **13** Hadad. Studies on comparative Semitic and historical linguistics are cited in vol. I.

4. Writing and epigraphy. On the structure of Syrian Semitic writing see *EHO*, and my restatement in *Archivum Linguisticum* 17 (1969), 155 f. Naveh, 'Script' (1970) is an excellent guide to the problems of the origin and development of Aramaic writing in the period covered by this volume and slightly beyond. On the development of the Jewish scripts (the so-called Square Hebrew) from the Imperial Aramaic see in more detail F. M. Cross's article in G. E. Wright, *The Bible and the Ancient Near East* (London, 1961), 133–202. General works on Semitic writing are cited in vol. I.

5. Dictionaries. See vol. I. The section on Aramaic in Köhler–Baumgartner is better than that on Hebrew. See further Greenfield, *JAOS* 82 (1962), 290 f. On a lexicon of the Aramaic inscriptions in Russian see Segert, *Archiv Orientální* 35 (1967), 463 f.

CORRIGENDA AND ADDENDA (VOLUME I)

REVISED LIST OF CONTENTS

(to show the serial numeration introduced in the second impression)

CORRIGENDA AND ADDENDA

p. 1 (bottom). Question the statement about ability to write; see A. R. Millard, 'The practice of writing in Ancient Israel', *BA* 35 (1972), 98 f.

p. 8. Add A. F. Rainey, *PEQ* 102 (1970), 45 f.

p. 11. For ידיו read ידעיו; for בעל read בעלא; for iv read vi.

p. 12. The reading in xlii was previously suggested by H. Michaud, *Sur la pierre et l'argile* (Neuchâtel, 1958), 58, note.

p. 13. At lv, for [yhaw], HWW read [yḥaw], ḤWW; for lxviii read lxiii.

p. 14. Par. 2; for ח read ה.

p. 19. Nimrud 2; for אהרי read אחרי.

p. 23. A second small fragment was discovered at Silwan at the same time; see now D. Ussishkin, *BASOR* 196 (1969), 16 f.

p. 25. Ophel; add R. Milik, *Revue Biblique* 66 (1959), 550 f. (with photograph).

p. 27. Par. 1; for קצרת read קצרם.

p. 28. Add L. Delekat, *Biblica* 51 (1970), 453 f.
Line 4 and p. 30, note 8. These statements are inaccurate; 1 pers. sing. perfects without [ī] are rare, but they do occur; e.g. Ps. xvi 2; Job xlii 2.

p. 36. Add B. Rocco, *Rivista Biblica* 14 (1966), 201 f. (small painted inscr.).

p. 51. A2 and note 2; for [sah] read [ṣaḥ]; add B. A. Levine, *IEJ* 19 (1969), 49 f.; D. N. Freedman, ibid. 52 f.; Y. Aharoni, *BASOR* 196 (1970), 16 f.; B. Otzen, *VT* 20 (1970), 239 f.

p. 53. Note 9; remains of a temple were unearthed at Arad, but it had been abandoned by this time, perhaps at Josiah's reform; see Winton Thomas (ed.), *Archaeology and Old Testament Study* (Oxford, 1967), 397 f.

p. 58. Khirbet Beit Lei; add F. M. Cross in *Near Eastern Archaeology in the 20th Century* (Glueck Festschrift, New York, 1970), 299 f.
Notes; for Polel read Poel.

p. 59. Well over 150; change to at least 250; see the list by F. Vattioni, *Biblica* 50 (1969), 357 f.; *Augustinianum* 11 (1971), 433 f.; see also M. Heltzer, *AION* 21 (1971), 183 f.

p. 64. Note 18; for Gedeliah read Gedaliah. Stamps; add A. D. Tushingham, *BASOR* 200 (1970), 71 f.; 201 (1971), 23 f.

p. 68. Add S. Yeivin, *PEQ* 101 (1969), 63 f.; R. B. Y. Scott, *BASOR* 200 (1970), 62 f.; Y. Aharoni, ibid. 201 (1971), 35 f.

p. 72. Bottom; for all other dialects read most.

p. 73. Middle; for grammer read grammar. Bottom; forms with infixed [t] are found in Ugaritic and twice on the Ahiram inscr. Like Ahiram, Moabite retains a 2-millennium feature which is lost in later 1-millennium Syriac Semitic dialects.

p. 74. For Anderson read Andersen; add G. Wallis, *ZDPV* 81 (1965), 180 f.; P. D. Miller, *Orientalia* 38 (1969), 461 f.; E. Lipiński, *Orientalia* 40 (1971), 325 f.

p. 75. Line 11; for עטרט read עטרת.
Line 17; for ההרמתה read החרמתה.

p. 78. Note 2; question the Aramaic influence in Job.

p. 81. Note 17; for [hahramtīh] read [haḥramtīh].

p. 82. Note 25; for ŠWH read ŠWḤ.

p. 86. Writing; add A. R. Millard, *JSS* 15 (1970), 2 f.; J. Naveh, *BASOR* 203 (1971), 27 f.

p. 88. For C1011 *passim* read C1101.

p. 89. *ANET* (Supplementary vol. 1969) contains photographs of the following Hebrew inscrs.; no. **8** Silwan (811); no. **10** Yavneh-yam (808); no. **13** Tell Arad C (807); no. **14** Gibeon (810; three); Chap. IV, Stamps (809; three royal from Gibeon); Weights (776; six examples).

p. 94. S. A. Birnbaum; this volume contains plates only; a volume of comment appeared in 1971. For G. W. read G. E. Wright.

p. 97. 1963; for Winnet read Winnett. 1964; for Mesad Hashavyahu, *passim*, read Meṣad Ḥashavyahu.

p. 98. For F. J. Anderson read F. I. Andersen.

p. 99. Gibson (forthcoming); *Archivum Linguisticum* 17 (1969), 131–60.

p. 102. For ידעין read ידעיו.

p. 105 (bottom). Drop Kh.B.L.A2 to next line.

pp. 108 f. These corrections should be made in Semitic terms: [māhun]; 'ŠN; ḤWW; ḤLP; ḤNN; ḤPR; ḤṢB; ḤRM; LḤM; MḤW; NDḤ; SḤB; ʿBŠ; [ʿayn]; ŠLḤ.

On a recently discovered 9-cent. fragment in Ammonite (the 'Citadel' inscr.) see S. H. Horn, *BASOR* 193 (1969), 2 f.; W. F. Albright, ibid. 196 (1970), 16 f.; B. Obed, *RSO* 44 (1969), 187 f.; G. Garbini, *AION* 20 (1970), 249 f.

A valuable new aid to the study of Hebrew epigraphy, Catalogue no. 100 of the Israel Museum, Jerusalem (*Inscriptions Reveal: Documents from the Time of the Bible, the Mishna and the Talmud*) was published in 1972. It contains photographs with short descriptions of most of the inscriptions in vol. I and of a number of inscriptions (particularly from Arad and from Kh. el-Qom near Hebron) too recently discovered for inclusion there, some of them as yet unpublished.

FURTHER BIBLIOGRAPHY

Gezer, Siloam, Lachish; H.-P. Müller, *Ugarit-Forsch.* 2 (1970), 229 f.

C1101: A. Lemaire, *Rev. bibl.* 79 (1972), 565 f.

Yavneh-yam: A. Lemaire, *Semitica* 21 (1971), 57 f.

Tell Arad: A. F. Rainey, *BASOR* 202 (1971), 23 f.; A. Lemaire, *VT* 23 (1973), 243 f.; V. Fritz, *Die Welt des Or.* 7 (1973), 137 f.

Seals: N. Avigad, *Glueck Festschrift* (1970), 284 f.; A. R. Millard, *BASOR* 208 (1972), 5 f.

Mesha: Y. Yadin, *BA* 32 (1969), 70 and *IEJ* 19 (1969), 18 f.; M. Miller, *PEQ* 1974, 9 f.

Amman: R. Y. Kutscher, *Qadmoniot* 5 (1972), 27 f.; E. Puech and A. Rofé, *Rev. bibl.* 54 (1973), 531 f.; F. Zayadine and H. O. Thompson, *Berytus* 22 (1973), 115 f. and F. M. Cross, *BASOR* 212 (1973), 12 f. (a second new inscr.).

Writing: L. A. Bange, *A Study of the Use of Vowel-Letters in Alphabetic Consonantal Writing* (Munich, 1971); T. Wahl, 'How did the Hebrew scribe form his letters?', *J. Anc. N.E. Soc. Columbia Univ.* 3 (1970–71), 9 f.

Language: K. Beyer, *Althebräische Grammatik* (Göttingen, 1969); B. S. J. Isserline, *Austral. J. Bibl. Arch.* 1 (1972), 197 f. For some criticisms of Beyer's procedures and a defence of my own in the Note on the phonology of pre-Massoretic Hebrew (p. xi) see J. C. L. Gibson, 'Inscriptions, Semitic', sect. II, *The Interpreter's Dictionary of the Bible: Supplementary Vol.* (forthcoming).

ADDENDA (VOLUME II)

No. **1** Barhadad. In an article which came to my attention after my manuscript had gone to press E. Lipiński proposes a new reading of the controversial l. 2 (*AION* 31 (1971), 101–4).

He reads:

בר עתרהפש ׀ [אש ר]ב

i.e. 'Barhadad, "son" of ʿAttar-hapēš, the great [man], king of Aram'. Following a remark by J. Starcky (in A. Dupont-Sommer, *Les inscriptions araméennes de Sfiré*, p. 135, n. 1) he dates the inscr. in the early 8 cent., about the same time as no. **5** Zakir, and therefore identifies Barhadad with Barhadad II, the son of Hazael; he understands בר in the sense of 'grandson', ʿAttar-hapēš being the previously unknown name of the usurper Hazael's father. But in a private communication of February 1974 Professor Lipiński informs me that he has abandoned this reading and now proposes:

בר עזר[ש]מש ז[י] ׀ אב

i.e. 'Barhadad, son of ʿI<u>d</u>ri-Šamš, who was the father of the king of Aram'. ʿI<u>d</u>ri-Šamš thus becomes the name of Hazael's father and the Barhadad of the inscr. is Hazael's brother. This revised reading demands a slightly earlier date for the inscr. in the latter half of the 9 cent. (Lipiński compares the script of the Amman citadel inscr.) Both of Lipiński's readings seem to me to give peculiar formulae, and I am inclined still to prefer Albright's interpretation and to keep to a date around 860 B.C.

Professor Lipiński argues for his revised reading in his forthcoming book *Studies in Aramaic Inscriptions and Onomastics* (Louvain), chap. I. I am grateful to him for letting me see a proof of this important work during a visit he made to Edinburgh in August 1974.

No. **5** Zakir: A. Jepsen, 'Zur ZKR-Inschrift Z.2', *Mitteil. Inst. Orientf.* 15 (1969), 1–2; J. F. Ross, 'Prophecy in Hamath, Israel and Mari', *Harvard Th. Rev.* 63 (1970), 1–28; Lipiński, op. cit., chap. I (a new translation).

Nos. **7–9** Sefire: Lipiński, op. cit., chap. III (several revised readings and a new translation).

No. **27** Hermopolis: E. Y. Kutscher, *Isr. Or. St.* 1 (1971), 103 f.; J. Naveh, ibid., 120 f.: J. A. Fitzmyer, *J. Bibl. Lit.* 93 (1974), 201 f.

No. **33** Nanasht 2. Lipiński, op. cit., chap. VIII reads

קדם אדר ספנו נוה

i.e. '. . . before an oak. Respect the precinct (of my tomb)'. This removes the difficult divine name. With נפש cp. no. **37** Daskyleion 2.

No. **37** Daskyleion 1. Lipiński, *VT* 23 (1973), 368 f. and op. cit., chap. VIII, interprets צלמה as a plur., ה standing for the Eastern Aram. emphatic ending [ē], i.e. 'These are the images which Elnaf, son of Ishyahu, made for his tomb'. The הו of l. 2 thus belongs to the father's name, which is Jewish. Elnaf was a wealthy Jew in the Persian administration who like many Jews in contemporary Egypt was clearly a syncretist in religion.

Neue Ephemeris für semitische Epigraphik. A first volume of this important repertoire, to be published occasionally, appeared in 1972, with studies on Phoen., Aram. (see below), and South Arabian epigraphy.

NEW TEXTS

A. Caquot, 'Une inscription araméenne d'époque assyrienne', *Hommages à André Dupont-Sommer* (Paris, 1971), 9–16 (a legal document containing a mention of the word 'mammon'; see further on this kind of text R. Degen, *Neue Ephem.* I, 49 f.; Lipiński, op. cit., chaps. IV–VI).

H. Lozachmeur, 'Un ostracon araméen inédit d'Éléphantine', *Semitica* 21 (1971), 81–94.

A. R. Millard, 'Some Aramaic epigraphs', *Iraq* 34 (1972), 131–7.

R. Degen, 'Ein neuer aramäischer Papyrus aus Elephantine', *Neue Ephem.* I, 9 f.

CRAIBL Jan.–Mars 1974 contains a preliminary report on a trilingual stele from Asia Minor (Greek, Lycian, Aram.), 4 cent. B.C.

FURTHER BIBLIOGRAPHY

Lachish altar inscription: this very difficult text, published by Dupont-Sommer in *Lachish* III (London, 1953), 358 f. and omitted in the Bibliographical notes, has recently been studied by R. Degen, *Neue Ephem.* I, 39 f. and A. Lemaire, *Rev. bibl.* 81 (1974), 63 f.

R. Degen, 'Zum Ostrakon CIS II 138', *Neue Ephem.* I, 23 f.

P. Grelot, *Documents araméens d'Égypte* (Paris, 1972). A full study of ostraca and papyri.

E. Lipiński, 'The goddess Athirat in ancient Arabia, in Babylon, and in Ugarit', *Orientalia hovaniensia Periodica* 3 (1972), 101 f. (on no. **30** Tema).

H. Tawil, 'Some literary elements in the opening sections of the Hadad, Zakir and the Nerab II inscriptions', *Orientalia* 43 (1974), 40 f.

J. C. L. Gibson, 'Inscriptions, Semitic', *The Interpreter's Dictionary of the Bible: Supplementary Volume* (forthcoming).

INDEXES

NAMES OF DEITIES

אדרסון (?) **33** 2
אוס(י)רי **23** A 2 **24** 1, 3 **29** 4
אל **7** i A 11 **13** 2, 11 **14** 22
אלור **5** A 1 B 20
אנרת **7** i A 38
ארקרשף **13** 11
אשירא **30** A 3, 16

בל **37** 3
בנת **27** i 7 ii 1, 12 iii 1
בעלחרן **17** iii 1
בעלשמין **5** A 3, 11, 12, 13 B 23 **21** 2 **34** 3
בתאל **27** iv 1

הדד **7** 1 A 36, 38 **13** 1, 2, 8, 11, 13, 14, 16, 18, 22, 23 **14** 2, 22
הנאלת **25** 1

זרפנת **7** i A 8

יהו **28** obv. 1, 4

כבבה **36** 3, 7
כדאה **7** i A 10

לצ **7** i A 9

מלכת שמין **27** iv 1
מלקרת **1** 3
מלש **7** i A 8
מרדך **7** i A 8

נבא **7** i A 8
נבו **27** i 1 **37** 3
נכל **18** i 9 **19** ii 9
נכר **7** i A 10
נר **7** i A 9
נרגל **7** i A 9
נשך **18** i 9 **19** ii 9

סבת **7** i A 11
ס[ן] **7** i A 9

עלין **7** i A 11

פתח **27** i 2 ii 2 iii 2 iv 2 v 1 vi 1

צלם **30** A 2, 3, 10, 12, 16, 17

קנואל(?) **14** 8

רכבאל **13** 2, 3, 11, 18 **14** 22 **15** i 5
רשף **13** 2, 3

שהר **5** B 24 **18** i 2, 9 **19** ii 1, 9 **33** 5 **34** 4
שנגלא **30** A 16

שמש **5** B 24 **7** i A 9 **13** 2, 3, 11, 18 **14** 22 **18** i 9 **33** 5 **34** 4

ת[שמת] **7** i A 8

PERSONAL NAMES

אבה **23** A 1, 2
אבי **20** 10, 11
אבסלי **23** A 2
אדן **21** 1
אדנלרם **6** i 1

אושע **28** obv. 1 rev. 7
אחשי **20** 10
אחתבו **23** A 1, 2
אחתסן **27** i 5
אטי **27** iv 3, 6

Truncated

PLACE-NAMES

SEMITIC TERMS

(Note: Only problematic or significant items are listed)

HEBREW BIBLE

OTHER REFERENCES

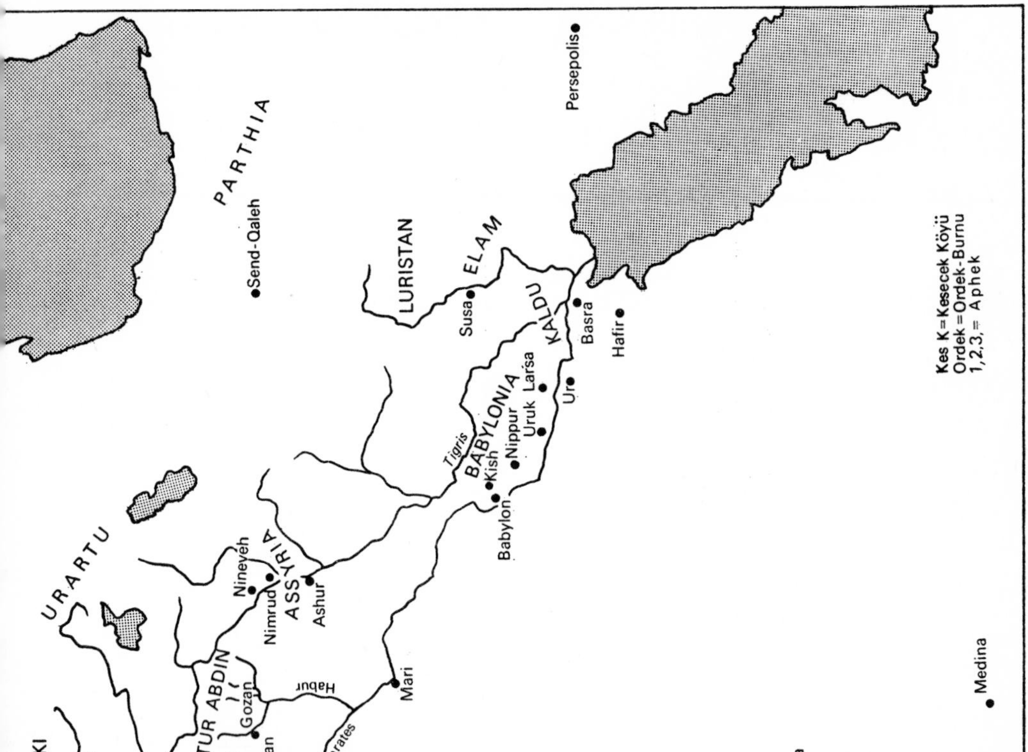
PARTHIA
Send-Qaleh
Persepolis
LURISTAN
ELAM
Susa
KALDU
Basra
Hafir
BABYLONIA
Tigris
Kish
Nippur
Uruk
Larsa
Ur
Babylon
URARTU
Nineveh
Nimrud
ASSYRIA
Ashur
TUR ABDIN
Gozan
Habur
Mari
Euphrates
Balih
Harran
Edessa
Hadattu
Carchemish
MUSHKI
KASKU
Hattusa
HITTITES
Halys
Melid
TABAL
KUMMUHI
GURGUM
Sam'al
Castobala
Karatepe
KUE
Kes.K
Cuzneh
Saraidin
CILICIA
HATTINA
Ordek
Arpad
Aleppo
Nerab
Sefire
HATARIKKA
Afis
HAMATH
Qarqar
Hamath
Orontes
Palmyra
Ugarit
Byblos
1
Sidon
Tyre
Acco
Damascus
SUBITE
Dan
Hazor
Ein Gev
2
Megiddo
Samaria
Deir Alla
Amman
3
Ashdod
Ashkelon
Gaza
Arad
KEDAR
Petra
Elath
Tema
Medina
PHRYGIA (MUSHKI)
CYPRUS
Migdol
Tell el Maskhuta
Saqqara (Memphis)
Scheich Fadl
Hermopolis
T. el Amarna.
Abydos
Thebes
Assuan (Elephantine)
Kes K = Kesecek Köyü
Ordek = Ordek-Burnu
1,2,3, = Aphek

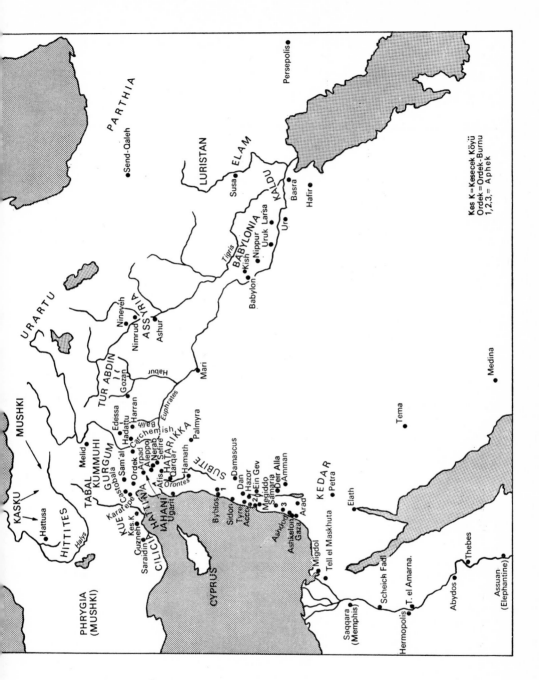

Table of relationships in the Hermopolis Papyri

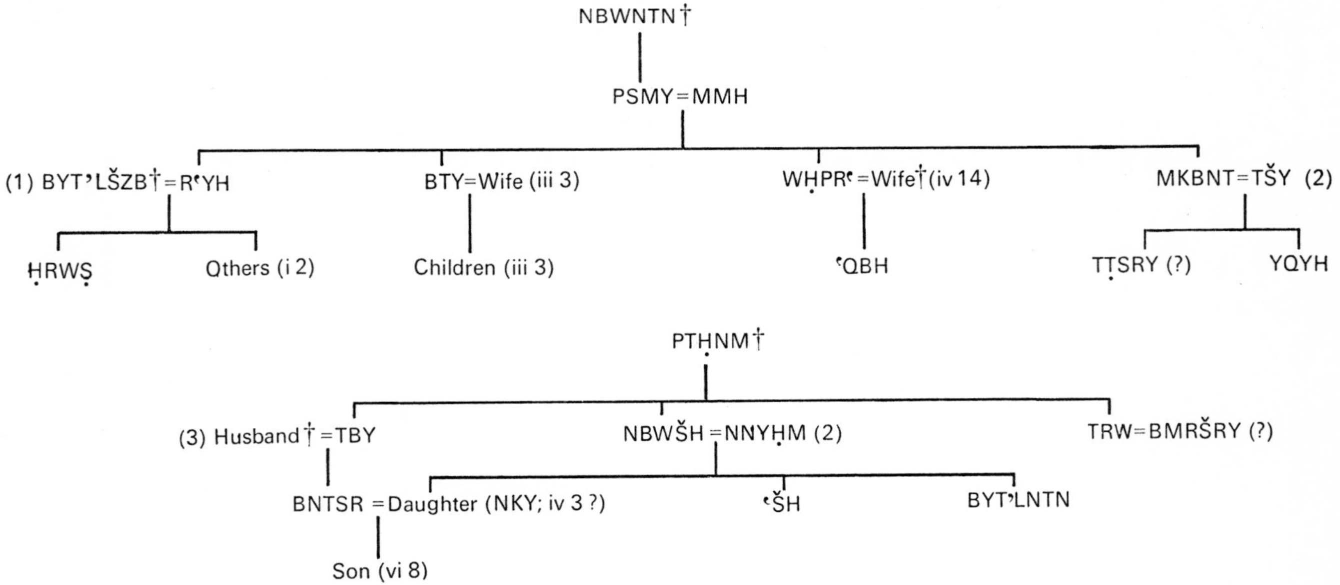

(1) TPMT and ' ḤTSN (i 5) may be relatives of his.

(2) Sisters. Other members of their family are mentioned in iv 3, 10f.

(3) The writer of vi may be a relative of his; also MKY (ii 9).

	Phoen. Tell. H. Cypr. Nor. Barh.	Haz. Ein G. Dan.	Phoen. Kil. i, ii	Zak. Lur.i	Ham. graf.	iA	Sefire. iC iiC	iii	Had. Pan. Barr.	Nin. wts.	i Ner. ii	Nim. ostr.	Nin. end.	Ash. ostr. Adon	Clay tab.	B-M pap
א																
ב																
ג																
ד																
ה																
ו																
ז																
ח																
ט																
י																
כ																
ל																
מ																
נ																
ס																
ע																
פ																
צ																
ק																
ר																
ש																
ת																

10–9 cents.   8 cent.   7 cent.   6 cent.

Table of scripts 10–6 centuries

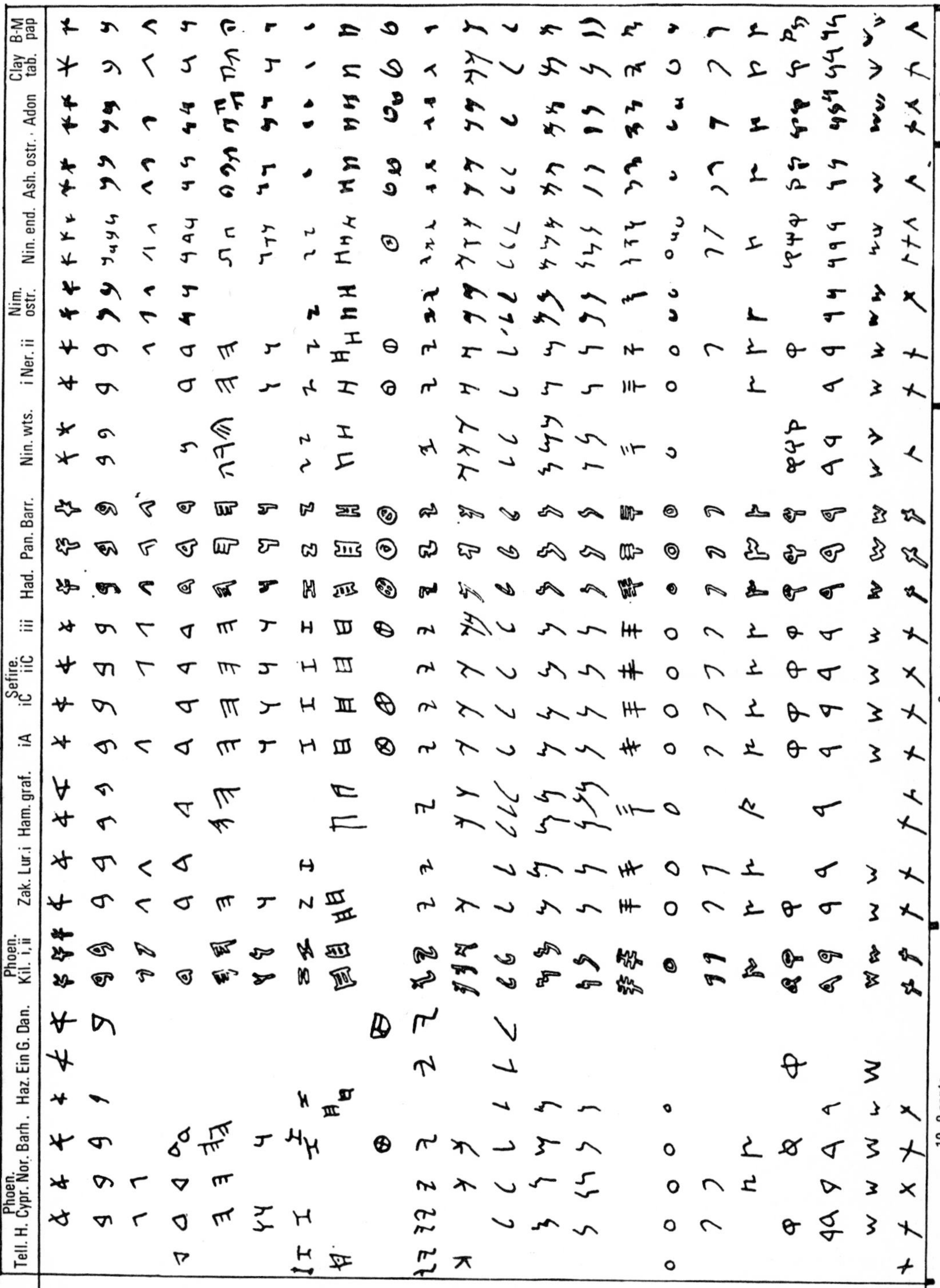

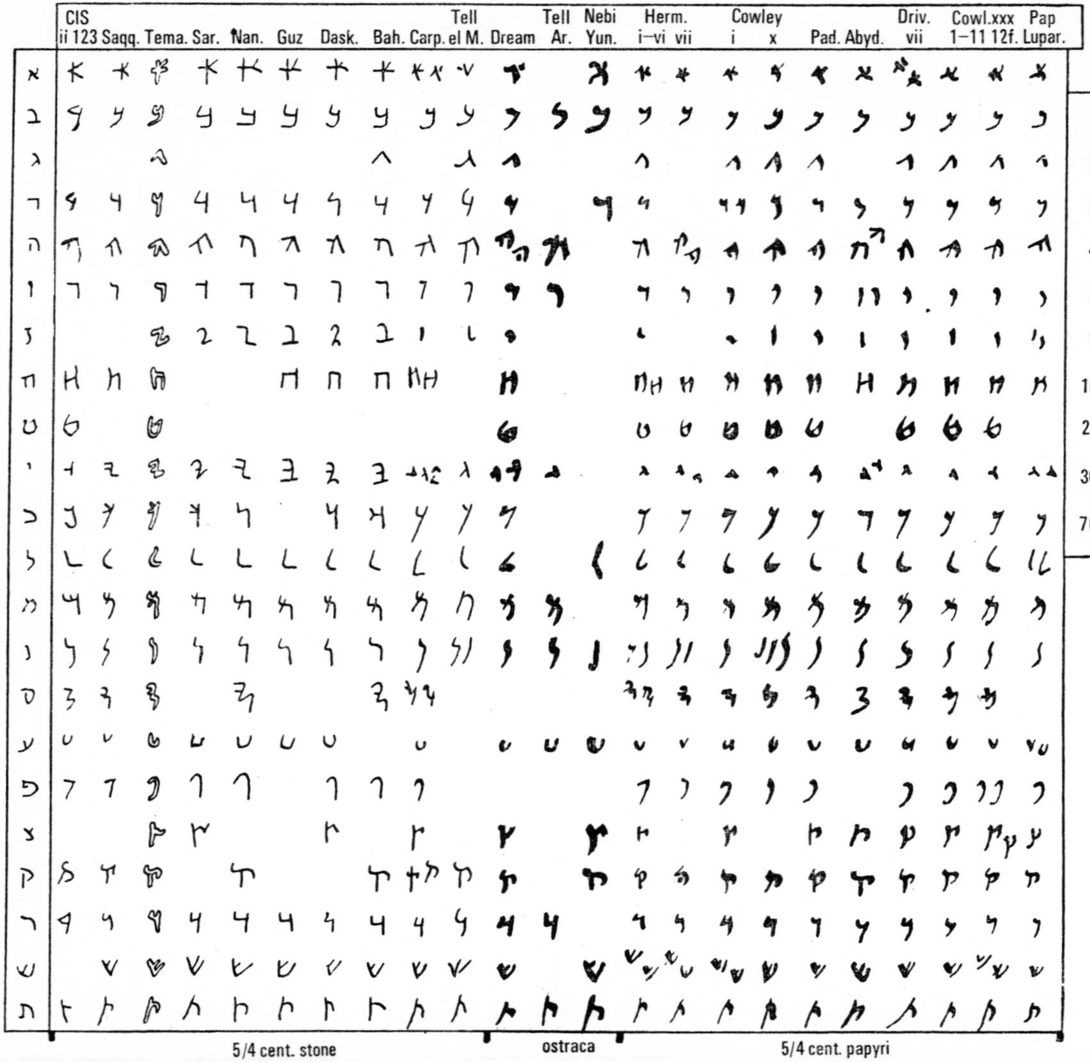

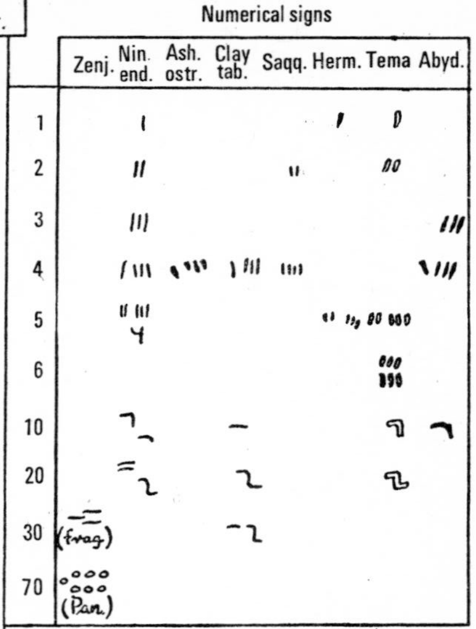

Dates

CIS ii 123	*c*.500 B.C.
Cowley i	495
Cowley x	456
Cowley xxx	408
Driver vii	*c*.410
Papyrus Luparensis	*c*.375–50

Table of scripts 5–4 centuries, with numerical signs

(a)

1

(b)

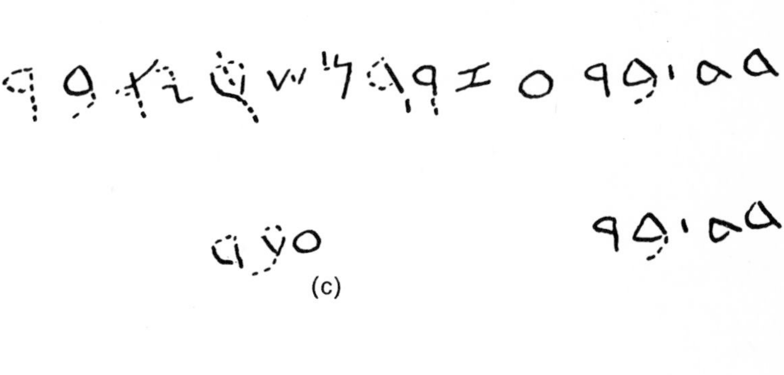

(c)

5

10

15

20

25

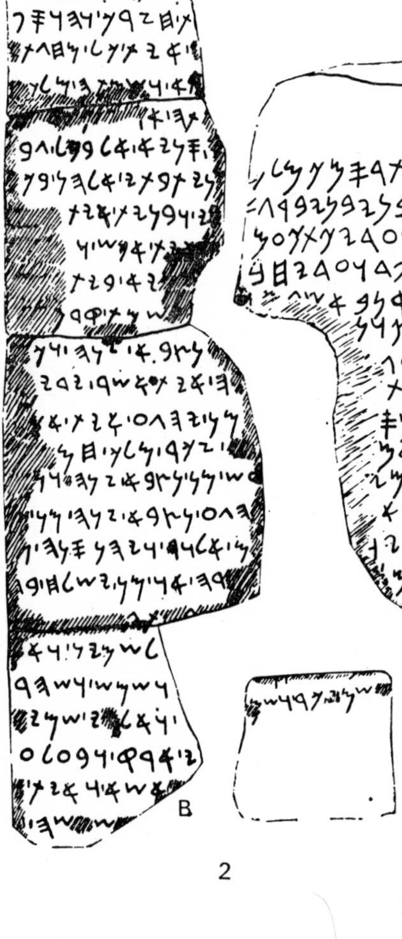

B

C

2

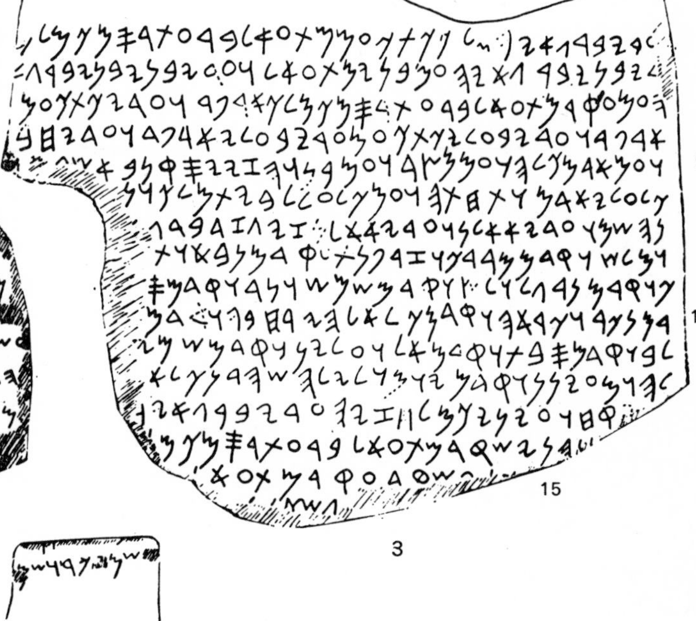

5

10

15

3

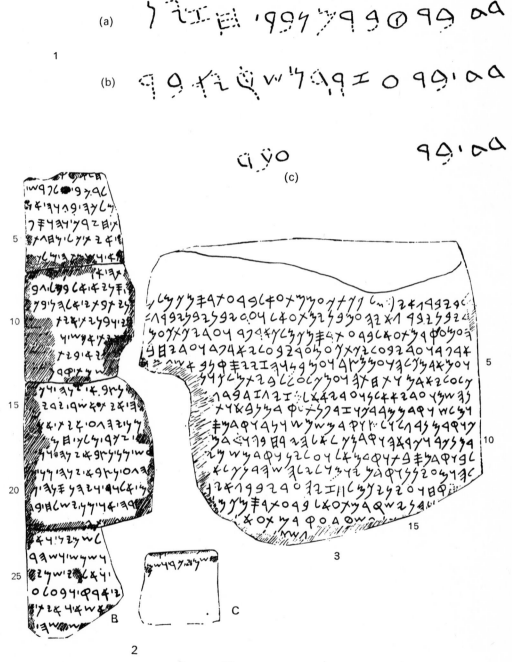

Figures 1–3

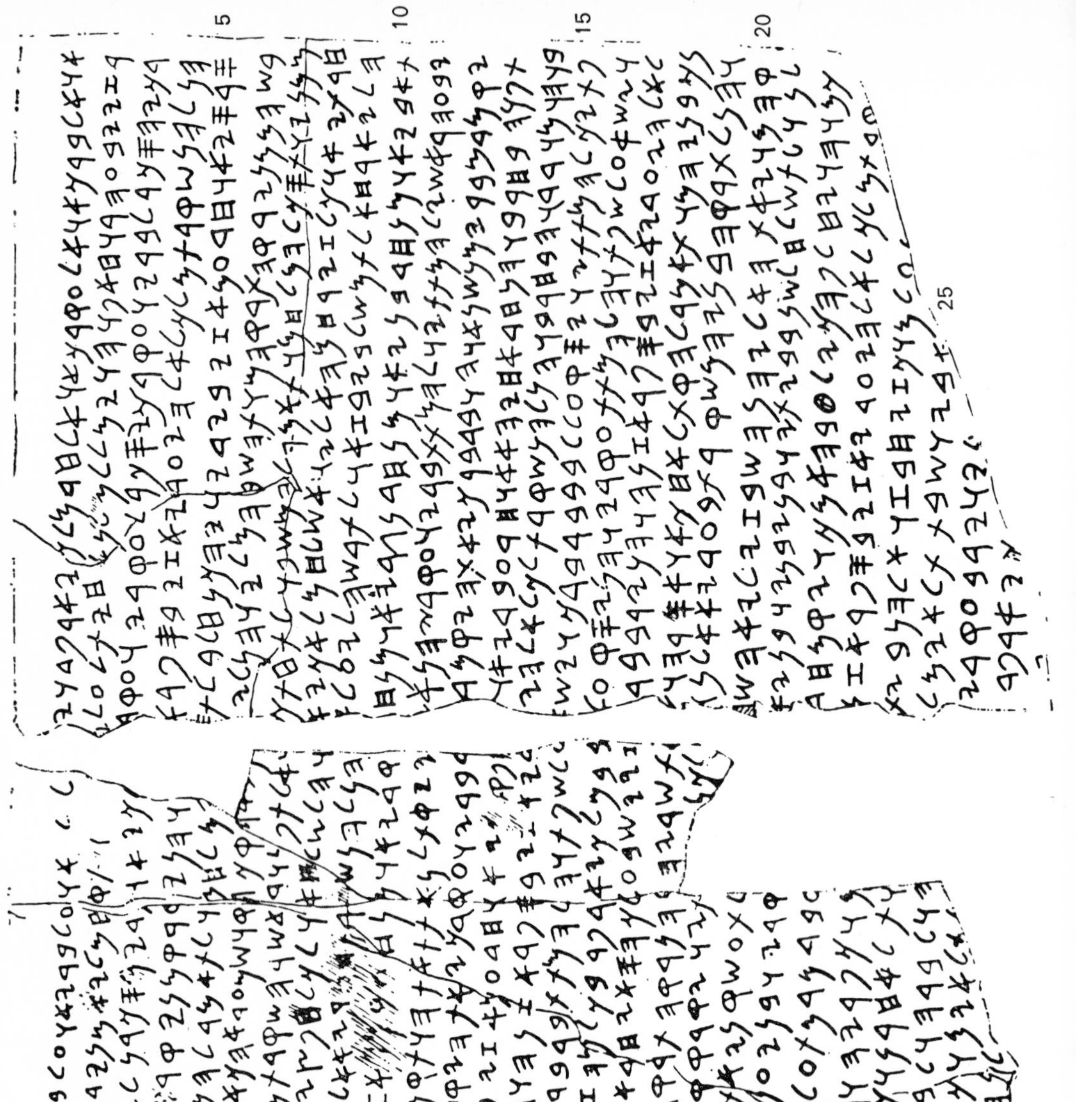

Figure 4

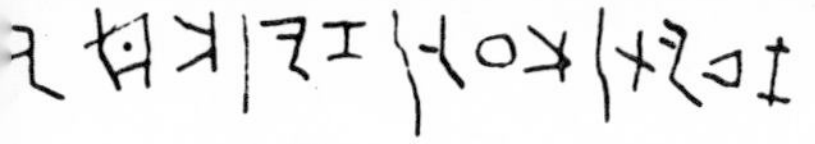

5

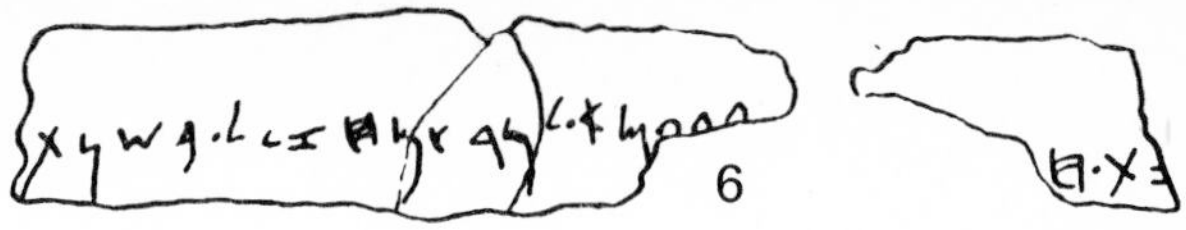

6

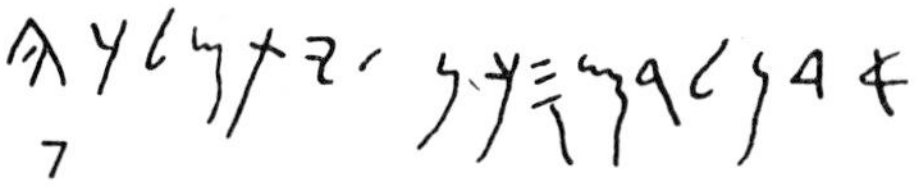

7

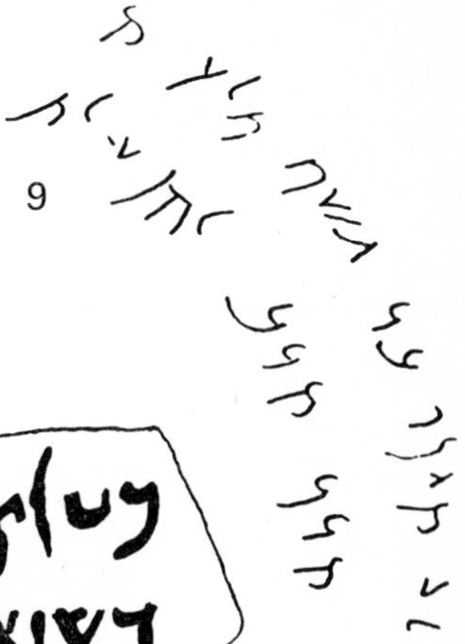

9

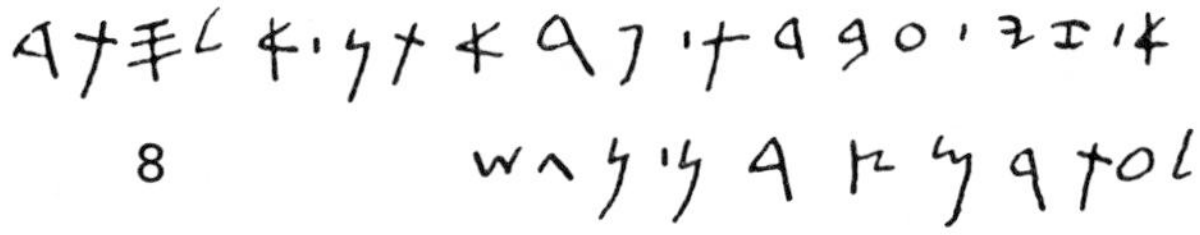

8

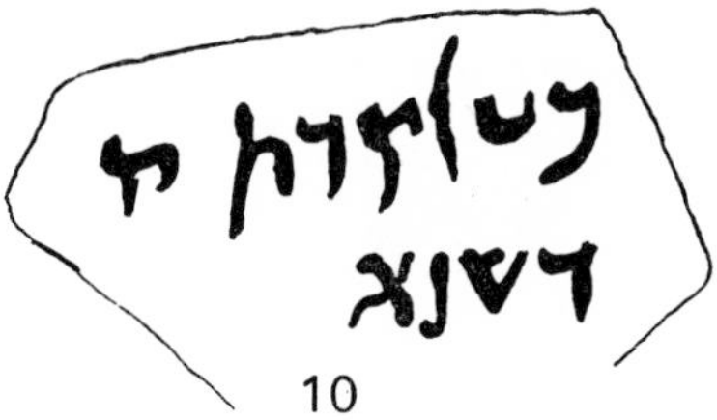

10

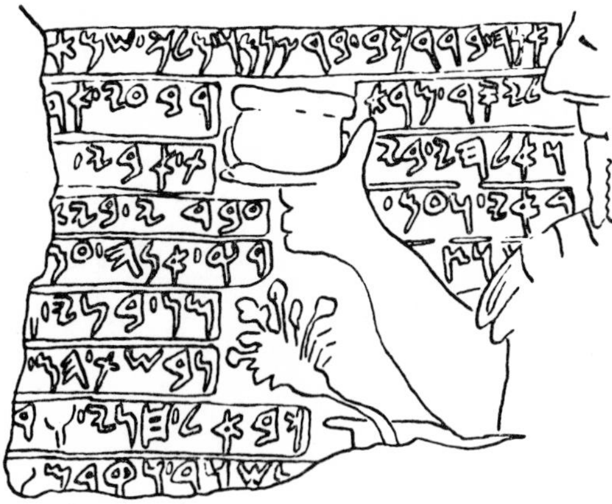

11

12

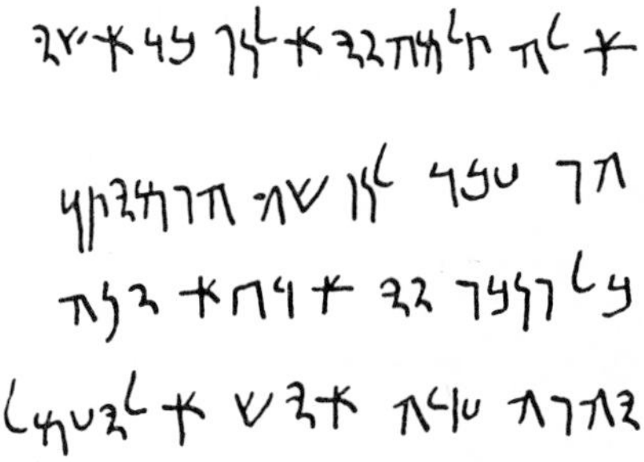

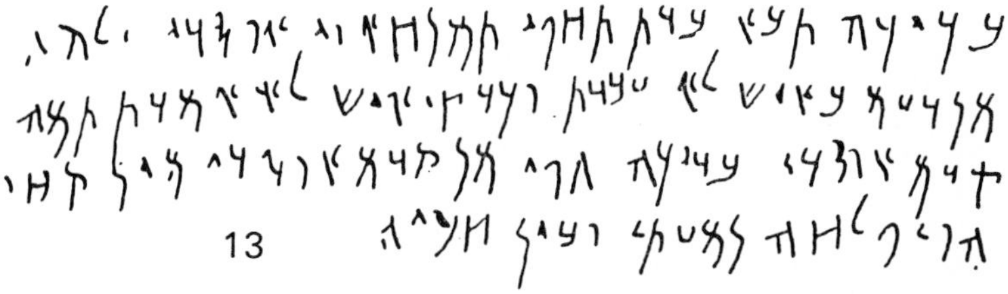

13

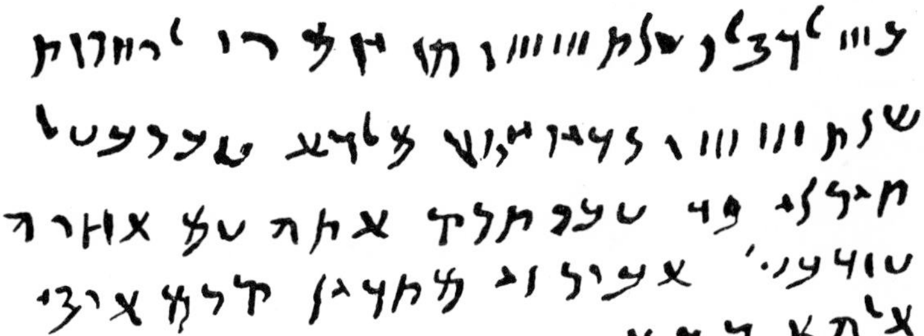

14

Figures 5–14

Figures 15–28

PLATE I

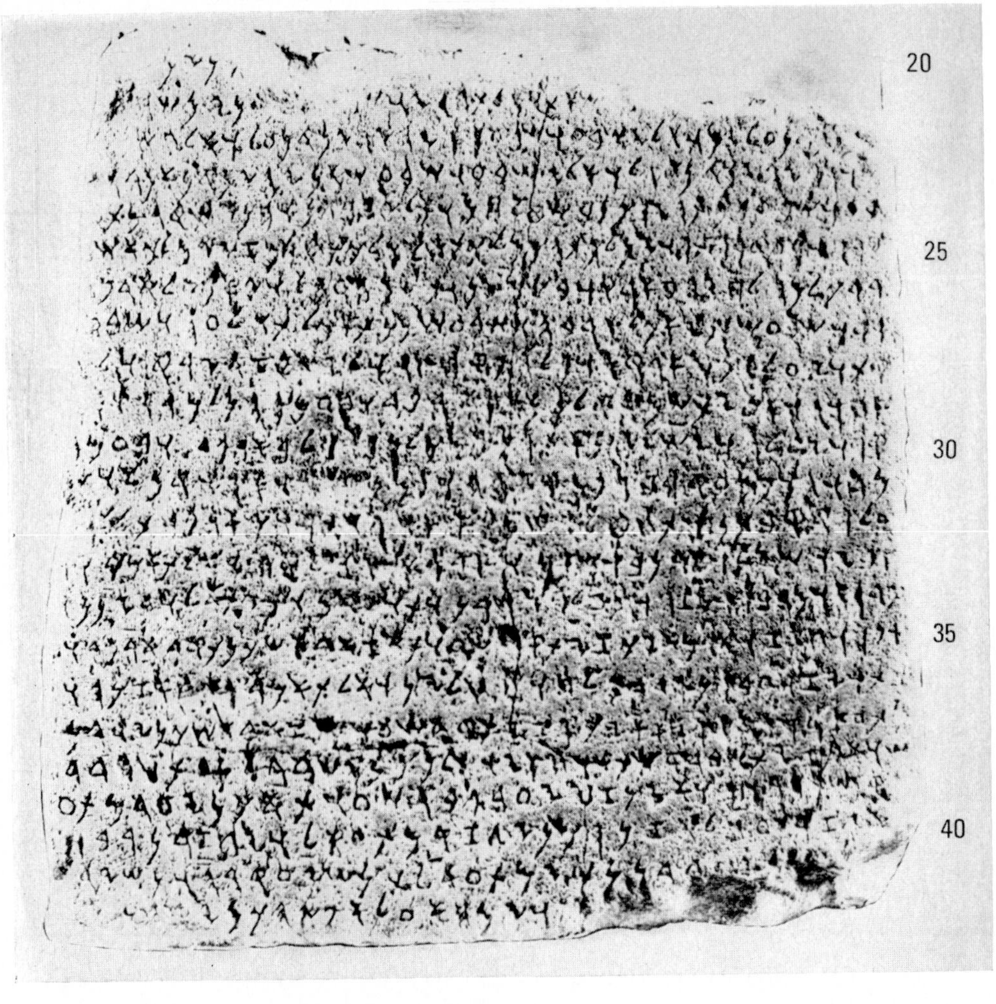

PLATE II

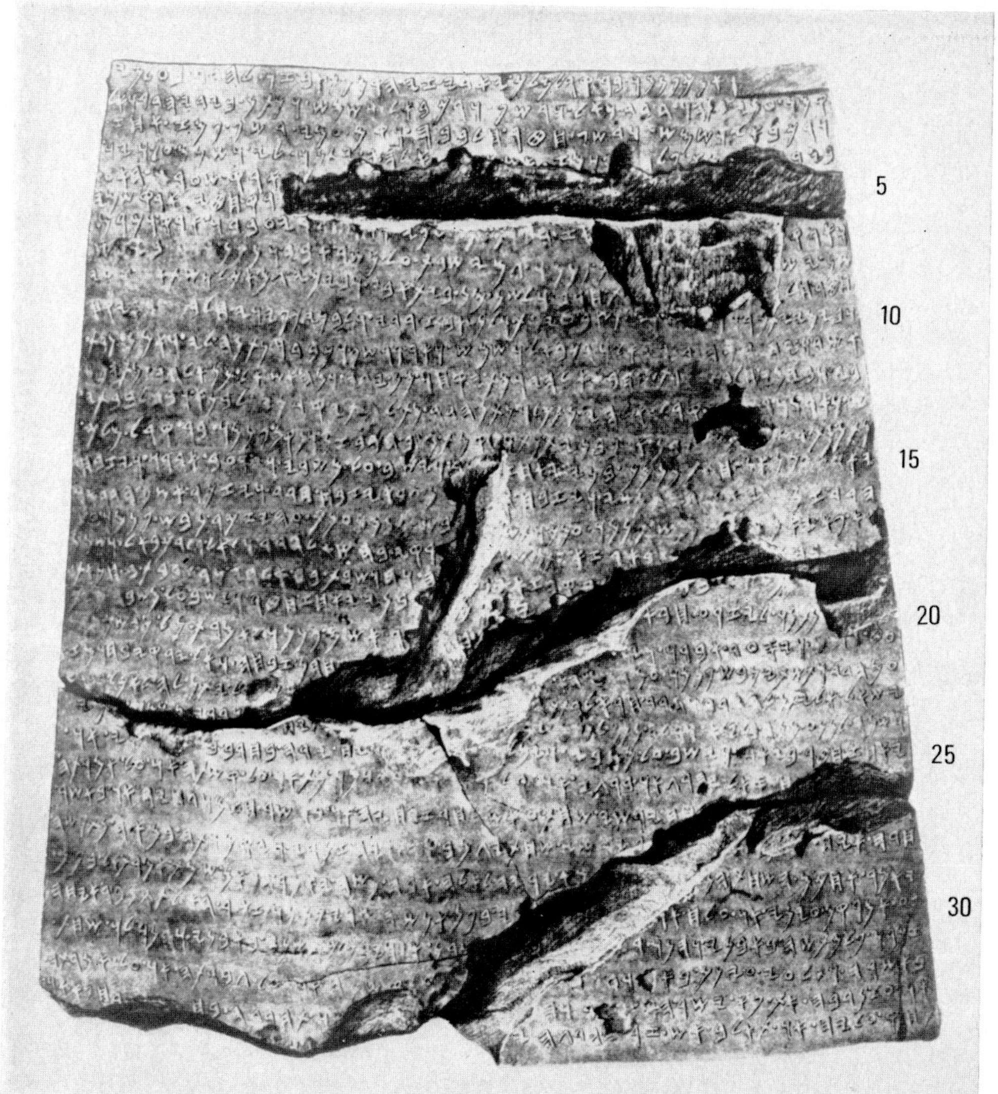

PLATE III

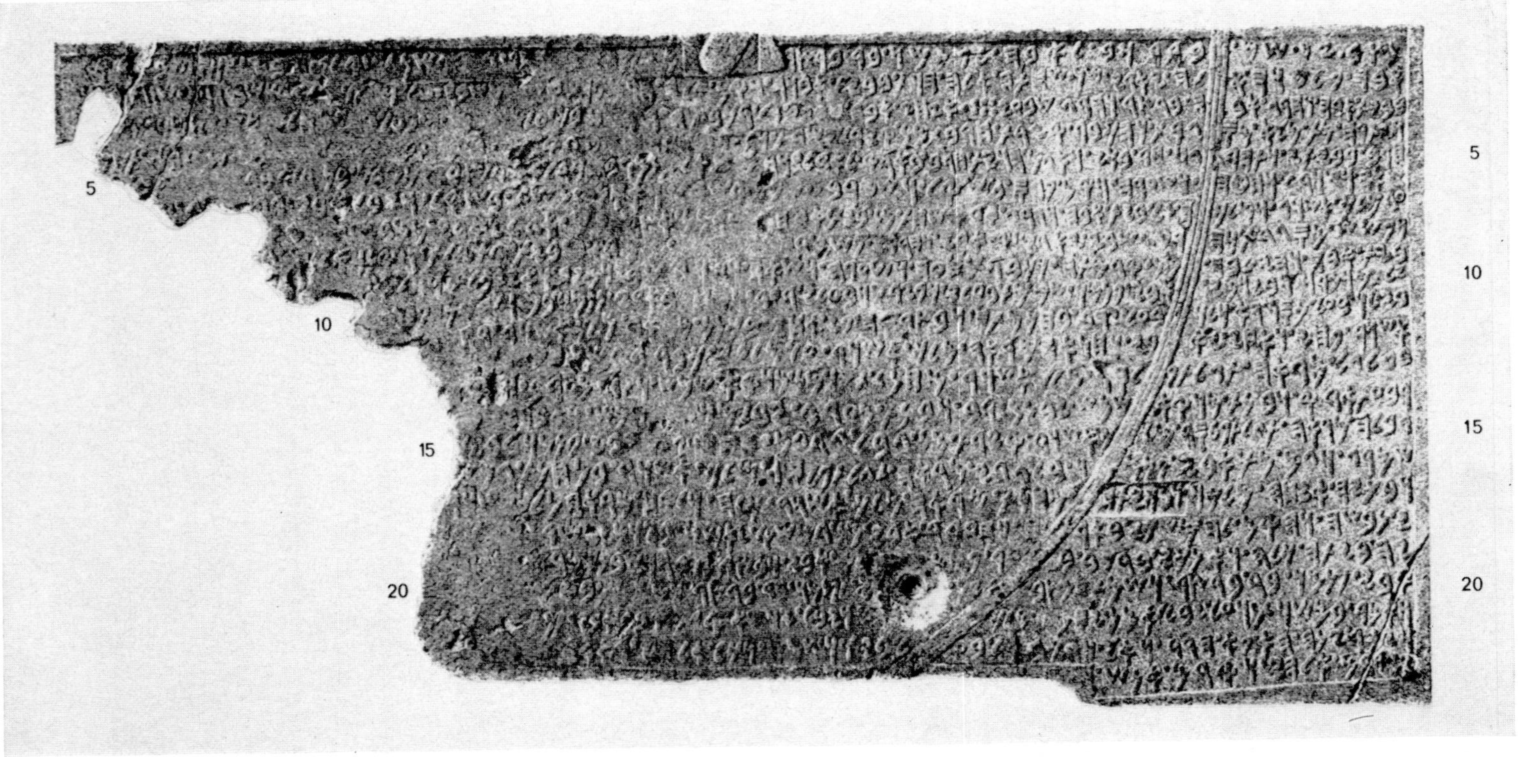

PLATE IV

PLATE V

1

2

PLATE VI

1

2

PLATE VII

1

2

PLATE VIII

PLATE IX

1

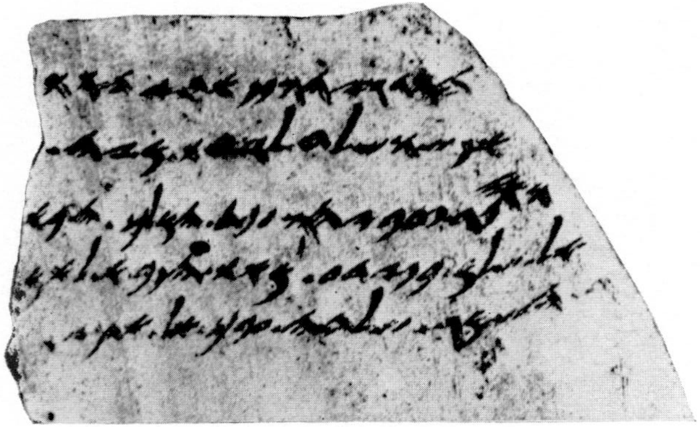

2 (reverse)

2 (obverse)

PLATE X

1

2

PLATE XI

1

2

PLATE XII